RADICAL
DISSENT IN
CONTEMPORARY
ISRAELI POLITICS:

RADICAL DISSENT IN CONTEMPORARY ISRAELI POLITICS:

Cracks in the Wall

David J. Schnall

PRAEGER PUBLISHERS
Praeger Special Studies

New York • London • Sydney • Toronto

Library of Congress Cataloging in Publication Data

Schnall, David J
    Radical dissent in contemporary Israeli politics.

    Bibliography: p.
    Includes index.
    1. Political parties--Israel. 2. Radicalism--
Israel. 3. Israel--Politics and government.
I. Title.
JQ1825.P37S36   320.9'5694'05   78-31209
ISBN 0-03-047096-X

PRAEGER PUBLISHERS
PRAEGER SPECIAL STUDIES
383 Madison Avenue, New York, N.Y. 10017, U.S.A.

Published in the United States of America in 1979
by Praeger Publishers,
A Division of Holt, Rinehart and Winston, CBS, Inc.

9   038   987654321

Printed in the United States of America

To Tova, whose love is my inspiration;
and to Eliezer Hillel, the product of that love

ACKNOWLEDGEMENTS

In any project as broad and extensive as this, there are numerous individuals who contribute of their time and effort from the first conceptualization to the finished product. It is impossible to acknowledge all to whom thanks are due and invariably some are inadvertently omitted. For this I apologize in advance.

There are several names, however, that must be mentioned for their particular contributions. Firstly, my good friends and benefactors: Mr. Harry Starr and Dr. Issai Hosiosky of the Lucius Littauer Foundation, Dr. Harold Cassidy of the Sigma Xi Scientific Research Society of North America, and the administration of the City University Research Foundation. Without their generosity and support, this volume could never have been undertaken.

Thanks must also be extended to those who aided my research while in Israel. These include Mr. Moshe Kohn of the Jerusalem *Post*, for his patience and gracious understanding, Mr. and Mrs. Moshe Gewirtz, and Rabbi and Mrs. Aaron Rakefet. I was allowed use of the facilities of the Hebrew University, Givat Ram Campus, under the auspices of the Davis Institute. Prof. Ehud Shprinzak of the Political Science Department read sections of an earlier draft of the manuscript and supplied valuable information and comments. Gratitude must also be expressed to the subjects of this study who were interviewed and whose cooperation allowed for the successful completion of this work. In an important sense, this book is as much theirs as it is mine.

Prof. John Entelis, a friend and instructor at Fordham University, was an inspiration for the project and also offered helpful comments. The final manuscript was typed and prepared by Bertha Shoulson, Florence Bergin, Catherine Clowry, Dolores Garcia, and Lorraine Ryan.

Finally, there is no way I can adequately express the importance of those to whom this volume is dedicated: they make it all worthwhile. Of course I take sole responsibility for any errors of fact or interpretation to be found in the following pages.

CONTENTS

I

THE CONTEXT

1

INTRODUCTION

Israeli politics have always been infused with at least the aura of ideological commitment. Born of all shades of religious, socialist, and revisionist thought, the state has depended upon the Zionist credo that its suvival is the key to Jewish well-being throughout the world. Strains were evident from the outset and confrontation—whether over military hegemony, German reparations, or the desecration of the Sabbath—have been violent and bloody.

To a certain degree, such confrontation is encouraged and institutionalized by the Israeli brand of democracy. Its proportional system of parliamentary representation implies the proliferation of political parties. Further, since the voter chooses party lists rather than specific delegates to represent him, these parties tend to be centralized and display relative ideological consistency. Institutions are often longstanding—many predating the founding of the state—and loyalties and commitments tend to run deep. Finally, since proportional representation allows a given party to win one seat by carrying about 1 percent of the general electorate, dissenters may be encouraged to stalk out on their own, taking their grievances to "the people."

Of equal importance is the ethnic polyglot that is Israeli society. Its non-Jewish population includes well-educated and skilled Palestinians, Druze and Bedouin tribes, and a variety of Christian groups of Oriental and Western derivation. Its Jewish population is a mixture of Western and European nationalities, as well as emigrants from African, Mediterranean, and Asian Muslim states. In addition, these immigrants display a variety of religious and confessional practices and commitments which range from strict, "ultra"-orthodoxy to frank agnosticism. As might be expected, such a mix is often associated with painful and unfortunate confrontations between these component groups.

Yet the day to day realities of developing a nation engulfed in a sea of enemies, cooperation imposed by government coalition, and beleaguered isolation resulted in a perceptible decline in ideological tension. Variously attributed to the institutions of the state, generational change, or simply "Ayn Breira" (we have little choice but to cooperate), differences rooted in religious belief, political commitment, or the "Jewish nature" were at least deferred. Young Israelis, derisively termed the "expresso generation," were characterized by a lack of Zionist spirit and pioneering zeal. They seemed, to their critics, content to relax, enjoy some measure of affluence and sip coffee on Tel Aviv's Dizengoff Street.

The events of 1967 and 1973, however, proved momentous in Israeli life and gave new strength to many facets of ideological commitment. The first war offered new confidence and status as military victor and occupier. It also presented a packet of opportunities for peace, problems of integration, and controversy over settlement and annexation versus the unilateral creation of a Palestinian state. A body of support developed about each alternative and around each debate.

The 1973 War had yet a different effect. Though it may properly be argued that Israel did not incur a military defeat in 1973, it is clear that neither did it gain the kind of elegant military victory to which it was accustomed. The battle was indecisive and protracted, resulting largely in a stalemate. Yet where the Arab states could not be said to have won a military victory, they do appear to have won a psychological one, a victory of morale. In Israel, the war was followed by recrimination, demoralization, and self-doubt. Longstanding military reputations were besmirched; a search for blame ensued, as did a begrudging respect for the "new Arab fighting man." Here too, undercurrents of dissent and controversy surrounded every new inquiry and discovery.

While Israeli politics have often been volatile and fiery, until the past decade their nature has generally been restricted to recognizable bounds. Radical and militant ideological dissent, when it occurred, was limited and rarely garnered the consistent support of even a minority of the population. During the 1970s, however, and particularly since 1973, salient forms of protest have surfaced. These appear to take exception to the very nature of Israeli life, its ideological underpinnings, and, in some instances, its very raison d'être. All argue that serious change is warranted.

The ideologies of seven such dissenting groups are the substance of this study. Their development, history, values, and tactics will be analyzed and described at length in succeeding chapters. It must be understood from the outset that this book is intended to be neither exclusive nor conclusive. The groups chosen for analysis are not the only pockets of protest to be found in Israel. Nor is their iedology static. Indeed, significant events that occur in the Middle East from day to day, in the late 1970s, have a profound effect on the belief systems of even the most casual and indifferent member of the polity. Undoubtedly, the groups to be discussed are quite fluid and dynamic.

It is for this reason that the emphasis of our study is upon ideology, for it is there that the most basic elements of political perception are to be found. Specific strategies change and coalitions vary regularly, but some measure of consistency may be expected to underlie it all. Further, almost by their nature, dissenters tend to band together in smaller groups, demand ideological purity and decry compromise in the name of practical gain.

It must also be admitted that the choice of these particular protesters was somewhat subjective. It seemed to the author that they comprised a fair cross-section of those who have lived on the fringe of Israeli politics. Further, they are among those who have gained the most notoriety or popularity (as in the case of Black Panthers or Gush Emunim) and have proven to be surprisingly durable over time (as in the case of Uri Avnery or Natore Karta). No doubt exception might be taken to the inclusion of one or another of them, though a replacement would be no less subjective.

THE PLAN OF THE BOOK

Unlike much of the literature regarding ideology, the intent of this study is highly descriptive and specific.[1] Rather than the creation of a far-ranging theory of the nature and function of ideology per se, we are concerned here with ideologies of a particular nature within a given geographical location, that is, radical dissent in Israel. Such a description will form the body of this book.

Most nations are underwritten by at least a moderate degree of two sociopolitical elements, both outgrowths of that ideology that flows from its mainstream. These are a broad consensus on (a) national goals and ends, and (b) legitimate sources of authority. In its most extensive form, therefore, ideology on a national scale may be said to fulfill at least one important function: the maintenance of the political system. While disagreement and debate may well exist—particularly in regard to specific details of this broad consensus—it will generally take a moderate and amiable form, remaining within recognized and acceptable limits. Change, where warranted, will generally be sought within the system and by means of legitimate sources of authority.

In addition, depending upon the resilience and depth of this consensus and the political structure which it reflects, such disagreement may engender a variety of responses. At a given time they will include: reform, indifference, cooptation, and possibly repression as well as several in between. The key is the continuation of the consensus and the willingness of the combatants to abide by the rules of the game even when the rules work against one or the other. Stability in government, peaceful succession of power, the continuation of various levels of stratification, or the assignment of status over time are reflections of such a condition.

However, it has also been evident that not all members of a given society abide by this broad consensus and the peaceful means of political action it generally implies. For some, the structures of the society are oppressive, alienating, or unresponsive. For others, there is a psychosocial need for collective action and mass confrontation which makes the everyday manner of doing things dull, uneventful, and unfulfilling. Theories of why individuals are attracted to such movements and their structure abound, but it is clear that here as well ideology plays an important role in simplifying the arguments being portrayed and adding both stature and passion to the nature of a movement in formation.[2]

Generally, dissent of this nature is termed radical, in the sense that it makes demands for change of a fundamental nature, outside the acceptable channels. While not necessarily associated with political violence and confrontation, such dissent often utilizes extremist tactics to portray its cause. This is because there is a fundamental belief that the structures for change within the traditional political system are either too slow or unresponsive to the type of comprehensive change that is contemplated. It is this type of dissent, that is, radical in that it does not accept the consensus that cements the political system, that forms the context of this book.

By and large, Israel is a society of broad and far-reaching social consensus. Some of the reasons for this will be discussed in coming chapters. The ideology which flows from its mainstream is Zionism, a state-building system of beliefs that predates the state by at least seven decades and has undergone several changes and permutations. Its political and social institutions are of comparative long standing, especially in relation to other new states. As used here, radical dissent is that which either does not accept the basic ideological tenets of political Zionism, or accepts them but under circumstances of such extensive and comprehensive change as to be outside of, and unacceptable to, the broad consensus of society.

For purposes of this analysis, three simple conceptual categories will be employed.[3] Each ideology will first be discussed in terms of its "world view." By this is meant the image of social and political reality to which it subscribes. Herein will be presented its perceptions of the natural and social order, the distribution of power within society, the nature of that power and that upon which the power depends. Succinctly, the world view is a descriptive statement of the present political and social environment.

A second ideological component is its set of "values and goals," prescribed for society. The ideology of dissent is often geared toward change, in this case broad and comprehensive change, and such values reflect the content and context of that change—from whence it shall come and in what order or priority. Values and goals of this sort are understandably fluent and often vague or ill-defined. While this must be considered in any attempt at categorization, it is this very aspect of ideology that gives it direction and shape.

Finally, a third component to be discussed is the "strategies for social change" by which these goals are to be realized. How change will come about, under what circumstances, and when, are all issues to be raised under this rubric. Further, it is here that the very practical aspects of political participation may be discussed. To what extent is activity within the traditional political system to be tolerated? What role shall be played by violence and militancy? What, if any, alliances might be properly formed and what duration or stability should such alliances have?

In pointed terms, these three components might be described in terms of a simple progression. The first, the "world view," is the assessment of "where we are"—roughly corresponding to the historical cognition discussed above. "Values and goals"—an ideology's evaluative element—describes "where we want to go" based upon that preceding assessment. Finally, the "strategies for social change" describes "how we can get there' and is linked to the passion, the propensity for action that gives ideology its dynamic force. Admittedly, these categories are subjective and tend to overlap; yet it is hoped that their use will clarify the research to be presented below.

The following two chapters set the stage for an analysis of dissenting ideologies. In the first, Zionism, the central ideology of Israeli politics, is discussed. It too is subjected to this categorical outline, despite the fact that Zionism is no monolith and its nuances have varied according to the particular spokesman. For this reason, emphasis is placed upon those elements that have summoned the greatest agreement and those that have been clearly central to its argument. The second of the two chapters presents a brief and cursory discussion of those major social and political institutions that create the environment within which each ideology operates. It is only by thus defining its context that dissent can be fully appreciated.

The thrust of the discussion then shifts from the environment to the ideologies themselves. They too, however, have been divided according to form. The first grouping comprises those that draw their foundation from some form of socialist thought. They vary among themselves as to the strength of their rejection of classic Zionism, the extremism they advocate and their commitment to an Israeli state. All included in this group, though, support the essential perspectives of Marxism as a political force. The second set of ideologies are less rooted in such a thorough ideological critique, but draw sustenance from a specific ethnic or religious community. Either defined by a sense of deprivation and repression, or spurred by an apocalyptic vision, such ideologies are more clearly nationalist in their orientation.

Finally, a concluding section is devoted to summary analysis and discussion. The ideologies are compared in the hope of allowing their differences and similarities to clearly emerge. That which is significant as well as that which is secondary, that which is well-worn as well as that which is novel—all are outlined, defined, and described. Here too the trichotomous categorical scheme is employed and it is about this format that the analytical discussion revolves.

This is followed by a concluding chapter, almost in the form of an epilogue. Much of the research for this study was done prior to the 1977 elections. This major event has been variously termed an earthquake or a hurricane, in that it shook from power the party that had held sway in Israel since the founding of the state. In its place, the Likud bloc, led by long-standing opposition leader Menahem Begin, has become the new political force in Israel. Its young administration has brought sweeping economic changes and a significant peace offensive which is inconclusive a year later.

It is largely for this reason that emphasis has been placed upon ideology in this study. It is a factor that tends to be longstanding and viable over time. While the fortunes and vicissitudes of any given movement may vary, its essential ideology will generally remain constant. The last chapter, however, attempts an assessment of ideological dissent as reflected in the 1977 elections and the events that followed on its heels. There is a discussion of the activities of each group in 1977, their prospects for the future, their successes and failures.

NOTES

1. The literature regarding ideology as an element in political science is considerable. Some of the leading contributions include George Lichtheim, *The Concept of Ideology* (New York: Random House, 1967), Robert Denewick et al., eds., *Knowledge and Belief in Politics: The Problem of Ideology* (New York: St. Martin's Press, 1973); David Apter, ed., *Ideology and Discontent* (New York: Free Press, 1964); Robert Lane, *Political Man* (New York: Free Press, 1972); Giovanni Sartori, "Politics, Ideology, and Belief Systems," *American Political Science Review* (June 1969), pp. 398–411; and Willard Mullins, "On the Concept of Ideology in Political Science," *American Political Science Review* (June 1972), pp. 498–510.

2. Good reviews of such theories may be found in Serge Denisoff, *The Sociology of Dissent* (New York: Harcourt, Brace and Jovanovich, 1974), and Gilbert Abcarian, *American Political Radicalism* (Waltham, Mass.: Xerox Corp., 1971).

3. This typology is based on Kenneth Dolbeare and Patricia Dolbeare, *American Ideologies: The Competing Beliefs of the Seventies* (Chicago: Markham, 1971). See also Lyman T. Sargent, *Contemporary Political Ideologies* (Homewood, Ill.: Dorsey, 1972).

2

ZIONISM AS IDEOLOGY

Zionism is one of the most complex and hotly debated concepts of modern history. Its manifestations have taken secular or religious, socialist or capitalist, radical or conservative form, while its contemporary value and direction is still a major issue in both international and sectarian forums. Sympathizers seek their roots in nineteenth century European nationalism as well as the words of the ancient Hebrew prophets. Detractors argue that it is a form of colonialism at best and racist imperialism at worst. Perhaps the most objective statement that can be made is that Zionism represents the dominant ideology of the state of Israel and even so innocuous a description is not without caveat and qualification.

The intention of this book, however, is neither to directly study Zionism nor the polemics that surround it, so much as to study the thought of those Israelis who have expressed radical political dissent. To be sure, such dissent is aimed at the political and social institutions of Israeli life as well as at the diplomatic and military stances of its leadership. Yet, because Zionism is the principle and rationale for much that occurs within Israeli officialdom and is indeed the stated raison d'être of the state, most dissent focuses upon it, using the ideology as a context for protest.

Generally speaking, radicalism in Israel is defined by its alienation from the Zionist mainstream. Given the brief history of Israeli politics, such radicalism is not common. Political life there, while often volatile and fiery, has generally remained within recognized bounds. Protest has been limited and rarely gained the consistent support of any specific sectors of the population. This is largely because of particular ideological imperatives peculiar to Zionism (to be discussed below), as well as institutional ele-

10

ments inherent in Israeli life (to be discussed in the following chapter). Consequently, any study of dissent in Israel must be preceded by a discussion of the Zionist idea which serves as its ideological context.

Choosing a starting point for the Zionist movement is no mean feat. One is well obliged to glance at the yearnings of exiled Jews after the successive destructions of their homeland by Babylonians, Greeks, Syrians, and Romans, which date to early Biblical times. Jewish communities flourished in the Diaspora some six hundred years before the common era and the Jewish homeland as an independent political entity was finally eliminated by the Roman legions in the wars of 70 and the revolt of Bar Kochba in 135 C.E. (common era). To a certain extent, Zionism is over 2,000 years old.

Though often used as a polemic instrument, this claim should not be taken lightly. If Zionism represents a national ideology, then it operated as a reflection of communal will long before the modern era. Jews in far-flung regions of the world prayed daily for the restoration of Jerusalem and the return to the land of glory. Though dispersed throughout Christian Europe, Moslem North Africa, the Middle East, and Asia, they shared common longings and liturgy that constantly reminded them of their obligations to "the land of our fathers."

Equally, though the Holy Land changed hands many times during these millenia, some Jewish presence always existed to keep alive the memories of earlier days. Impoverished communities of scholars and the pious—some in Jerusalem, more in the Galilee—prayed for the Redemption that would surely be at hand and hoped to be near the Temple Mount in Jerusalem at the triumphal arrival of the Messiah. These faithful were occasionally joined by cognate spirits from Europe and the Middle East, particularly with the fall of Muslim Spain and the onset of the Inquisition. To speak of Zionism but to ignore the moving words of Halevi and Nachmanides or the mystical yearnings of Karo and the Luria-Alkabets families is to assume a very simplistic approach to the issue.

Nevertheless, Zionism as a modern political movement had its genesis in the great movements of national liberation and unification at the end of the nineteenth century. It was then that it assumed its secular thrust and moved from the realm of the liturgical to the world of the actual. Rather than pray for the return to Zion, the modern political Zionist proposed to do something about it, to hurry the Messiah along, as it were.

At first, we can see that Zionist activism assumed two forms, the polemic and the pioneering. The former organized bodies, conferences, and congresses, making representations to the various nobility of Europe and collecting funds to run their operations and subsidize emigration to

Palestine. The latter were those who undertook the arduous journey to a barren and hostile land that seemed anything but "promised." By no means is it easy to label the Zionists of that day, however, as many of the organizers also intended to or actually did emigrate while many of the settlers were also active organizers and fund raisers.[1]

Migration to the Holy Land was obviously prerequisite to its reestablishment and consequently was a main goal of Zionist activism. These migrations occurred according to certain outside influences—in addition to motivations of ideology—and are thus divided into periods of migration or aliyot. The first aliyah includes that portion of the Jewish population to relocate in Palestine during the latter part of the nineteenth century until, roughly, 1905. The earliest settlements included Petah Tiqvah in 1878 (although discontinued and moved elsewhere because of malarial epidemic), Yesod Hamaaleh in 1883, and Mishmar Hayarden in 1884.

Another means by which one might differentiate Zionist leadership and the thought it represented is by the country of its origin, most specifically whether it was West European and American or East European. Generally accepted as the father of Zionism, Theodore Herzl best represented the former. Educated and literate, his identifications with Judaism were tenuous at best and he had little understanding of the mentality or motivations of his East European brethren. Moved more by the Dreyfus affair and the resurgence of anti-Semitism in France and Germany, Herzl viewed a Jewish homeland in highly rational terms.

It was his belief that the cause of Jew hatred stemmed from the innate jealousy that existed between the dominant culture and its Jewish minority. Lacking a place of refuge or a homeland of their own, Jews were left to the mercy of their "hosts" with no means of self-defense other than accommodation to their demands, no matter how repressive and cruel they may be. Remove Jews from Europe and one will have removed anti-Semitism as well. Imbued with the spirit of enlightened liberalism, Herzl further believed that one need only convince the world (both Jewish and non-Jewish) of the justice and rationality of his scheme in order that it might rush to his side in support.

Naive though he may seem in retrospect, Herzl did succeed in organizing a World Zionist Congress in 1897, at which time he was confronted with the full force of East European sentiment, a force with which he had not reckoned. To these activists, rebuilding Zion was a holy, indeed messianic task, though their rhetoric and approach was a good deal more secular. Coming from the ghettos of the czar, they were far more in touch with Jewish tradition and spoke with authority of the millenia of longing. A

Jewish homeland, for them, was more than a rational solution to a problem imposed by the gentile world; it was the fulfillment of an age-old dream. Herzl's assertions that Palestine need not be the place where this dream was actualized, but that Uganda or the Argentine might do as well, were scandalous in their eyes.

The East European contingent was led by the scholar and essayist Asher Zvi Ginsburg who wrote under the pen name "Ahad Ha'am" (one of the folk). To him the Jewish homeland would be not a refuge but a show place, and far more than merely a political renaissance. Included, he argued, must be a cultural and humanistic rebirth to link this new entity with the great Jewish commonwealths of the past. To create just another state, modeled on the culture of Western Europe, would be a sacrilege and merely reflected the extent to which Herzl and his kind were alienated from their Jewish roots.

The theoretical debate between the followers of Herzl and those of Ginsburg was never resolved so much as mooted. With the onset of the second aliyah (about 1905), a new form of Zionist settlement became prominent in Palestine. Born in Eastern Europe, it carried forth the traditional elements that belied its proximity to centuries of Jewish oppression. Yet it also displayed a set of influences that were more contemporary and secular. The leadership of the second aliyah consummated a marriage of Jewish nationalism with radical socialism.

In practice this implied the abandonment of bourgeois living for the life of the laborer and agriculturist. A free and communal life style was introduced in which cooperative achievement and the elimination of private ownership were emphasized. Under the influence of these settlers, the first kibbutzim were established and sociopolitical patterns set which would mold the life of the future state. Successive migrations during and immediaterly after World War I would strain to fit the socialist-Zionist mold and much of the political leadership to this day is either of the second aliyah or cut in its image.

In addition, many of the major political institutions of Israeli society were organized under the tutelage of these settlers and will always bear their mark. The Histadrut, Israel's massive labor union, as well as most of the political parties, were founded during this period. Their structures indicate the strong and often conflicting impacts of Zionism—a nationalist ideology with elements of Jewish tradition and messianism—and radical socalism. It may be interesting to note, in this regard, that most of Israel's political structures were already in existence well before the founding of the state. Its leadership cadres were gaining valuable political experience within the councils of the respective parties, the Histadrut, and the ubiquitous Jewish Agency, the shadow government of the Jewish population in pre-1948 Palestine.

While the functions and operations of these institutions will be discussed in the following chapter, it is necessary to mention the influence of one more aspect of European Jewish life on the development of political Zionism, that of organized religion. The debt political Zionism owes to Jewish tradition and biblical sources has been already noted. It must be understood, however, that the bulk of Zionist leadership was by no means of orthodox demeanor. Quite the contrary, they were primarily secularists whose sentiments were often antireligious.

Nevertheless, Zionist feelings made inroads within the religious camp as well. Traditional rabbis such as Kalischer and Alkali predated Herzl in their calls for settlement in the Holy Land. Several religious sages joined the East European camp of the secularists, which soon came to call itself Hovivei Zion (Lovers of Zion). However, the full union of nineteenth century Orthodox Jewish life with Zionist nationalism was effected by the creation of the Mizrahi Party at the Vilna Convention of 1902.

The prime movers of this party were Rabbi Isaac Reines and his younger colleagues, Meir Berlin and Y.L. Fishman. The essential philosophy of the movement was that the restoration of Zion was a religious duty and a holy task. To deny this labor was to ignore the many exhortations to love and defend the land of Israel. Further, there was no reason why one had to wait for the Messiah, but rather he might be hurried along by the efforts of mere mortals. More practically, there existed a fear that should there be no presence of Orthodoxy within the ranks of the Zionist movement, the new nation might be left entirely to the administration of freethinkers.

Mizrahi created many structures similar to those organized by secular Zionist groups, but they remained under Orthodox jurisdiction. These included a formal political party, strictly religious suburban and agricultural settlements, banks, and youth movements. Indeed, Mizrahi suffered an internal rift over the question of socialist influence within Zionist ranks. The parent body opposed the shift to the left, arguing that it was both unwise and un-Jewish. A young workers' wing supported greater emphasis on labor and established its own cooperative communities and kibbutzim to show that one might be strictly Orthodox and adhere to socialist economic principles.

Yet the acceptance of Zionism was by no means universal among European Jewry's religious leaders. Many were ambivalent at best, while others hotly opposed the entire national enterprise. Arguing that redemption was a divine prerogative, the attempt to create a national homeland prematurely was usurpation of the highest order and deserving of severe punishment Further, should the divine redemption occur, it would be led by the strictly traditional communal leadership, not by a group of non-observant, secular, and assimilated Jews—as many Zionist leaders were perceived.

This perspective pervaded the bodies of rabbinic leadership throughout Eastern Europe's Hassidic communities, as well as the non-Hassidic Agudah movement in Lithuania and Germany. It was also characteristic of the thinking of many in Palestine's older Jewish communities, whose presence, particularly in Jerusalem, predated the Zionist settlements of the late nineteenth and early twentieth centures. Aside from the contempt with which they held these socialist radicals, the Orthodox communities of Palestine often looked upon the new settlers as competitors for the meager charitable support coming from European Jewish sources. While this type of opposition still exists in certain sectors (to be discussed later), it is held by only a minority of Jewry's Orthodox today.

Finally, it is impossible to exaggerate the importance of the holocaust as an influence in the emigration to and formation of latter-day Zionism and the state of Israel. The fifth aliyah (ca. 1931–38) was comprised of refugees from Nazi terror in Austria and Germany. Indeed, in many senses, these emigrants were not running to, so much as running from, and their ties to the ideology and structure of political Zionism were negligible. Equally, this was largely a middle-class and professional population to whom socialism had little appeal. They consequently settled in the cities, continuing bourgeois life styles similar to those they knew in Europe.

The enormous extent of Jewish suffering during Hitler's rule of Germany is too familiar to be repeated here. Aside from the liquidation of fully one-third of the world's Jewish population, the holocaust had severe social and cultural effects on the quality of Jewish life all over. The European Jewish community which was destroyed was one of the most productive and prolific of any national entity the world had seen. In all fields of endeavor—medicine, philosophy, the arts, theology, and the sciences—Jews in Europe had been exemplary. Suffice it to say that from this community stemmed such luminaries as Heine, Marx, Freud, Einstein, and Buber.

It is crucial here to realize that the holocaust radically affected the nature and thrust of the Zionist movement. No longer was the issue one of ideological debate or pioneering settlement. The very survival of the world's Jewish community was at stake. To a large extent, emigration to Palestine was the final choice for millions of East European Jews and illegal activity as well as diplomatic maneuvering assumed a tragically frantic pace. Parenthetically, it may be added that, given the strict limitations on Jewish immigration imposed by the British Mandatory power, it was often difficult for Palestinian Jews to determine who the real enemy was, the Germans or the English.

These, then, were the major influences in the structure of Zionist thought and the birth of the Israeli state. Founded on the contradictory bases of West European liberal nationalism and East European Jewish tradionalism, the movement was soon engulfed by socialist thought of several shades. Equally, the events of 1933–45 seemed to confirm all that earlier Zionists feared: the danger of Jewish existence being dependent upon the good will of the dominant gentile culture. It was in the shadow of this natonal catastrophe that the state was established and its influence has been felt in the character and mentality of its people.

WORLD VIEW

As should be evident, Zionist thinking is by no means a monolith and this brief presentation of its highlights should be understood with this qualification in mind. Nevertheless, several traits, common to most Zionist thinkers, do emerge. It is upon these that we shall dwell.

Writing during the late nineteenth and early twentieth century, one theme that occupies most pioneers of Jewish nationalism is the precarious position of Jewish life in Europe. Much hope had been placed on the emancipation of European Jews in the wake of the French Revolution and the growing influence of liberalism, particularly in France, England, and Germany. Nevertheless, the Dreyfus affair and the growing influence of anti-Semitism in German politics of the late nineteenth century gave the lie to these highly touted ideals.

This evaluation weighed heavily on the minds of early Zionists.

> Wherever they live in appreciable numbers, Jews are persecuted in greater or lesser measure. Their equality before the law, granted by statute, has become practically a dead letter. They are debarred from filling even moderately high offices in the army or in any public or private institutions. . . . In Russia special taxes are levied on Jewish villages; in Rumania a few persons are put to death; in Germany they get a good beating occasionally; in Austria, anti-Semites exercise their terrorism over all public life.[2]

The natural response was a radical rejection of the culture and environment within which the Jew was forced to live. This might result in responses other than Zionist, however. It is well known that for many the persecutions of Europe led to emigration to America. It is estimated that between 1880 and 1920 some two million European Jews reached the shores of the United States. For others, change was indeed necessary, but their overt ties to the lands of their birth and rejection of all things Jewish led to participation in the myriad radical movements of Eastern and Central Europe. Thus, they were to be found in the forefront of the abortive Russian Revolution of 1905 as well as its successful offspring of 1917. Jews had always lived under adverse conditions and those of eighteenth century Europe were not sufficient to foster a renewed sense of nationalism.

One more aspect had to be added to the Zionist world view, therefore. It was necessary to argue that despite the years of exile, travail, and misfortune, despite the dispersions and destructions, the Jews were still one people. Further, they were still essentially the one people that they had been some two thousand years earlier when first forced to leave their homeland. Despite the secular rationalism that was current among most Zionist leaders, this bit of romantic mysticism served as an important ideological component.

> We are a people—one people. We have sincerely tried everywhere to merge with the national communities in which we live, seeking only to preserve the faith of our fathers. It is not permitted us. . . . In our native lands where we have lived for centuries we are still decried as aliens, often by men whose ancestors had not yet come at a time when Jewish sighs had long been heard in the country. . . . We are one people—our enemies have made us one whether we will it or not, as has repeatedly happened in history. Affliction binds us together and thus united, we suddenly discover our strength.[3]

Thus while not willing to accept a racial epithet for the Jewish people, Zionism nevertheless requires that they be identified as a single entity— avoiding the perplexing problem of precisely describing that entity. The Jews are a people, inexorably united despite and perhaps because of nineteen centuries of anguish, prejudice, and disability. To think of their eventual assimilation into an alien national culture—whether it be in a Western capitalist state or a European socialist one—flies in the face of reality, not to mention the lessons of history. The only answer is the unification of these people (or as many of them who care to "return") within the confines of a state of their own. They might thus be finally liberated and allowed to "normalize."

They were still, indeed, kindred to their ancestors with national yearnings, much the same as their predecessors. There is only one land that might satisfy the long-held hopes and desires.

> Whether it is our misfortune or whether it is good fortune, we have
> never forgotten Palestine and this steadfastness which has preserved
> the Jew throughout the ages and throughout a career that is almost one
> long chain of inhuman suffering is primarily due to some physiological
> or psychological attachment to Palestine. We have never forgotten it
> nor given it up. . . . And whenever they got a chance, the slightest
> chance, there the Jews returned, there they created their literature,
> their villages, towns and communities.[4]

It should be recalled that the unquestioned demand for Palestine as
fulfillment of the Jewish dream was not always universal. In Herzl's early
writings, he considers the possibility of similar fulfillment in Argentina and
the British territory of Uganda. The key here was the development of a
Jewish homeland so as to remove them from the environs that had spawned
anti-Semitism. The specific locale of that homeland was not always important.

This concern was often the cutting edge between Zionists of East and
West Europe as well as those of religious or secular demeanor. The nature
of the relationship between the Jew and his intended homeland was incorporated into the Zionist world view. The essential question is whether
the movement shall remain a rational approach to solving the Jewish
problem in Europe or whether there was a positive claim to the promised
land. For many, this claim was more than merely a collective memory. In
its most extreme religio-mystic manifestation

> Eretz Israel is not something apart from the soul of the Jewish People; it
> is no mere national possession, serving as the means of unifying our
> people and buttressing its material or even its spiritual survival. Eretz
> Israel is part of the very essence of our nationhood; it is bound organi-
> cally to its very life and inner being. Human reason, even at its most
> sublime, cannot begin to understand the unique holiness of Eretz Israel;
> it cannot stir the depths of the love for the land that are dormant within
> our people. . . . Jewish original creativity, whether in the realm of ideas
> or in the area of daily life and action, is impossible except in Eretz
> Israel.[5]

Thus there is an inexplicable tie between the Jew and his land that the
centuries have not erased. The Zionist move is not one that merely strives
to eliminate anti-Semitism by means of removing the Jew from the sight and
mind of the Gentile. It is rather a positive means toward a recognized end,
the reestablishment of the Jew in the land that nurtured him and his culture.
Whatever are his accomplishments in the dispersion, they pale by compari-

son to his potential within his homeland. Further, consciously or unconsciously, the love and desire to return burns brightly within him. Needless to say, not all Jews, nor even all Zionists agreed with this evaluation of Jewish life.

Finally, a basic component of Zionism is the result of the influence of radical socialism and Bolshevism, especially in the minds of the Eastern European contingent. Following the Marxist lead, blame for the precarious and generally penurious condition of European Jewry was placed upon the rise of capitalism and the irrational competition between those of the working masses. Rather than seek out the Jews as their natural allies, the oppressed proletariat was placed in a position of conflict with them and forced to see them as rivals for a limited number of jobs.

Further, because of historical circumstances—generally not of his own doing—the Jew has been alienated from the land as well as those industries that are at the center of production. Instead, he was relegated to labor at the periphery of economic life in such secondary trades as the needle and tobacco industries. In this sense, the Jew has been separated from "nature" and will not fulfill the significant historical role that is within his potential.

> The moral of this story told by dry statistics is, that as long as the Jewish People remains remote from nature and basic industry, Jewish economic life will remain stagnant, Jewish culture will be at a low ebb, and the political welfare of the Jews will remain a plaything of chance. These figures force upon us the conclusion that in international Socialism, the class struggle and the revolution, the part played by Jewish socialism will be as significant as the Jewish needle and flatiron are when compared to the non-Jewish tractor, locomotive or steamship. Such is the chronic malady of Jewish history.[6]

From all perspectives, then, Jewish weakness is a function of the secondary and dependent role that Jews play in gentile society. Whether for rational, socialist, liberal, or religious reasons, it is proper that Jews seek their own emancipation so that the malady of anti-Semitism be finally eliminated. In general, this national liberation is directed toward Palestine.

VALUES AND GOALS

Quite clearly, the primary and all-embracing goal of the Zionist movement prior to 1948 and its successors after 1948 is the establishment and reinforcement of an independent Jewish state. Only with a national entity will the Jew be safe from the attack and control of the gentile enemy. Only in a state of his own will the Jew begin to resume a normal life style, master of his own destiny and beholden to no one. Only within the bounds of his own land will the Jew resume his touch with nature, assuming positions of influence as well as a significant role within industries of consequence. Finally, only in a Jewish homeland will Judaic religion and culture fulfill its historic mission as both a national creed and a universal "light unto the nations."

This deceptively simple concept, the re-creation of a Jewish common-wealth, was by no means universally defined. It is not entirely clear whether all Zionists anticipated a fully independent Jewish state with its own political, military, and diplomatic apparatus. Many in the earlier period might well have been satisfied with a national refuge, ruled by some foreign power, with varying degrees of autonomy given to Jewish authori-ties over local and internal matters. Indeed, little more than this was promised by the British in the much heralded Balfour Declaration of 1917. From that time until the founding of the state, the Jewish settlement operated on the basis of considerable domestic independence within the context of the British Mandatory Power.

With the onset of World War II, however, it became increasingly evident that such a state of affairs was ultimately unsatisfactory, especially in light of the infamous White Paper of 1939. Issued in the wake of Arab nationalist upheavals during the late 1930s, the British limited therein the Jewish right to emigration from Europe to Palestine and the ultimate size and property of the Jewish population of Palestine during the next decade. With Europe becoming a Jewish graveyard, such limitation was obviously unacceptable. Only an independent national entity, with authority over such crucial matters as the number of immigrating Jews, could solve the impending doom of European Jewry.

The demand for a Jewish commonwealth rested upon two vital props. The first was the ultimate negation of the Diaspora, the galut. Thus, while immediate emigration to Palestine was not always an acceptable goal (particularly in such states as America, where Jews had attained a fair degree of prosperity and freedom) nevertheless, Zionism required ac-ceptance of the proposition that Jewish life in the dispersion was bent on ultimate disintegration and secular assimilation.

Such negation took several forms. For some it represented intellectual and spiritual matters. Prevented from full participation in the cultural life of their native lands, Jews could never fulfill their potential in the academic and professional world. An era of discovery was passing them by because of the irrational disabilities under which they were forced to operate.

Similarly, their religious and spiritual growth had been arrested and deformed because of the need to accommodate to an unnatural state of social and cultural dependence.

For others in Eastern and Central Europe, the negation of Diaspora life took a more immediate and chronic form. They suffered not only intellectual and religious inconvenience, but also physical and economic distress. For them the goal of statehood represented liberation from the passions of the mob and from official government policies of discrimination and oppression. In Eastern and Central Europe, the Zionists were more likely to take the plunge that emigration to Palestine represented. They simply had less to lose.

Parallel to this ideological prop was the prophetic message which demanded the "ingathering of the exiles." The messianic era has been traditionally defined as one in which Jews would return from the lands of their dispersion and gather once more to live the primeval existence in the land of their birth. Indeed, traditional Jews pray daily that the Lord

> bring us home in peace from the four corners of the earth, and make us walk upright to our land. . . . Sound the great trumpet for our freedom; lift up the banner to bring our exiles together, and assemble us from the four corners of the earth. Blessed are Thou O Lord, who gathers the dispersed of thy people Israel.

Here was an arena in which the religious and secular among Zionist theorists could agree. Whether conscious or dormant, much of the Zionist goal was messianic. The causal factors were not identical, but Zionists of all stripes who advocated a rebuilding of Zion hypothesized the movement of many Jews to their own land, fulfilling an ancient prophecy.[7]

While most agreed upon the overall goal of a national enterprise, however, considerable disagreement ensued over the nature and form that such a state should take. For those whose primary interests were the removal of Jews from the control of unsympathetic gentile authorities, such considerations were secondary, if not altogether irrelevant. Allow Jewish autonomy over an area of their own and nature will inevitably take its course with little planning or anticipation needed.

Such a perspective was common among those who saw the Jewish problem in essentially negative terms. Thus:

> The whole plan is essentially quite simple, as it must necessarily be if it is to be comprehensible to all. Let sovereignty be granted us over a portion of the globe adequate to meet our rightful national requirements; we will attend to the rest. To create a new state is neither

ridiculous nor impossible. . . . The governments of all countries scourged by anti-semitism will be keenly interested in obtaining sovereignty for us.[8]

Similarly, Zionists in the United States tread softly on the area of Jewish identification with a foreign sovereignty, for two related reasons. In order to gain respectability among American Jews who were just becoming comfortable with their new-found status as free citizens, no full-scale negation of the bounties of this new Diaspora could be made. Equally, despite Jewish patriotism and participation in American war efforts, the charge of dual loyalty and cosmopolitanism was never far from the surface. Consequently, the society contemplated in Palestine had to be one of free and democratic structures to which those Jews who so desired might emigrate.

Therefore it was necessary to emphasize that Zionism

is not a movement to remove all Jews of the world compulsorily to Palestine. It is essentially a movement to give to the Jew more, not less freedom; it aims to enable the Jews to exercize the same right now exercized by practically every other people in the world: to live at their option either in the land of their fathers or in some other country. . . . [Zionists] believe that only in Palestine can Jewish life be fully protected from the forces of disintegration; that there alone can the Jewish spirit reach its full and natural development.[9]

Significantly, however, a powerful strain of East European Zionism took note that there was more to the Jewish national renaissance than merely the development of a state operated by or for Jewish people. Rather, a Jewish state could only earn its title by being a great center of Jewish culture and learning. It was neither possible nor preferable to transfer the masses of European Jewry to the new state if they sought only alleviation of their physical and material ills. They would find little solace in the wilderness of Palestine and would likely add little to the great cultural rebirth that was contemplated. More than the liberation and emancipation of the Jew, this strain of Zionism looked toward the liberation of Judaism. All else was petty nationalism and little more than the outgrowth of nineteenth century European culture.

In this sense, even a formal national entity is unnecessary and inadvisable. In any event, the negation of the Diaspora as a central goal is erroneous. Thus:

For this purpose Judaism can for the present content itself with little. It does not need an independent state but only the creation in its native land of conditions favorable to its development: a good sized settlement of Jews working without hindrance in every branch of civilization. . . . Then from this center, the spirit of Judaism will radiate to the great circumference, to all the communities of the diaspora to inspire them with new life and preserve the over-all unity of our people.

With such a development as an immediate goal, it was assured that eventually the level of culture and society would develop the inevitable structures for the formation of a political state. Such a state would be "not merely a State of Jews but a really Jewish State."[10]

The goals of Zionism are at once clear and unified, yet vague and debatable. Among its leaders there was little question of the need for a homeland and ultimately for a state for the purposes of physical survival. Yet the quality and nature of that enterprise and indeed whether that should be a topic of discussion at all was a most lively issue. The forces of history, however, pushed a good part of the debate into the background. The nature of Jewish survival took second place to the survival of the Jew.

STRATEGIES FOR SOCIAL CHANGE

In many ways it is difficult to differentiate clearly between the overriding goals of the Zionist movement and its tactical program for their accomplishment. The establishment of a Jewish state and its secure continuation have always been of transcending value, yet in many ways it was seen as essentially a means of the greater end of ameliorating the tragic situation of Jews throughout the world. The renewal of a Jewish commonwealth, as has been shown, was viewed by some to be secondary to the nature of Jewish society to be created there. Finally, the goal of a homeland often took second place to the need for refuge. It may well be that had realistic options been available to refugees just prior to and during World War II, the impetus for emigration and the ultimate establishment of a Jewish state might not have arisen.

For those of a socialist bent, Zionism, in the sense of the restoration of a Jewish political entity, was both goal and strategy. Parallel was the similar goal-strategy of the class struggle and the restoration to the Jew of a direct contact with the vital means of production. Only thus would the Jewish enterprise enter the flow of history as defined by Marxian theory and indeed lead the march to internationalism. Short of this, the Jewish state would be little more than one more bourgeois nation-state.

By the same token, socialism was a strategy for the successful development of a characteristically Jewish society in which justice would prevail and oppression be eliminated. It is difficult to decide which goal took precedence and which was seen as means to an end. Hence:

> It seems very clear: From now on our principal ideal must be Labor. Through no fault of our own we have been deprived of this element and we must seek a remedy. Labor is our cure. The ideal of Labor must become the pivot of all our aspirations. It is the foundation upon which our national structure is to be erected. . . . We need a new spirit for our national renaissance. That new spirit must be created here in Palestine and must be nourished by our life in Palestine. It must be vital in all its aspects and it must be all our own. What we need is zealots of Labor—zealots in the finest sense of the word.[11]

For most, however, the concept of Jewish statehood was primary and strategies were introduced to bring about that eventuality as smoothly and efficiently as possible. Yet, here too there was considerable debate. Little consensus existed over such issues as emigration versus political autonomy, diplomacy versus self-help, and centralization versus independent action. Equally, much disagreement ensued over the wisdom of a Jewish military corps in Palestine, the relationship with Arab settlers there, and the extent of socialist, religious, and Western Jewish influence. Thus, while a major goal was fairly clearly defined, its means was much the subject of lively discussion.

In addition, one might spot the inherent differences in approach between those of Eastern and Western Europe. The former were more given to calls for self-help and far less confident in the actions of organized political or diplomatic bodies. The latter, despite protestations to the contrary, were imbued with the spirit of constitutionalism and liberalism. Present cogent and irrefutable arguments before the forums of the world and its leaders would inevitably follow.

This Western perspective was most noticeable in the writings of Herzl. Thus, on the question of what ought to take precedence, immigration and colonization or a formal grant of autonomy by a European power, Herzl opted for the latter by means of a Society of Jews contracting for the whole of the Jewish nation. Thus:

> Infiltration is bound to end badly. For there comes the inevitable moment when the government in question, under pressure of the native populace—which feels threatened—puts a stop to further influx of Jews. Immigration, therefore, is futile unless it is based upon our guaranteed autonomy. The Society of Jews will treat with the present

authorities in the land under the sponsorship of the European Powers, if they prove friendly to the plan.[12]

Nevertheless, these words were not generally heeded. To the contrary, emphasis was largely placed upon the emigration of European Jews to Palestine in various forms of agricultural enterprises. For many (especially those of the second aliyah), migration to Palestine was the fulfillment of a Zionist dream. For others—such as those of the last aliyot prior to World War II—it was out of dire physical necessity. In any event, Herzl's words proved almost prophetic. A Society of Jews was created, under the title of the Jewish Agency, which operated as a spokesman for the Jewish settlement in Palestine and for its shadow government. As well, feeling threatened by the influx of Jews to Palestine, the local Arab leadership pressed for the promulgation of the British White Paper in 1939, which limited Jewish migration severely.

It is interesting to note that the perception of a society that speaks for and acts on behalf of world Jewry outlived even the movement to found a Jewish state. With the creation of Israel, the Jewish Agency did not cease to exist but ultimately became a quasi-official organization which serves as fund-raiser, agent, and representative of the state to the Jews of the Diaspora. Its influence will be discussed in the coming chapter.

The state, as well, has strained to present itself as the protector of Jewish rights throughout the world and the rightful legacy of those who have been cruelly treated and brutally exterminated in the past. This has been reflected in government policy, such as the acceptance of reparation payments from West Germany and the year-long trial of Nazi war criminal Adolf Eichmann. It remains a major factor in Israeli foreign policy to the present.[13]

Finally, a good part of the strategy to bring about a secure and autonomous Jewish homeland derives from the philosophy of self-help. Indeed, this may be seen as a natural outgrowth of the Zionist creed. Based in large measure upon a disparaging view of Jewish life under the influence of foreign powers and rooted in the desire to recreate the Jewish commonwealth, it is only natural that independent action and self-initiated policy should be a major tactic. Too long has the Jewish minority in any given land reacted to official government decree and the passion of the mob. Too long has the Jew waited for the sympathies and pathetic good will of the gentile who dominates his life. Creating a Jewish national enterprise requires creating a new Jewish personality.

It was this perspective that reflected a certain restless quality within the movement and ultimately spawned a mentality that was fertile ground for terrorism and militancy.

> From a political point of view, propaganda is less productive than action. Create facts and more facts—that is the cornerstone of political strategy. Facts are more convincing than phrases. . . . The same is true of Zionism. The practical colonization work in Palestine with its experiences, its sacrifices, its inevitable mistakes, has created these political facts which have paved the way for our present status. No matter how small and weak the Jewish colonies might be—no matter how great the shortcomings in their system of colonization—they did more towards enlightening the Jewish nation than a thousand beautifully-worded programs and diplomatic negotiations.[14]

Thus it is clear that even as the views and goals of the Zionist thinkers have varied, so too have their strategies. They have advocated peaceful means as well as aggressive ones. They have abided by the formal political and diplomatic rules of the game and they have bent them. The overriding interest appears to have been the perceived needs—spiritual and physical—of the Jewish people and their ultimate survival. Although the ideology perforce underwent change with the creation of the state, much that is said and done today bears the mark of the earlier pronouncements, either as motive or rationale.

Several points may be made by way of concluding this brief overview of Zionist ideology. In the first instance, it must be recalled that this chapter has dealt primarily with the thinking of Zionist leaders in the formative years of the movement, that is, before the creation of the State of Israel. The major overriding concern was the development of a territory which might serve as either homeland or refuge and almost all other concerns were subordinated to that.

It is not unreasonable to argue, however, that once the major goals of an ideology have been accomplished, its perspectives will be forced to change and accommodate new realities. Short of that, the ideology itself would expire, and with it the movement it spawned. For this reason, the changes in Zionist ideology with the creation of the state of Israel have been left for the next chapter. There, the major institutions of the Zionist state will be discussed, as well as the manner by which they fulfill many of the original goals and strategies propounded by the movement, or, indeed, counter them.

Equally, this point has become a major platform from which movements of dissent in Israel evolve. It is argued that since the major intention of the Zionist movement was the creation of an essentially Jewish state, Zionism as an ideology should have been laid to rest in 1948. Its continuation past its natural function relegates it to either a state religion, justifying the political actions of its leadership, or a vestige of the past. Further, the argument goes, its continuation merely hampers the rational actions of an otherwise typical political entity in the world arena. Such insights, however, will be presented at length in later sections of this work.

It is also evident that Zionism has never been a monolithic code. Its exponents and interpreters have come from all walks of Jewish life and have justified its goals for a myriad of sometimes mutually exclusive reasons. To some, Zionism represented little more than an alternative to the meager life style of the European Jew. Those who were satisfied with their homes would not be interested in migration and indeed opposed Zionism as a threat to their new found status in society. Those whose lives were indeed difficult might migrate to a Jewish homeland to start anew with few debilities.

For others, Zionism represented the fulfillment of an apocalyptic dream. The dream was either presented in religious or socialist terms: the "return to Zion" and the "ingathering of the exiles" on the one hand, the "conquest of labor" on the other. The new Jewish home was to be either a theocratic society or a workers paradise. In any case it was the Jewish incarnation of Eden in the modern world.

Further, there were those among Zionist leaders who had second thoughts about the wisdom of massive migrations to the ancestral homeland without regard to the nature of that settlement. Rather than a state of Jews, they were concerned to create a Jewish state, that is, a national form which would be peculiarly Jewish in its character and structure. Only in such a setting would Judaic culture blossom and fulfill its inherent potential. The movement, they argued, should support not merely the emancipation of Jews but the emancipation of Judaism.

It should be no surprise, therefore, that dissenting forms would later come to exist within the structures of the Jewish state, given the varying motivations and goals of the movement that spawned it. Indeed, the several groups which form the subject of this study carry much that is traceable to the contending strains of the Zionist movement. Thus among our subjects will be found those whose protest is based upon the strength of their socialist convictions as well as those who either attack or radically support Zionism from religious beliefs. Equally, dissent is based upon the needs and demands of ethnic groups who feel that their presence has been ignored because of the nature of Zionist ideology. Each will be explored in detail below.

Prior to such analysis, it remains to present a brief overview of the institutions and structures of the Israeli state. Only then will it be possible to understand the impact and direction of dissenting ideologies within the context of their protest. While the emphasis of this presentation will necessarily be placed upon the operations and direction of these official institutions, an attempt will also be made to outline their histories and missions. This follows in the next chapter.

NOTES

1. This brief discussion of the history of Zionism is based on the following sources: Walter Laquer, *A History of Zionism* (New York: Holt, Rinehart and Winston, 1972); *The Zionist Idea*, ed. Arthur Hertzberg (New York: Atheneum, 1975); and Howard M. Sachar, *A History of Israel* (New York: Alfred A. Knopf, 1976).

2. Theodor Herzl, "The Jewish State," in *Theodor Herzl: A Portrait for this Age*, ed. Ludwig Lewisohn (New York: World, 1955), p. 246.

3. Ibid., pp. 238, 251.

4. Chaim Weizmann, "Statement Before the Palestine Royal Commission: November 25, 1936," in *Chaim Weizmann*, ed. Meyer Weisgal (New York: Dial Press, 1944), p. 311.

5. Abraham Kook, "The Land of Israel," in *The Zionist Idea*, ed. Arthur Hertzberg (New York: Atheneum, 1975), pp. 419, 420.

6. Ber Borochov, *Nationalism and the Class Struggle* (New York: Young Poale Zion Alliance of America, 1937), p. 69.

7. Philip Birnbaum, ed., *Daily Prayer Book* (New York: Hebrew, 1949), pp. 76, 88. For an explication of this point, see Hertzberg, op. cit., pp. 80–100. It is interesting to note that Rabbi Kook assumed the position that those who worked for the rebuilding of Zion, no matter what their motivations or beliefs, were the instruments of the divine Redemption.

8. Herzl, op. cit., p. 212. It is not intended to imply that Herzl had no vision as to the nature and shape of a Jewish state. Rather, the form was quite secondary to the foundation of the state itself, in contradistinction to the thought of Ahad Ha'am, for example, as discussed below.

9. Louis Brandeis, "The Jewish Problem, How to Solve It," in *Brandeis on Zionism: A Collection of Addresses and Statements by Louis Brandeis* (Washington, D.C.: Zionist Organization of America, 1942), pp. 24–25.

10. Ahad Ha'am, "The Jewish State and the Jewish Problem," in *The Zionist Idea*, ed. Arthur Hertzberg (New York: Atheneum, 1975).

11. A.D. Gordon, "People and Labor," in *The Zionist Idea*, ed. Arthur Hertzberg (New York: Atheneum, 1975), p. 374.

12. Herzl, op. cit., p. 254.

13. For a good analysis of this point see Michael Brecher, "Images, Processes and Feedback in Foreign Policy: Israel's Decision on German Reparations," *The American Political Science Review* (March 1973), pp. 73–102.

14. Leo Pinsker, *Road to Freedom: Writings and Addresses by Leo Pinsker* (New York: Scopus, 1944), p. 91.

3

THE SOCIAL AND
POLITICAL ENVIRONMENT

The previous chapter outlined the development of Zionist thinking through the foundation of the state. It stopped there because a fundamental change took place perforce in 1948. The primary goal of the Zionist movement had been the creation of a Jewish state—its form, nature, and structure being subject to debate until that point. With the declaration of the state and its successful defense from attack by the Arab forces, Zionism as an ideology faced a crisis. It could either be laid to rest, its goal having been realized. Alternately, it could shift its focus and attempt to fulfill newer and more necessary functions.

In fact, it chose a form of the second path. Rather than atrophy, Zionism was transformed from a state-building ideology to the political orthodoxy of an established national enterprise. By so doing, its form was substantially changed. Many of the old arguments and factions decayed for lack of relevance. Others flourished and took on new meaning. Further, Zionism itself became much less a dynamic and in many ways turned into a catchall or justification for largely political or economic decisions.

Further, differences which had been muted in the name of state-building and military crisis were now allowed to come to the fore as legitimate outlets of official ideology. With the formation of the state, parties and factions were institutionalized within its political framework. Thus, differences of approach and personality would now be punctuated and perpetuated by their parliamentary inclusion. Inconsequential as these differences may have been at their inception, they now developed constituencies of their own and often begot still greater multiplicity after the creation of the state.

Such political and ideological strain was exacerbated by a major social event: the massive migrations of displaced persons from the liberated death camps of Europe and from the now unfriendly Arab lands of the Middle East and North Africa. The new arrivals were neither prepared for a pioneering life in a secular socialist state, nor particularly committed to any form of Zionist ideology. Assimilating these newcomers in the midst of war and the first stormy years of statehood put unusual strains on the institutions of the new state as well as on the doctrine of "ingathering the exiles." These strains are felt to this day.

As a result, the Israeli political system gives the appearance of instability. Its numerous factions and parties naturally led to the use of proportional representation (P.R.) even before the birth of the state. By offering the possibility of parliamentary inclusion to even the smallest faction, such an electoral system often institutionalizes political differences in itself. As a function of such a structure, no individual party has been able to garner a majority of votes, though prior to 1977, Mapai and its various alignments had won between 33 and 40 percent of the popular vote. As a result, successive governments have been carefully balanced coalitions, whose strength depends upon the negotiating skill of the partisan leadership. Similar procedures have contributed significantly to instability in France and Italy.

By consequence, countervailing trends had to develop to cement both the governmental and social fabric of the infant state. Considerable resources had to be expended to alleviate the problems caused by migrations so as to integrate new arrivals and acquaint many who had lived in far less developed polities. Equally important, a set of precedents and constitutional forms had to be devised in order to set recognized bounds to the nature and context of debate and opposition.

Interestingly, the many issues of procedure and definition that beset the state contributed to the decision not to promulgate a written constitution. Perhaps it was thought that wounds and confrontations were still too fresh to allow the type of negotiation that a written document might require. Rather, time would be the universal healer and major issues would pale with its passing. Apparently, sufficient time has not yet passed to allow the introduction of a written document. Indeed, the unwritten form has cultivated its own judicial and political adherents who probably would prevent its commitment to writing in any event. It should also be recalled that oral law has a long and honored position in Jewish culture and history.[1]

Thus, on the one hand, protest and dissent are built into the fabric of Israeli political, social, and institutional life. Nonetheless, structures exist to mitigate the power and dull the thrust of such strains. This chapter presents the historical and political development of the major institutions of Israeli government and society. Further, particular attention will be given to the impact of these respective institutions in the contribution to or blunting of contemporary dissent. Only then will the context of dissent be sufficiently clarified so as to allow an intensive presentation of the ideologies which have grown about it.

It should first be noted that several ideological elements have been emphasized in the post-1948 period, elements that play a role in terms of foreign as well as domestic policy perceptions. In the first instance, the conception of ingathering the exiles has been transformed. While still placing emphasis upon the desire for aliyah (immigration to Israel), it has not worked that way. Prior Zionist commitments notwithstanding, large numbers of Jews, especially from the West, have not migrated to Israel, and of those who have, significant proportions have returned. Yet more disturbing is the current spector of "yerida" (emigration of natives from Israel), all giving lie to this basic Zionist tenet.[2]

As a result, the thrust of this ideological component has shifted somewhat to include the quality of life in the Jewish state, as well as its relationship with Jews of the Diaspora. It has come to mean that there exists a mutual identification of all Jews, no matter what the extent of their dispersion or assimilation into their native societies. Further, despite apparent debilities or indifference, all Jews recognize their basic desire to "return" to their homeland at some point in the future and consequently must support the needs and demands of Israel. Finally, this component of contemporary Zionism has come to imply the belief that all Jews upon their arrival in Israel can and will live free and equal lives regardless of their prior status or disabilities. Factionalism and socioeconomic cleavages, therefore, have no place in the Jewish state.

Of equal importance is the Israeli perception of its external political situation. Embodied in the Hebrew phrase "ayn breira" (there is no alternative), it implies that while there may be a legitimate place for internal dissent and dissatisfaction, it must be voluntarily suppressed in the face of overwhelming diplomatic and military pressures exerted by the Arab world. Beset by a siege mentality—which may well be an accurate assessment of reality—there is little room in Israel for protest and faction outside the established mainstream.

JEWISH SELF-GOVERNMENT: 1920–1948

Unlike the political systems of most other new states, Israel's did not develop after its own foundation. Rather, most of the major political and social institutions of the Jewish national enterprise predated 1948. Virtually every aspect of governance—domestic, military, diplomatic, religious, or social—is either a direct continuation or an immediate successor to some structure established under the British Mandate or before. As a result, it has been argued that Israeli inclusion as a developing nation is deceptive because most of its public sector has been well developed for decades.

That these structures owe their precedent to the mandatory period does not mean that they necessarily trace their heritage or source to British tutelage or practice. Indeed, they were often established with begruding consent or despite the efforts of the mandatory power. Particularly in the post-World War II period, Jewish self-government was a bone in the throat of the British, who might have preferred a less sophisticated and well-accepted Jewish representation in world forums. Further, the final British pull out from Palestine may well have been intended as an impetus for disorder and civil war, in the hope that the United Nations would request an extension of the British administration as trustee.

Consequently, an outline of government and politics in Israel must begin with a brief discussion of the Jewish experience with self-government in the prestate period. As known, it was the British who wrested Palestine from the Ottoman Empire and occupied it at the end of World War I. In 1917, the famous Balfour Declaration was issued, in which the British Government indicated its interest in the creation of a Jewish homeland in Palestine. Though an independent state was not necessarily implied within this document, hopes soared for Zionists both inside and outside Palestine. Our discussion begins with this period, therefore.

With the decision to award the Palestine Mandate to Great Britain, the League of Nations directed the World Zionist Organization to serve as a Jewish Agency in securing the cooperation of Jews interested in supporting a national home, no matter what their present place of residence. In addition it was the role of this agency to cooperate with the British in the development and operation of the Jewish settlement in Palestine (the Yishuv). This proved to be a difficult task because of the overt political affiliations and sympathies of the Zionist organizations.

If the national enterprise was to be successful, it would have to call upon the considerable resources of all Jews, those who intended to migrate to Palestine as well as those whose future plans did not include such relocation. More pointedly, it was vital to call upon at least the financial and philanthrophic aid of Zionist and non-Zionist alike, particularly among affluent American Jews whose early response to Zionism was cool at best. A formal commitment to the Zionist organization would be distasteful to many.

As a result, numerous meetings and conferences were held during the first decade of British administration in order to seek a formula for the broadening and expansion of the Jewish Agency that would be acceptable to Zionist and non-Zionist alike. Such a proposal was tentatively sketched at the Zionist Congress of 1925 and approved by that same body at its 1929 meeting. At the outset, a rough equity was to exist between Zionist and non-Zionist members. It would be the task of the new Jewish Agency to handle the programs of immigration and settlement, redemption of public lands and their development as agricultural centers using Jewish labor and colonization, and the cultural and educational revival of Hebrew and Judaica in the Yishuv.

Nevertheless, the Zionist organization retained influence over vital aspects of development in Palestine and its relationship with the new Jewish Agency was never clearly outlined. Chaim Weizmann, later to become the new state's first president, moved from his position as head of the Zionist Organization to president of the Jewish Agency. While the latter assumed control of the Keren Hayesod (Fund for Foundation), the Jewish National Fund, the land reclamation and management agency, remained under the management of the Zionist Organization. Further, while the various departments of the Jewish Agency were to function as the administrative and diplomatic arms of the Yishuv, the proportional participation of non-Zionist elements was quickly reduced. By 1937 they constituted a small and largely unimportant minority within the agency.[3]

As its procedures developed, the Jewish Agency became the spokesman of the Yishuv to the world. Its political section operated as a virtual foreign ministry, while its immigration department bargained with the British for increased immigration quotas and was charged with the settlement and provision for these immigrants until the labor division could find them jobs. It is clear that while the thrust of these activities may have been aimed externally, their impact was also keenly felt in the domestic life of the Jewish community. In many ways, the Jewish Agency retained much of this impact even after the establishment of the state.

Yet a second institution was established to administer the more internal, day to day operations of the Yishuv. As early as 1918, arrangements for elections to a National Community Council were made, although religious opposition to extending suffrage to females slowed the progress of such elections. In addition, provisions were made for general, direct, secret balloting by proportional representation—a tradition that established the nature of electoral politics to this day. Candidates were to have a reading and writing knowledge of Hebrew and be residents of Palestine for at least twelve months, while a residency requirement of six months was imposed upon voters.

A 314 member assembly was elected, representing some 20 parties ranging from the economic Right to the socialist Left and from ultra-orthodox rabbinic leaders to freethinkers. Called Asefat Hanivharim (the Elected Assembly), it was to be the grand congress of the Yishuv, with taxing and legislative power. The Assembly elected its own National Council (Va'ad Leumi) whose 36 members were entrusted to execute the decisions of the general body and draft a constitution for its approval.

The Assembly was required to meet at least once each year and hold elections every three to six years. Between sessions, the National Council operated under delegated authority and an approved budget. The Council, in turn, assigned the administration of communal affairs to an executive body nominated and elected by the Council. Though these organs operated consistently from 1920, continued Orthodox opposition and a controversy with the British over taxing rights delayed British recognition until 1927 and prevented the full usage of taxing powers until 1932.

Thus the primary thrust of the Va'ad Leumi was domestic and its task was the smooth administration of the Jewish settlement in Palestine. Its powers complemented those of the Jewish Agency and their internal relations were in the main harmonious. Nevertheless, in time, the Jewish Agency and its leadership overshadowed the Council. Two reasons are immediately apparent for this development.

Firstly, the major personalities of the Jewish national movement involved themselves in the Jewish Agency and the Zionist Organization, perceiving these as the primary institutions within which the battle for statehood would be waged. While vital, the internal operation of the Yishuv may have been viewed as of secondary or at least less visible importance. Secondly, as events proceeded—particularly regarding the fate of European Jewry—the questions of immigration and settlement, the intransigence of the mandatory power, and the deterioration of relations with the Arab peoples became overriding issues, which often pushed domestic issues into the background. Herein may be seen a source for the general tendency of modern Israel to delegate secondary status to domestic social and economic policy.[4]

With the close of World War II and the full disclosure of the Nazi atrocities, the Jewish Agency increased its pressure externally for international support and stepped up its illegal immigration activities. The latter had been severely restricted by the British White Paper of 1939 and the incongruity of opposing the British in light of its anti-Nazi war effort. Operating in a more clandestine and militant manner, Jewish terrorist organizations performed individual acts of destruction and extremism, such as the bombing of the King David Hotel in Jerusalem. In any event it became increasingly clear to the British that the present status of its mandate was untenable and it petitioned the UN to find an equitable solution to the Palestine problem in 1947.

With the British withdrawal imminent, the Va'ad Leumi and the Jewish Agency's Executive Committee formed an emergency committee in October 1947. Under its auspices, a legal code and proposed constitution were drafted, a civil service roster was introduced, and increased recruitment for the military force was undertaken. An interim functional government was established in March 1948, in the midst of a burgeoning battle with Arab forces. Its executive council approved a provisional government, which took power with the declaration of the state in May.

This first official governmental form, however, was understood and intended to be provisional. Its main agencies were transfers of departments that had existed under the Va'ad Leumi, the Jewish Agency or the mandatory power. Thus, thirteen ministries were created, including labor, health, religious affairs, finance, trade, education, and culture, in addition to the usual departments of foreign and political affairs and defense. During the ensuing months of Arab-Jewish war, the national government was able to establish a Supreme Court, collect taxes, issue currency, and establish procedures for the election of a postwar Constituent Assembly. While conflicts existed between the various military establishments within the infant defense force, the authority of the provisional government was not questioned.

On January 25, 1949, national elections were held. Continuing the electoral traditions of the Zionist Organization and the elected Assembly, a system of proportional representation was utilized, whereby election to the new Parliament was according to party list rather than individual names. The size of this unicameral legislature was set at 120, the number traditionally attributed to the size of the Great Assembly (Knesset), which served as a judicial-legislative body in ancient Judea under the Biblical figures Ezra and Nehemiah. Twenty-one parties competed for these 120 Knesset seats, a plurality of 46 seats being awarded to Mapai, the centrist Labor Party which took 35.7 percent of the vote.

It was this party that was called upon to form a coalition government, an occurrence consistent in Israeli affairs until 1977. As the leader of Mapai, David Ben-Gurion reached agreement with the leadership of several smaller parties, including the Religious Front. One of the most important decisions made by this government, the outgrowth of long and protracted debate, was not to enact a formal written constitution. Instead, a Transition Law was promulgated in 1949 (known as the "small constitution"), which outlined the institutional context of future governments, while the actions of this first Knesset (Parliament) became the precedents for the evolution of the state of Israel.[5]

THE KNESSET

Understanding the institutional structure of Israeli politics requires a dicussion of its three primary elements. The first, which serves as the context for the other two, is Israel's Parliament or Knesset. The second is its leadership, the coalition government, which serves at its head, while the third is the complex party system from which Knesset members are elected and cabinet ministers are recruited. Though much actual power inheres in the role of the latter two, the Knesset is formally the ruling force in Israel.

This stems from several facts. In the first instance, the Knesset is patterned in many ways after the British Parliament. Its functions are broad and varied, ranging over domestic and foreign affairs. It confirms the government and selects Israel's president, a largely ceremonial position somewhat corresponding to the British monarchy. It passes on government policies and programs and levies taxes. Its control extends to most aspects of the economy and it is charged with the appropriation of monies for government operations.

Of similar importance is the fact that the Knesset is virtually unfettered and unrestricted in its actions. Since both the government and the president are its creations, they have no power for dissolution. Only the Knesset itself can vote to dissolve before the expiration of its formal term in office, which has been set at four years, through usage until 1958 and by legislation thereafter. Indeed this legislation is not absolute and may be superseded by a subsequent act of the Knesset.

By that same token, laws of the Knesset are not subject to the review or formal limitation of any other government body. Unlike the American practice of judicial consideration as to the constitutionality of legislation, the Israeli judiciary has no such power and must operate only within the legal framework of the legislature. This, of course, is complemented by the fact that Israel has no written constitution, as earlier mentioned. Thus, by function alone, the Knesset is Israel's supreme political body.

Internally, the Knesset has its own procedures, conventions, and division of labor. These too are set and evaluated by internal review. The chairman of the Knesset is its Speaker, who serves as the executor of these "house-keeping" functions, and as such wields considerable power. Though he does not participate actively in debate, it is he who rules on matters of protocol and propriety, delegating priorities as to speakers, alloting their time on the podium, and carrying out the Knesset's agenda.

While members may appeal the Speaker's ruling to a special Interpretations Committee, that group can only establish precedent but may not overrule the Speaker's past actions. In addition, the Speaker sits as a member of that committee and his power is thus further extended. It may be noted that part of the prestige adhering to the position of the Speaker is due to the personality and considerable talent of its first occupant, Joseph Shprinzak, who held the position from the foundation of the state until his death on January 28, 1959.[6]

As with other legislatures, the Knesset size of 120 members is too unwieldy for direct action to be taken by its full membership. Rather, the body is divided into several standing committees roughly equivalent to the various agencies and ministries of the government. By no means are these departments tied to the deliberations of the committees, yet the actions of the latter and their investigations weigh heavily on policy in both procedural and substantive terms. Committee hearings are held in secret and members may ask any information of the relevant ministers.

While a full discussion of each standing committee is beyond the province of this brief description, it is worthwhile to note the activities of the House Committee whose importance is so outstanding that it is known popularly as the "Small Knesset." Parallel roughly to both the Committees of Rules and Ways and Means in the U.S. Congress, the House Committee regulates the procedures of the Knesset and its other committees, as well as deciding which committee shall discuss new pieces of legislation. Because of the very sensitive position it holds, therefore, its membership has been expanded to 23 members—larger than the membership of any other—to include as broad a partisan representation as possible.

Finally, it should be noted that seniority is a major component of influence in parliamentary affairs in Israel. Positions of power are based on years of service and tenure in office. Similarly, placement on strategic commitees and influence within party caucuses depends upon such seniority as well. This has been a source of conflict. Younger members of Knesset have regularly attempted to press for greater influence and power. Much of this depends, however, on placement upon party lists, an issue to be discussed below. Thus, while the object of the conflict is partisan, the Knesset is the arena upon which the battle is played out.

THE CABINET

It appears that the Knesset is the supreme power in Israeli political life. Much of its influence is defrayed, however, through its delegation to the cabinet which serves as the focus for this power. As in other parliamentary regimes, the cabinet sets priorities, initiates both foreign and domestic policy, and is charged with final responsibility for implementation. Rather than act on its own, the Knesset at large and its various committees generally react to decisions made by the cabinet or by specific ministers within it. In this sense, Israel's prime minister, as head of government, has enormous influence. Though the state has a formal presidency, its most important function is the selection of a Knesset member to lead the next government, following an election.

In the past, this has been a rather automatic affair. One party has always won a clear plurality and its leader was charged with the mission of forming a cabinet. Until the 1977 elections, the moderate Labor Party (Mapai) served in this capacity and its leaders, David Ben-Gurion, Moshe Sharett, Levi Eshkol, Golda Meir, and Yitzhak Rabin have served as head of government. For the first time in Israel's history, however, Labor was reduced to opposition status in 1977, losing its plurality to Likud, the right-wing bloc whose leader, Menahem Begin, has now acceded to the prime ministry. Nevertheless, his choice as head of government as well was not a matter of discretion but rather a function of this partisan leadership.

Despite the hegemony of the Labor Party through 1977, however, never has any electoral bloc won a majority of seats in the Knesset. Consequently, all of Israel's governments have been comprised of carefully balanced coalitions. One party has always held a lion's share of the seats and therefore has commanded the majority of the government portfolios. Nevertheless, specific and often sensitive ministries have been apportioned to minority delegates as a price exacted for participation and cooperation. The best example of such ministerial maneuvering is the position of the National Religious Party, whose participation in governments since the formation of the state has been rewarded by a powerful hold on the departments of social welfare, religion, and the interior.

Given the hybrid nature of Israel's governments, collective responsibility has been difficult to enforce. Cabinet members are expected to support government policy both in Parliament and outside it, their personal or party positions notwithstanding. This principle has little legal or constitutional grounding, however, and the intensity of partisan loyalty has often made it difficult to strictly enforce. Indeed, the breach of collective responsibility was the formal reason given for the dissolution of the Rabin government during the winter of 1976–77, precipitating Labor's downfall in the spring elections. Several instances of a similar breach in the past resulted in merely mild rebukes or public statements so that despite lip service to the principle, its adherence has not been consistent or clear.[7]

It should be noted that there is no formally constituted number of ministries and many departments have been created or abolished as the need arose. In the early years of the state, for example, there existed ministries of minorities (to deal with internal Arab affairs) and war sufferers (to handle problems of liberated death camp survivors). These were ultimately eliminated, while the problems of development and immigration forced the establishment of ministries of development and information.

Through need and practice, however, certain ministries have greater political importance than others, either because of their strategic importance in Israeli affairs or because of the nature of the individuals who have held the positions. In particular, the Departments of Defense and Finance have played an extensive role in policy making with the Ministry of Foreign Affairs lagging somewhere behind. Thus, the Labor Party was always careful to hold these positions for their own members and it has not been uncommon for the prime minister to serve as minister of defense as well, a political ploy close to the heart of the late David Ben-Gurion. The 1977 cabinet, however, included Moshe Dayan as foreign minister, that is, a Laborite in a Likud-led government.[8]

Finally, it is important to note that much of the work of the cabinet is accomplished not on the individual ministry level but rather within the context of special ministerial committees. Though they do not have formal legal recognition, such committees have remained fairly constant and allow the organization of policy into broad issue areas. These are economic affairs, foreign affairs and security, domestic affairs, and services and legislation. While the committees are largely self-directing, they are subject to the supervision of the cabinet as a whole and a member always retains the right to bring issues and questions before the entire administration.

THE PARTY SYSTEM

As implied above, much of the flavor and thrust of political life in Israel is provided by the political parties. The current brand of democracy is much different from that of the United States or Britain but similar in many respects to the continental forms of France or Italy. Thus, there is a multitude of parties that vie for election by means of proportional representation. Voters do not choose individual candidates, but rather party labels which then provide members of Knesset according to the percentage of vote garnered. Conversely, party candidates do not represent specific constituencies or geographic entities, but rather draw from a national electorate. As such—with rare exception—they do not have definitive political personalities to the voters, apart from their party affiliation.

Such an electoral system has profound implications for party structure and organization. First, it means that Israeli parties are likely to be highly ideological, because voters make their choices not on the basis of candidate appeal but rather from party platforms. The latter, therefore, must have consistent meaning in order to sustain voter loyalty. By the same token, such parties are likely to be highly centralized, enforcing partisan ideology on all members and particularly on the parliamentary delegation. Since the individual politico depends upon the party for his position and future, he has little choice, generally, but to conform.

Thus on the one hand, it will appear that the Israeli system of proportional representation and party dominance may proliferate ideological conflict and increase the number of combatants on the political field. Individuals or groups with claims to dissent may be encouraged to take their grievances to the electorate rather than accommodate them to the programs of an existing party. Such action is often curtailed, however, by the fact that most Israeli parties are long-standing operations, predating the existence of the state itself. Partisan loyalty is deep and long lasting, with rather stable patterns of voter activity. Simply running a competing list is not a real alternative.[9]

There is a more tangible reason for voter and member loyalty to partisan affiliation. Unlike the American political party, Israeli parties offer significant material benefits to their members and can enforce conformity by threat of withholding them. In the words of one analyst, the parties of Israel

> are "total" not only in the sense of offering their adherents a program extending over a wide range of problems but also in the sense of attempting to influence the lives of their adherents . . . by direct action. By at once dispensing personal bounties and demanding constant allegiance expressed in the daily mode of living one might almost say they attempt to run the lives of their adherents.[10]

Consequently, much dissent or open factionalism is diffused or perforce, submerged.

Because of the importance of partisanship in the formation of coalitions and the overall making of policy, one's status within the party will largely determine official standing and position. Committee assignments, portfolios, diplomatic posts, and so on, depend generally upon partisan standing, which in turn is related to seniority. There has been a natural tension, as a result, between the younger members, often Israeli-born with military backgrounds, and the much older party regulars reared in Europe and trained in the pioneering days of the prestate period. Though the government has often been characterized by its considerable age and tenure in office, the inevitability of mortality has allowed younger partisans to come to the fore of late.[11]

While several smaller parties have won parliamentary inclusion— some of which will be the subject of later chapters—there have been four major partisan blocs: that of the Right, the center, the Left, and the religious communities. The dominant party until 1977 was Mapai, the Labor Party whose size, orientation, and position as coalition leader placed it in the center of the Israeli political spectrum despite its mildly socialist flavor. Until the last election, a coalition government in Israel was inconceivable without Mapai and national leadership, therefore, was recruited from the party's ranks. The direction of a new government was dependent upon the partner that Labor would seek in its new coalition.

The right-wing bloc, variously identified as revisionists, General Zionists, Liberals, Herut, and presently Likud, had ever been relegated to opposition status. Led by firebrand former revolutionary Menahem Begin, the bloc's ideological fervor would not allow it to negotiate to the degree coalition partnership required. In addition, lingering personal feuds and dislikes became institutionalized in the early period of the state, keeping the right out of Israeli government until its victory in 1977 and Begin's assumption of the premiership.

Mapai generally found the left more compatible as a coalition partner. Made up primarily of the Achdut Ha-avoda wing and the Mapam Party, its orientation was both Marxist and nationalist, with much emphasis upon the increasing role of the public sector in the economy and collective labor and agriculture modeled after the innovations of the kibbutz. This segment of the Israeli left, unlike its Communist colleagues, was quite proud of the role it had played in the building of the state, remains ever loyal to the government, and is proud of the role its sons have played as founders of the military officer corps.

Given the affinity for labor-socialism inherent in the ideologies of many of Mapai's leaders, it is no surprise that the party entered into coalitions with the forces of the nationalist left several times during the state's first three decades. Indeed, what with internal rifts among all the members of this left-wing conglomeration, new electoral lists were really often retreads of Mapai affiliates. The coalitions stemmed from the same souces and were of such similar nature that of late the entire bloc, including Mapai, simply referred to itself as the Labor Alignment, with little formal party distinction. It should be noted as well that in the dark days of spring 1967, even the right-wing opposition was called into coalition with the Labor Alignment to form a Government of National Unity, a partnership which was dissolved with the departure of the Right some two years later.

Finally, being a nation with an established faith, it is not surprising to find a religious bloc within the Parliament. In one form or another, this religious bloc has had some representation in most of Israel's governments. Flexible on international and economic issues, it has insisted upon exclusive control over such ritual questions as dietary laws, Sabbath closings, personal status as Jew or gentile, and questions of marriage and divorce. The senior coalition partners have generally been willing to concede these issues in return for the loyalty and amenability of the religious bloc. It is telling that the National Religious Party is also to be found in coalition with the 1977 Likud government. The religious establishment is examined in closer detail below and the implications of its position will be discussed in suceeding chapters.

QUASI-GOVERNMENTAL AGENCIES

In addition to the formal political institutions which comprise Israel's national government stand two important agencies whose status is somewhat removed from the official center but whose influence is highly significant nonetheless. These are the Histadrut, Israel's mammoth labor union, and the Jewish Agency, which serves as the state's representative to Jewish communities in the Diaspora. Both these structures are somewhat peculiar to Israel in that they predate the founding of the state, act with considerable independence from governmental direction and have discretion and initiative—a unique situation for such structures in modern politics.

The Histadrut is Israel's labor federation within which workers participate as members of their trade. The concept of labor is broad, however, so that many elsewhere considered professionals are included as well. This reflects the limited gap between occupational classes in official Israeli ideology. Established in 1920, the Histadrut provides many benefits traditionally assigned to labor federations. It influences official wage policy and represents its membership in labor disputes and negotiation. Indeed, it exceeds similar structures elsewhere in the far-reaching social and health services it offers, often making its members dependent upon its patronage and good will.

Yet the unique nature of the Histadrut as a trade union has more to do with its mission and economic activity. From the very outset, it has seen as its task to insure productive positions for members of the Jewish work force. Clearly influenced by the perceptions of labor Zionism, Histadrut leadership has traditionally taken upon itself the practical aspects of settling a largely urban and bourgeois series of migrants into laboring status, often in rural or fringe areas. Particularly in its formative years, the oganization serviced European and later Oriental settlers by implementing the concept of "Avodah Ivri"—Hebrew labor. Often this meant social and economic action which excluded the Arab peasant or working class.

In more recent years, the Histadrut has assumed a position still more unique for a formal labor union. It has embarked upon large-scale and highly significant entrepreneurial practices that touch almost every branch of the Israeli economy. These include collective agricultural units, co-operative farms, commercial cooperatives, and the holdings of Hevrat Ovdim, a subsidiary unit of the organization at large. The first two have traditionally been oriented toward agriculture, although industrial enter-prises have become increasingly more important aspects of the economy in recent years. Both the cooperatives and the collectives formally cling to the structures of socialism that were the legacy of their founders, though it is not unusual to find significant practical changes, such as greater legiti-mation of private ownership and hiring seasonal labor.

The two other forms of Histadrut enterprise are still further removed from what might be expected of a trade union. Commercial or producer cooperatives include small workshops involved in skilled or specialized crafts, as well as large utilities and transportation facilities. In some sectors these enterprises dominate their market. For its part, Hevrat Ovdim repre-sents the Histadrut in corporate form. It owns manufacturing and mining operations, construction companies, and various service enterprises. Each member of the Histadrut holds a share in Hevrat Ovdim, which is governed by those who also form the leadership of the whole organization. Thus, aside from being Israel's national labor union, the Histadrut is also its major employer, an irony not lost on many of its working class.

Finally, the impact of Histadrut activities upon political life should not be underestimated. It is clear that in a nation led to its independence by a labor bloc and directed by a similar coalition during its first three decades, a major share in the execution of national policy and ideology will be held by its trade union arm. Suffice it to say that all members of the Labor Party are also members of the Histadrut and that there is often considerable overlap in their respective leaderships.

Further, Histadrut elections are conducted in much the same manner as national elections. Just as parties appear as such on Knesset ballots, so too do they register for Hiustadrut elections. The union's leadership is generally a reflection of the political configuration nationally, and policy follows. It is not unfair to conclude, therefore, that the lines of direction and authority run both ways in relations between the government and its union and that Histadrut has a form of influence and independence not to be found among similar institutions elsewhere.[12]

Alongside the Histadrut stands a second quasi-governmental institution with major influence upon Israeli political and social life, the Jewish Agency. As noted above, prior to 1948, the Jewish Agency served as the spokesman of the Palestinian Jewish community to the world. In this capacity, it represented Jewish interests with foreign governments, served as a conduit for foreign donations and fund raising activities, and undertook thorny domestic problems in the areas of settlement, immigration, and employment. It might have been expected, therefore, that the need for such a body would be obviated by the creation of the state, its activities superseded by formal governmental structures designed to fulfill these vital functions. Nevertheless, the Jewish Agency continues to exist and has shown remarkable vitality and flexibility in its attempt to redirect its energies and redefine its raison d'être, that is, to justify its own existence.

To understand the present mission of the Jewish Agency one must return briefly to Zionist ideology, post-1948. Officially, Israel still sees itself and the Jewish people at large, as one. This concept of "peoplehood" preempts any other national identification or ethnic affiliation. They have learned through long and bitter experience, the argument goes, that the peoples of the world, no matter how friendly and liberal they may appear, are not well-disposed toward Jews and cannot be depended upon for Jewish security and well-being. Thus, out of voluntary acceptance or gentile animosity, Jews throughout the world are one.

Further, Israelis are the vanguard of this people, fulfilling a proper destiny by building the Jewish state. A primary function of such a vanguard is to protect Jewish needs and interests throughout the world and serve as their representative in international forums. Implicit in this thinking is a rejection of the Diaspora, that is, a refusal to legitimate Jewish life outside of Israel. Only within its borders can the Jew be secure and free to develop his natural talents to their fullest. The ultimate purpose of Jewish life, therefore, must be aliyah (emigration to Israel). If not carried out voluntarily, such emigration may be forced by gentile pressure, in any event.

Nonetheless, the state has had to live with several harsh realities which contradict, yet coexist with, this ideological position. First, there are large, powerful, and wealthy Jewish communities throughout the world— the largest in the United States, Canada, and Western Europe, while smaller groups are found in South America, South Africa, Eastern Europe, and Asia. Many within these communities show no intention to migrate and appear to live happy and secure lives. Further, of those who have migrated, many choose not to live in Israel or live there briefly and then move elsewhere. This has been noted in Americans who have emigrated to Israel and then returned, and Russians who leave the Soviet Union and either avoid Israel altogether or remain only as a way station to the United States.

A second reality is the political and economic relationship between Israel and the larger Jewish communities of the Diaspora, principally the one in the United States. Rather than serving as the shield and protector of these communities, the relationship often appears to be the reverse. Israel surfaces as the ward, dependent upon contributions and sympathetic pressure upon American policy makers. The existence of an Israel lobby in Washington has long ago been noted. Indeed, of late, distinguished members of Diaspora Jewish communities have grown restive with Israeli leaders and have pressed for greater influence upon Israeli foreign and domestic policy. Considerable furor has been raised among American Jews over the question of dissent in this area—its legitimacy and desirable parameters.[13]

Despite the unrealistic nature of some of its ideological goals, however, attempts are regularly made to make them operational and to popularize them abroad. Much of this task has now fallen to the Jewish Agency. Thus, while it once served as a spokesman for the Jews to the world, it now serves, in part, as an Israeli spokesman to Jewish communities in the Diaspora. Exporting Zionism, the Jewish Agency provides information and program material, sponsors lectures and classes, provides speakers, and publishes a variety of magazines and journals. It also serves as a clearinghouse for Zionist activities not officially under its rubric and monitors school and community programs as well as public actions and policies.

Aside from these ideological functions, the agency is also empowered to promote and direct aliyah. Prospective emigrants are interviewed by agency officials, attempts are made at finding housing and employment for them, and various financial arrangements are made to ease the burden of taxation and the expense of moving. This particular function obviously has considerable impact upon social life in Israel, as it affects competition at home and has fostered some resentment, both in native Israelis and in new immigrants.

In addition, the Jewish Agency has far-reaching influence in the matter of fund raising within Jewish communities throughout the world. While many Jews of the Diaspora are clearly not prepared to undertake a move to Israel, they exhibit their support through donations, of considerable size. Aside from aiding in the collection and consolidation of such funds—along with structures such as the United Jewish Appeal or Israel Bonds Commission—the Jewish Agency also plays a major role in their dissemination in Israel. Political parties, for example, receive support according to their proportionate strength in the Knesset. This obviously enforces the status quo and underwrites the activities of major parties, while making independent political movement a risky enterprise, at best. Thus, in many ways the Jewish Agency has come to represent the pragmatic arm of Zionist ideology and the financial stamp of approval from world Jewry to Israeli political leaders. It seals the mutual identification of Jews throughout the world and translates it into practical terms, no matter how unrealistic the proposition may at times appear.[14]

SECONDARY INSTITUTIONS

Finally, two other institutions, somewhat removed from the center of formal power, have a considerable impact upon the political and ideological environment in Israel. These are the national defense forces and the religious establishment. Both have significant influence regarding the self-image and goals represented by Zionism. Both have equally significant influence on the quality and pursuit of day to day life in Israel.

Perhaps more than any other national institution, the Israel Defense Force (Zahal being its Hebrew acronym) enjoys the widespread support of the population. Despite the recriminations and official inquiries immediately following the 1973 War, there is still a general consensus that Zahal has done an outstanding job in guarding the security and well-being of the Israeli people against overwhelming odds. Most Israelis perform their military and reserve duties proudly and few are the cases of conscientious objectors or draft dodging—though legitimate exemptions are available on physical or religious grounds.

Zahal is a citizen army in which some 80 percent of the adult male population participates. Though the precise tenure of full-time service has varied according to perceived need, it is presently 36 months for men and 24 months for women, at age 18. In addition, men must perform annual reserve duty averaging roughly 30 days to age 49, with some provision thereafter for civil defense duties. As might be expected, such conditions— virtually universal service, 2 to 3 years at age 18 and annual reserve duty for some 30 years following—often have a disruptive influence upon normal family relations, education, and the pursuit of professional or business interests. In general, the society has had to accommodate.

As a military force, Zahal has distinguished itself on several fronts. It has proven itself highly mobile—both in its ability to assemble its forces as

well as in its incredible speed in pursuit—noted particularly in the Sinai
Desert theater. Its intelligence corps has exhibited surprising accuracy,
while the air force, following the principle of "preemptive defense" (read:
first-strike capacity) has more than once eliminated enemy forces while
they were still on the ground.

Perhaps reflecting the creative mobility and flexibility of its columns,
the Israel Defense Force is an unusually informal affair, lacking the outward signs of military discipline and deference toward superiors. Insignia
are often absent from the uniforms and saluting is minimal. In addition,
subordinates regularly call their officers by their first names, reflecting a
cameraderie and unity of cause. Further, given the regularity of reserve
duty, it is not uncommon for military life to bring old friends together or to
reverse the roles and status generally assumed as civilians.

Aside from its primary purpose, which is of course military, Zahal also
serves several secondary functions which make it a vital aspect of the
Israeli political world. The first is historical, for the Israel Defense Force
harkens to the very base of the Jewish national experiment. Forged as it
was in the struggle for independence, the early Israeli fighting force was
very much an ad hoc affair. The bulk of its troops were organized under the
Haganah, which was the major military wing of the Jewish Agency and the
Yishuv, in pre-1948 Palestine. Its officer corps, however, grew from a
special shock brigade known as the Palmach. Rather elitist and partisan,
the Palmach was not altogether willing to be brought under a general
command, but preferred considerable autonomy and its members displayed a singular allegiance to the unit.

Parallel to these forces stood an array of terrorist and guerrilla organizations which assumed several titles (such as Irgun Zvai Leumi, Lohamei
Herut Yisrael) and organizational forms. Indeed, Menahem Begin, 1977
Prime Minister, directed one such group. The struggle to unify these
legions, avert civil war in the midst of the battle for independence, and the
very lively series of personality conflicts that reflected these grasps for
power are topics of heated debate even today—in the coffee houses of Tel
Aviv as well as the halls of the Knesset.

This continued and active interest in the struggle for independence,
along with the universality of miltary service and the respect in which it is
held, has contributed handily to contemporary Israeli society and culture.
Surrounded by enemies on all sides, Israel has become a garrison state
having to prove its battlefield prowess four times in 30 years—not including
regular guerrilla attack, border skirmishes and bloody terrorism. Guns and
military hardware are a commonplace and a familiarity with arms, unknown in two millennia of Jewish history, is now quite characteristic.

A certain cockiness, as well as a well-developed sense of independence, has also been noted and may be correlated to the role of the military in Israeli life. Suffice it to say that every veteran can find satisfaction and status in his reminiscences of military life and many look forward to reserve duty as a change of pace from the mundane world they know. There can be little doubt a major cultural contribution can be attributed to Zahal in its influence upon popular culture.

More directly, however, Zahal has undertaken the task of integrating and assimilating immigrants to Israel from a variety of cultures and lands. To a great degree, it is looked upon as the major institution of social unity, teaching the language, culture and mores of Israel to those of the economically and technologically superior societies of the West as well as to those whose prior Middle Eastern or North African living standards were well below Israel's. Camaraderie, unity of purpose, and esprit de corps are expected to overcome gaps of culture and society in forging one people.

Finally, the army has increasingly become the training ground for political leadership. As the old guard slowly passes from the scene and the years progress, the parties have had to reassess their leadership recruitment process. No longer can the experience of pioneering settlement or political agitation in Eastern Europe be the sole standard for selection. The new generation, largely in their fifties, is generally Israeli-born, with common ground in the military.

Several outstanding examples come immediately to mind. Moshe Dayan, Yitzhak Rabin, Shimon Peres, Ezer Weizmann, indeed even Chief Rabbi Shlomo Goren all distinguished themselves in the military prior to entering public life. It is no accident as well, that next to that of prime minister, the Ministry of Defense is the most powerful of all cabinet posts—a point punctuated by David Ben-Gurion's insistence upon holding both positions during his tenure in office. Thus it is clear that the Israel Defense Force represents a vital institution of political, social, and popular cultural influence, aside from its primary military function.[15]

By the same token, organized religion plays a major, yet less direct role in the cultural, social, and political life of the nation. An officially Jewish state, Israel has an established rabbinate and, through its Ministry of Religious Affairs, also underwrites the confessional authorities of its Christian, Muslim, and other minority faiths. Because of its favored position—and the fact that it has generally been a resented minority in the past—Judaism has taken a special form in Israel.

As noted above, the Jewish religious elements in Israel have been organized into a variety of political parties. The largest and most moderate of these, the National Religious Party, has served as partner in virtually all of Israel's governments. Its ability to align itself with both right- and left-wing coalitions stems from a simple proposition. Its general position on national, diplomatic, and economic issues has been quite flexible, allowing its senior coalition partner considerable freedom. In return for such loyalty and autonomy, the religious bloc has insisted on virtual monopoly over several areas of major concern.

The first among these involves the question of personal status. The religious bloc has maintained power over marriage, divorce, and conversion to Judaism. Consequently, there is no such thing as a civil wedding ceremony in Israel. Jews may be married and divorced only by rabbinic decree, while those of other faiths fall under the similar jurisdiction of their own religious authorities; there is no official accommodation for intermarriage. Interfaith couples must be married elsewhere, generally in Cyprus, and then may return to Israel, where government authorities will honor their foreign wedding certificate.

Equally important, identification as a Jew or a gentile may be attained only by means of the traditional standards of birth or conversion. Serious questions of legitimacy and family integrity, which weigh heavily in these areas of status, are also under rabbinic jurisdiction. The issue has taken on special meaning as a result of the displacements of World War II and the difficulty of obtaining documents of death, marriage, divorce, and so on. It erupted into a controversy of major proportion in recent years as the rabbinate has been forced to more clearly define the parameters of who is a Jew.

There are two more facets of this question that have major practical ramifications. First, the religious establishment has legitimated only the Orthodox Jewish tradition and has struggled to prevent the acceptance of marriages, divorces, and conversions under non-Orthodox auspices, as well as the development of non-Orthodox synagogues and religious institutions. Such internal conflict is confusing to the secular Israeli who understands little of the nuances that separate Judaism's various denominations. It is frustrating as well to many of Israel's American-Jewish supporters whose own religious affiliations are non-Orthodox at best and minimal at worst. Equally, the establishment of Orthodoxy implies the general propagation of tradition's strictest interpretation—often viewed as oppressive by Israel's none too religious majority.

Second, in a parallel vein, it is valuable to note the Israeli promulgation of a basic law unique in modern statecraft. Known as the law of return, it was passed in the wake of World War II. Unable to find refuge anywhere, millions of European Jews were brutally exterminated under the Nazis. After the war as well, there was no welcome harbor for thousands of stateless persons, fresh from the German death camps. Many were kept in detainment camps while the UN debated the fate of the Palestine Mandate and the British patrolled the waters of the Mediterranean, attempting to halt blockade runners.

As a result, one of the first actions of the new state was to assure that Jews would always have a place of refuge should the unthinkable occur once more. Jews of any background and nationality may enter Israel and become citizens immediately. Non-Jews applying for citizenship must undergo a more traditional waiting period and naturalization process. Thus, here too, one's definition of "Jew" and the manner by which the title may be assumed, has tangible and immediate consequences.

Aside from these very general and comprehensive issues, the religious establishment has also made itself felt in specific areas of social and domestic legislation. The raising of pigs, for example, is forbidden except in very limited areas of non-Jewish residence. Pork, bacon, and so on cannot be officially sold at Israeli restaurants—though it is available on a covert basis. Sabbath legislation has also been passed and public conveyances, theaters, and many service operations are closed from sundown Friday to an hour past sunset on Saturday. In a society in which Sunday is a regular working day this is a considerable concession to a religious minority.

In addition, the National Religious Party has been able to establish its control over several vital ministries during the past three decades. In return for its partnership, the party has consistently placed its leaders at the head of the Ministry of Religion, the Ministry of the Interior, and the Ministry of Religious Affairs. As might be expected, positions of such a sensitive nature have allowed the party to strengthen its electoral status as well. Indeed, its remarkable ability to win support among a part of the Arab electorate in Israel is partially attributable to the largess it dispenses.[16]

This, then, is the institutional context within which the subjects of our study operate. It is here that they draw their perspective and indeed from these that they dissent. Exception is taken to virtually all that has been discused above, such as the history and formation of Zionist theory, Jewish settlement patterns in Palestine, economic institutions, the decision-making process, the religious establishment. Some begin from the vantage of socialism while others operate within traditionally religious parameters. Some call for the complete elimination of the present political and social systems while others believe that significant change may yet come from within. To a one, however, they agree that serious change is required lest the present path lead to political, military, and cultural destruction.

If the above review was brief, it was intended to be exactly that. Many significant institutions—both major and minor—have not been included. This is not to imply anything about their importance but the review is a reflection of the perspectives of those who protest Israeli life. It is from among these above agencies that ammunition is drawn for protest and it is at them that the sharpest barbs are aimed.

The following sections will describe these protest movements and define their ideological positions. The first are those whose underpinnings are one or another brand of socialist thinking. They range from evolutionary liberalism to radical, Trotskyist activism, with several shadings between. The second group of dissenters posit no such specific economic philosophy but they come to their dissent from ethnic or religious ideology. Nonetheless, these too offer strategies of radical change for the nature and context of Israeli life. It is a tribute to the elasticity and open nature of the Israeli political system that it has tolerated such protest in the face of its brief but beleaguered history.

NOTES

1. On the Israeli constitution, see Emanuel Rackman, *Israel's Emerging Constitution* (New York: Columbia University Press, 1955).

2. See Aaron Antonovsky and David Katz, "Factors in the Adjustment to Israel: Life of American and Canadian Immigrants," *Jewish Journal of Sociology* (1970), pp. 77–87; see also Harold Isaac, *American Jews in Israel* (New York: John Jay, 1967); and Leonard Weller, "The Adjustment of American Jews in Israel: First Phase of a Longitudinal Study," cited in Leonard Weller, *Sociology in Israel* (Westport, Conn.: Greenwood Press, 1974), p. 35.

3. Marver Bernstein, *The Politics of Israel* (New York: Greenwood Press, 1959), p. 27. Also see Moshe Burstein, *Self-Government of the Jews in Palestine since 1900* (Tel Aviv, 1934), and Arieh Tartakover, "The Making of Jewish Statehood in Palestine," *Jewish Social Studies* (July 1948), p. 210.

4. For a discussion of Jewish self-government in this light, see Nadav Halevi and Ruth Klinov-Malul, The Economic Development of Israel (New York: Praeger, 1968), pp. 35–38.

5. Howard M. Sachar, *A History of Israel* (New York: Alfred A. Knopf, 1976), pp. 354–57.

6. For an analysis of the role of the speaker in the Israeli Parliament see Oscar Kraines, *Government and Politics in Israel* (New York, 1962), and Asher Zidon, *Israel's Parliament in Theory and Practice* (Jerusalem: Achiasef, 1955).

7. On collective responsibility, see Bernstein, op. cit., chap. 5.

8. It has been noted, however, that the influence of the foreign ministry is often largely superficial. Its research capacity and general domestic influence have often been underutilized. In this vein, see Lewis Brownstein, "Decision-Making in Israeli Foreign Policy: An Unplanned Process," *Political Science Quarterly* (Summer 1977), pp. 259–79.

9. David M. Zohar, *Political Parties in Israel: The Evolution of Israeli Democracy* (New York: Praeger, 1974). It is interesting to note that even David Ben-Gurion fared poorly in his

attempt to break with the Labor Party and form Rafi—an independent list of his own—during the mid-sixties. Surely a lesser Israeli statesman would do no better.

10. Benjamin Akzin, "The Role of the Parties in Israeli Democracy," in *Integration and Development in Israel*, ed S.N. Eisenstadt et al. (New York: Praeger, 1970), p. 19.

11. On the politics of seniority in Israel, see Yuval Elizur and Eliahu Salpeter, *Who Rules Israel* (New York: Harper and Row, 1973).

12. Much has been written on the Histadrut and its influence in Israeli affairs. Brief summations may be found in Halevi and Malul, op. cit., chap. 3; David Horowitz, *The Economics of Israel* (London: Pergamon, 1967); and J.J. Lowenberg, "Histadrut: Myth and Reality" and Milton Derber, "Histadrut and Industrial Democracy," chapters in *Israel: Social Structure and Change*, ed. Michael Curtis and Mordecai Chertoff (New Brunswick, N.J.: Transaction, 1973), pp. 249–77. For a general review see Aharon Becher, *Histadrut: Progam, Problems, Prospects* (Tel Aviv: International Department of the Histadrut, 1966).

13. This in particular has been a major issue in the development of Breira, an avowedly disenting organization made up largely of American Jewish intellectuals. See, for example, William Novak, "The Breira Story," *Genesis 2* (March 16, 1977); see also *Proceedings* of Breira's First Annual Membership Conference (February 20–22, 1977); and the new Breira newsletter, *InterChange*. In opposition to the movement, see Rael Jean Isaac, *Breira: Counsel for Judaism* (New York: Americans for a Safe Israel, 1977), and Rael Jean Isaac, "The Rabbis of Breira," *Midstream* (April 1977), pp. 3–17.

14. On the Jewish Agency generally, see Jewish Agency, American Section, *The Story of the Jewish Agency for Israel* (New York: Jewish Agency, 1964). A more contemporary view may be gained from Ernest Stock, "The Reconstitution of the Jewish Agency," *American Jewish Yearbook*, 1972, pp. 178–93.

15. This brief description and analysis of the Israel Defense Force was culled from the following sources: Yigal Allon, *The Making of Israel's Army* (London: Vallentine, Mitchell, 1970); Shimon Peres, *David's Sling: The Arming of Israel* (London: Weidenfeld and Nicolson, 1970); Ben Halpern, "The Role of the Military in Underdeveloped Countries, ed. John Johnson (Princeton: Princeton University Press, 1962); and Amos Perlmutter, *Military and Politics in Israel* (New York: Praeger, 1969).

16. For the role of religion in Israel see Ervin Birnbaum, *The Politics of Compromise* (Rutherford, N.J.: Fairleigh Dickinson University Press, 1970); Emile Marmorstein, *Heaven at Bay* (London: Oxford University Press, 1969); S. Clement Leslie, *The Rift in Israel* (New York: Schocken Books, 1971); and S.Z. Abramov, *Perpetual Dilemma: Jewish Religion in the Jewish State* (Jerusalem: World Union of Progressive Judaism, 1976). It may be noted that Shulamit Aloni, an attorney and civil libertarian, has recently performed a number of civil marriages under a "common law" statute. Their legal standing has yet to be tested.

II

THE VIEW
FROM THE LEFT

4

URI AVNERY: HAOLAM HAZEH

Haolam Hazeh—"this world"—is the name of a sensationalist, gossipy, and often lurid Israeli periodical. Its editorial policy has been one of libertarianism, journalistic attack upon leading political figures, and exposé. Accused of libel and sedition, the magazine, nevertheless, has a healthy following among younger Israelis—especially in the military—as well as unlikely establishment figures. Vehemently opposed to the close relationship between religion and state, *Haolam Hazeh* has been violent in its attacks upon various rabbinic functionaries and spokesmen for the religious parties and their representatives.

Haolam Hazeh is also the original name of a political party that won a single seat in the 1965 Knesset elections and doubled its parliamentary delegation in 1969, but was unable to carry the requisite number of votes for even one seat in the 1973 election. Known variously as Koach HaChadash—the new force—or Meri, an acronym for the Israel Radical Party, the undisputed leader and ideologue for this political organization is the magazine's founder and editor, Uri Avnery.

In many ways, Avnery is one of Israel's most durable and articulate gadflies, having been involved in various protest and peace movements since before the formal founding of the state. Though demurring from electoral activity prior to 1965, he was closely involved with attempts at Arab-Jewish unity and has attempted to create alliances with several youth-based leftist and libertarian organizations. A sensitive and intelligent author, Avnery has developed a following among European and American readers, to whom he presents arguments more radical than those published in Hebrew for Israeli consumption.[1]

Born Helmut Oystermann, of middle-class parents in Hanover, Avnery was given a liberal German primary education. He felt the early fury of the Nazi regime in his first year of high school. Taken as an omen of things to come, the Oystermann family emigrated to Palestine in 1933. Though only a teenager, Avnery soon became involved with the Irgun Tzvai Leumi, one of the major Jewish terrorist groups which operated in the prestate period. Though odd beginnings for a major peace activist, Avnery refers to his Irgun activities as "pure bliss. My life was circumscribed by a certainty I never knew again: We were doing the right thing."

Avnery left the terrorists, however, in the wake of a split over the alliance with the British and the Second World War. The Irgun would later regroup and become a major element in the Jewish military forces of the 1948 War. However, Avnery had become sufficiently estranged and doubtful of the justice of its cause to look for a very different alternative. This he sought in the formation of a group known as the Palestinians but popularly referred to as B'Ma-avak (In the Struggle), after the title of its irregularly published organ.

It was the goal of the B'Ma-avak group to popularize the idea that the creation of the state of Israel would signal as well the creation of a new Hebrew nation related to, yet apart from, the historical entity known as the Jewish people. This new nation, rather, would have far more in common with its Arab neighbors who, albeit unwittingly, were in common cause against British imperialism. To this end Avnery wrote a booklet entitled "War and Peace in the Semitic Region," an argument for the creation of a binational secular state.*

Despite his misgivings, Avnery joined the Jewish forces in the 1948 War and was to become a platoon leader in a much-storied brigade known as Samson's Foxes, whose primary theater of operation was the Negev Desert. Once again, his political proclivities notwithstanding, Avnery takes obvious pride in his military exploits, the notoriety attributed to his brigade, and the wounds he sustained due to battle. Yet, his observations of the development of political and social institutions during the war led him to be even more skeptical of the directions that the new state would take.

---

*Though the terminology and rhetoric was different, this proposal paralleled closely the opposition of Mapam, the left-wing Zionist Socialist Party, to the UN Partition Plan. Originally bent on binationalism, Mapam soon made peace with partition and subsequently joined the ruling labor alignment. Avnery indicates no contemporaneous knowledge of the Mapam position, much less affiliation with it. It seems likely that its socialist ideals would have been foreign to a libertarian like Avnery, at this juncture at least.

The memoirs of his war experiences made him a popular journalistic figure during the early years of statehood and gave him the capital to purchase a small, family-oriented magazine known as *Haolam Hazeh*.

During the fifties, Avnery continued his interests in a binational peace alternative and was instrumental in attracting peace activists of all stripes. The group's best known member—with the possible exception of Avnery himself—was Natan Yellin-Mor, a former leader of the terrorist Lehi organiation, who was sentenced to eight years in prison for his part in the assassination of UN mediator Folke Bernadotte.

It was through this group that Avnery publicized his concept of a Semitic union between Israel and its Arab neighbors, to normalize relations between the various powers and allow for a cooling of international tensions. This, it was alleged, was the only way for peace to come. Published in a 126 point "Hebrew Manifesto" (the use of the term Hebrew to differentie from the word Jewish with its Diaspora connotation), the program argued for a federation of Palestine, a regional Semitic Confederacy, and the repatriation of Arab refugees. Semitic Action carried little weight beyond its own circles but allowed for an airing of disparate ideological views.*

At various times, Avnery has flirted with socialists of moderate degree, New Left youth activists, representatives of Oriental Jewish protest groups, and individuals with little or no formal ideological obligations. During this period, he also learned that his magazine's popularity might be increased were it to be peppered with sensational news items, especially concerning sexual aberrations attributed to high government figures, various forms of scandal, and pictures of nude women. Despite Avnery's iconoclastic political and social positions, the magazine became a national success and an official source of embarrassment.

In 1965, the government responded to this annoyance when a particularly obscene item intimating the sensual appetites of one religious party leader was published. A bill to deal harshly with the media in the area of libel suits was introduced. Though primarily aimed at *Haolam Hazeh*, the implications of the law were to virtually remove any defense from all

---

*Here too, the thrust of Avnery's actions parallel closely those of a group known as the "Canaanites" which called for a grand confederation of states and provinces stretching from the Tigris River to the Suez Canal. Pluralist in nature, the result was to be an Eretz Hakedem ("land of the East") or Brit Canaan (Canaanite Covenant). Ironically, this expansive view led many of the group's members to join the Land of Israel Movement, a militant expansionist organization of the post-1967 War period and forerunner to Gush Emunim.

journals so accused and thus limit the freedom of Israel's active press. In response, many liberal intellectuals, young voters, and readers of *Haolam Hazeh* supported Avnery's last-minute bid for a Knesset seat. It was primarily on this issue that he was elected in 1965 with some 1.2 percent of the vote.

Despite the erratic and sometimes excessive nature of his journalistic actions, Avnery surprised many by the conscientiousness of his Knesset tenure. He had one of the best attendance records of any Parliament member and made numerous speeches in that capacity. Nevertheless, he remained consistent in his demands for the development of a peace front, the disestablishment of religion, and the control of the black market, these especially in the wake of the 1967 War. Though none of these issues was particularly popular and Avnery made little effort to join in coalition with other parliamentary delegations, whether major or minor, the position offered him great visibility. Coupled with the ever-increasing popularity of his magazine, Avnery was lionized by liberal and New Left elements in Europe and the United States.

The increase in his popularity was also reflected, after a fashion, within Israel. In 1969, Avnery was returned to the Knesset and the Haolam Hazeh Party list was also able to capture a second parliamentary seat. This was awarded to Avnery's long-time friend and business associate Shalom Cohen, an Oriental Israeli of Egyptian descent. As coeditor of *Haolam Hazeh*, Cohen had used the magazine as a forum for issues of concern to Israel's Sephardic population, a matter close to Avnery's heart. By 1971, however, Cohen and Avnery parted ways, the former to join the new Black Panther Party, which attempted more directly to deal with the social and economic status of Israel's Sephardim.[2]

In preparation for the 1973 elections, Avnery made several overtures toward left-wing and dissenting elements within the Knesset. The intent was to create a united left and offer a realistic alternative to the Labor Alignment. The move, however, was not to be realized, partly for ideological reasons, but largely due to questions of personality. Avnery was only able to ally his Haolam Hazeh List with left-leaning members of Maki (the original Israel Communist Party) and Siach (the Israeli New Left) to form Meri—the Israel Radical Party.

These political machinations proved futile, however, and were neutralized by the effects of the October 1973 War. The elections that took place in the wake of the war found the Israeli electorate with little time for what was considered the frivolous positions taken by Avnery. Haolam Hazeh failed to win a single seat and Avnery was returned to private life.

Though some have chastised Avnery for "playing the political game" at the expense of ideological purity, he has responded that he is an eminently practical individual with real alternatives for peace and consequently plans to continue his parliamentary career in future elections.

WORLD VIEW

Uri Avnery has taken an independent stand on a variety of issues ranging from personal status and civil rights to Israel-Arab relations, from the separation of religion and state to the elimination of Zionist influence within the state. In each area, he takes a dim view of the extant social and political institutions, claiming that they serve to exploit a myth that is no longer relevant to the national and regional reality Israel must face.

As presently constituted, therefore, Israel represents an aberration superimposed upon its geographic location. It is a state based upon Western principles of governance foreign to its region. Primary influence is wielded by non-Israelis—generally residents of the Western Hemisphere or Europe—who maintain foreign control by virtue of large capital outlays and donations. Internally this is reflected in Zionist imperatives that require Israel to be Jewish, making regional integration almost impossible.

This latter item, the ideological components of Zionism, are particularly noisome to Avnery. It is his contention that Zionism as a meaningful ideology died with the creation of the state. The present era is characterized as post-Zionist. Avnery is careful to indicate that he is not anti-Zionist "for one cannot be opposed to something that no longer exists." Thus:

> What is today Zionism has nothing to do with Zionism as such. It is clearly an instrument of Israeli government policy. Out of classical Zionism came the creation of the State of Israel. With that creation Zionism as such, became an historical fact; it ended in 1948. It became a state religion after that. What was an ideology is now an empty shell, empty of any practical content. That's why someone can be a Zionist leader and live in America.[3]

In this light, Avnery is emphatic about the manipulative role that Israeli leaders have played in thwarting peace and oppressing their citizens in the name of a dead ideology. All real power, he argues, is concentrated in the hands of the leaders of government, the political parties, and the mammoth trade union, the Histadrut. Within this ruling elite—which seems to perpetuate itself in form if not in person—there appears little flexibility or desire for change. In political, economic, and foreign affairs, the individual has no alternative to the traditional or established.[4]

The leadership seems steeped in stagnation and unable to respond creatively to the problems and complexities of the Middle East problem. It has missed many opportunities for peace because of its incapacities to decide upon positive solutions and alternatives implied in the conquests of 1967. He notes, with unabashed pride, that

> on the fifth day of the Six-Day War, I wrote an open letter to the then Israeli Prime Minister Levi Eshkol. I proposed that he turn with a dramatic gesture, to the Palestinian People whose homeland had just been conquered by the Israeli Army and propose the immediate establishment of a national Palestinian State. . . . The essence of Eshkol's view was that of a seasoned businessman, a master of negotiations: All the territories are in our hands, we hold all the cards, time is working for us, every day our hold on the territories is growing stronger. . . . Today it is clear that this was an historic mistake.[5]

The religious establishment, in particular, has been the target of Avnery's scorn. To him it represents the most obvious and distasteful example of foreign rule in Israel. Most Israelis, to his mind, are indifferent to the traditions of Jewish ritual and the secularization of the state has been long ago established in Western democracies. In Israel, religion is a vestige of time past and the result of the influence of things peculiarly non-Israeli. Equally, it represents one more opportunity for the political leadership to exercise sovereignty at the expense of the citizenry.

As a social force, religion in Israel is alleged to be but one more Zionist prop. Through it, the Zionists have been able to claim the world wide unity of the Jewish people, an argument to which even the most agnostic of Zionists must resort for the purposes of self-definition. This is punctuated by the requirement that all marriages and indeed the very elements of personal status and civil liberty are subject to rabbinic determination. The establishment of religion in Israel is, therefore, another serious obstacle to the integration of the state into its region.[6]

Ironically, as cynical as Avnery appears to be in reference to the quality of Zionist leadership and ideology, he remains highly optimistic as regards the inherent nature of the Israeli population. The attractive qualities are a native informality and a healthy, perhaps exaggerated, sense of freedom and independence which Avnery senses in the Israeli public. In particular, he notes these characteristics among the military, the very institution often charged with the creation of social consensus within Israel.

The leadership, however, is selfish and obstructive. In his view,

the political circles of Israel are more chauvinistic than the general public, because they are far more imbued with the traditional Zionist attitudes. In spite of everything the Israeli public is still remarkably sensible and the younger the age group, the less chauvinistic it is. The army, the youngest institution in the country, is on the whole more sober and sensible than both the government and the public.[7]

Though not committed to a Marxist view of history, Avnery has also argued that much of the government's control is predicated upon its virtual economic hegemony. Thus, Zionist domination depends upon the ability to channel foreign currency to the various political parties according to their size. This gives each a stake in the continuation of the system, and despite alleged opposition within the establishment, no alternatives are forthcoming. "Power," in Avnery's formulation, "always flows from up—down and never the other way. This is because money always flows from above." In this regard, the means of production are far less important than the flow of capital—largely from abroad.

A second economic prop which upholds the system is the massive "black market," a market which, Avnery estimates, has accounted for some 30 to 40 percent of Israel's gross. This creates a cycle of funds completely outside the formal network of taxation and government operation, yet circulated by the same people who man these networks. The funds could easily be controlled, he alleges, but for the interference of the political leadership. "The owners of this immense black capital are part of the power structure themselves."[8]

As a result, it is difficult to characterize the economic system of Israel. Despite vehement arguments to the contrary, it is neither capitalist nor is it Communist socialist. He pointedly details the extent of the confusion as an economic mixture. Thus:

There is no capitalism in Israel for whatever one does depends totally upon the government. There is no credit outside of it and by controlling credit, the government holds all the cards; the richer you are the more dependent. The control is not less than in the Soviet Union yet it is not socialist because there is virtually no planning in the economy at all. Such a mixture is unique to Israel.[9]

Finally, Avnery senses a change among Arab leaders living under Israeli rule. Apart from the development of a militant Palestinian nationalist movement and the hostility of Arab states, there is a new toughness, which he imputes to the quality of West Bank leadership. This quality will also force the Israeli Zionist leadership to reappraise its stance. Failure to do so, aside from being political and diplomatic folly, will only lead to future fiascos in the relationship between Israel and its Arab minority. Examples of this alleged new awakening are seen in the electoral gains of the Arab-focused Communist Party (Rakah), especially in the West Bank municipalities, and in the massive and bloody general strike, known as Land Day.

The change in leadership, rather than being social or even political, was more generational and attitudinal. The former element is of particular importance.

> within the large and rich families, authority has gone from the old fatalists, immersed in the customs and ceremonies of yesterday, to the young, energetic and rebellious, part of the new winds blowing through the Palestinian People, many of whom also studied at Arab universities.

Equally, this new group of Arab leaders has left behind many of the earlier means of political action within the Arab villages. Perhaps the most disturbing of these were the deep fissures and internal fractionalization that were a vestige of the feudal past, as much as the result of attempts by Jordanian and Israeli masters to prevent unification. Despite a formal prohibition on political activity among West Bank residents, leaders of the various municipalities have maintained close ideological and personal contact, a factor which Avnery infers to mean real political cooperation. The inability of the Israeli leadership to formulate a creative response to these developments is but one more example of the stagnation and weakness that characterizes it.[10]

VALUES AND GOALS

It is clear, then, that Avnery assesses Israeli society and government as overbearing and oppressive, with undue influence wielded by foreign, that is, non-Israeli though Jewish, elements. Zionism, to him, is an ideology devoid of content and relevance, as is the religious establishment in Israel. It is no surprise that he has been the most consistent and durable figure in the movement for radical change both in the form and content of Israeli political institutions.

His most cogent remarks have concentrated upon the area of Arab-Israeli relations, in which the first and perhaps only priority must be peace. Though concessions must be made by the Arab powers as well, a lasting peace settlement requires a systematic and far-reaching Israeli initiative. Major changes—both external and domestic—must come before any movement, from either the Arab states or the Palestinian people, may be expected.

The changes that Avnery desires amount virtually to an ideological and political turnabout. Israel must mute its ties with world Jewry, abandon the establishment of religion, and forsake its "irrational" insistence upon a Jewish state. Until that point, the state can never hope to integrate itself into a region that is suspicious of Judaism as a foreign force and Israel as an expansionist enemy. In addition, the problem of Palestinian nationalism—the crucial one in Avnery's thinking—will never be ameliorated as long as the possibility of a non-Jewish majority is not at least considered.[11]

Even as it is necessary for Israel to lose its religious and ideological ties with Jewry, so too is it essential that she abandon her virtual solitary dependence upon the forces of the West, most notably the United States. Avnery arrives at this conclusion not from any commitment to oppose Western influence in the region or to champion the cause of the Third World versus imperialism, but from a largely pragmatic understanding of international affairs. The American decision not to continue support for South Vietnam in the spring of 1975 is seen as evidence that the dependence upon a foreign power for survival is folly.

In Israel's case, reliance upon American aid may not lead to the fall of the nation, but severely impairs its freedom of movement and prevents it from assuming a normal diplomatic life with its neighbors. It behooves Israel to initiate a direct settlement with the Arab world, unimpaired by American involvement.

> A state that relies on foreign aid for its very existence and security must set itself as a supreme and decisive objective the task of reaching a situaton which will enable it to live in safety even without that aid. . . .
> The Israeli-Arab War is what creates Israel's absolute dependence upon the United States. Peace between Israel and the Arabs would to a great extent terminate that dependency. . . . The logical conclusion is clearly [that] the State of Israel must switch to a policy of direct approach to the Arab World.[12]

The content of the peace initiative that Avnery seeks is quite specific and detailed. He fully supports the creation of a Palestinian state within the boundaries of the presently occupied West Bank and the Gaza Strip, apparently having soured on the thought of creating a binational, secular, and unpartitioned entity in Israel-Palestine. He notes, somewhat sardonically, that while this is now common talk among "doves" even within the centrist parties, it was his position since June 1967. The two new states, Israel and Palestine, "would share a common capital in Jerusalem and be bound together by a 'special relationship.' The predominantly Jewish State would keep its ties with World Jewry as would the Palestinian State with the Arab World."[13]

The creation of such a state would have both long-range and short-range consequences. In the long range, it would serve as the basis for renewed diplomatic relations between Israel and its Arab neighbors, the main bone of contention, Palestinian nationalism, having been satisfied. It would also lead to a loose confederation of Middle Eastern states in economic and political affairs, not unlike that which presently exists in Western Europe. Such a development would insure the international integrity of the region and neutralize both American and Soviet influence there.[14]

In an immediate sense, the creation of such a national entity would institutionalize the Palestinian movement, stabilize it, and bring its moderate leadership to the fore. It would consequently decrease the incidence and influence of terror within the Palestinian camp, for the institutional leadership of such a state would have a natural stake in its orderly maintenance. Avnery compares the creation of a Palestinian state with the Zionist Biltmore Conference of 1943. There, partition was accepted on the assumption that a smaller state was better than none, over the objections of extremist elements within the Zionist ranks.

Terrorism, Avnery asserts—whether Palestinian or Israeli—only flourishes when it gives vent to the deep-seated feelings of a large segment of the population within which it operates. It will then be aided and abetted by them and romanticized both inside and outside its own camp. One who would eliminate the power of terrorist actions must drive a wedge between such organizations and the populations who sympathize with them.

> This means that the only effective way of liquidating the terror is to "get the fish out of the water"—that is to detach the terrorism from the sources of its nourishment and to exclude the terrorists from the community in whose name they are acting. This can be done in one way: to satisfy the basic demand of that community.

It is not unlikely, however, that a minority of extremists would remain, no matter how profoundly such demands were satisfied. These, determined to fight to the last despite the creation of the Palestinian state, might seriously impair the viability of the fledgling republic and serve as a security threat to Israel.

Should this situation arise, the threat would not be to the State of Israel but to the new Palestinian State and its rulers. Should there be a struggle, it would be a civil war, and the new regime would be interested in working with Israel to eradicate the evil. The same Palestinian community which is now adoring the Fedayeen and praying for their success would regard them as disturbers of the peace, separatists and destructionists.[15]

It is evident, then, that Avnery's values are not those of formal ideological formation, i.e., Marxist, socialist, or Zionist, but appear to be grounded in practicality and pragmatism. He wishes to allow an integration of all states in the Middle East, yet recognizes the importance of Israel's relationship to world Jewry; he seeks the creation of a Palestinian state not in the name of national liberation or even humanitarian ideals but rather for the sake of Israel's peace and stability. Those elements that prevent the development that he seeks must be laid respectfully but emphatically to rest.

Recognizing the unique nature of the Israeli enterprise, especially in the post-Zionist era, he cautions patience but resolution. In his view:

this State must stand on two legs. One is its special relationship with the Jewish People. The other is its relationship with other States in the region who also have much in common with the Israeli nation. One cannot contradict the other. The extent to which it does is a function of the "world picture" created by Zionist ideology, an ideology which must be allowed to die its natural death.[16]

STRATEGIES FOR SOCIAL CHANGE

For Avnery, the realization of his overriding goal, a true and lasting peace, is predicated upon several tactical changes in the very nature of Israeli society. Peace presupposes the Israeli willingness to accept a proper and normal role as a Middle Eastern nation. In addition, it requires a programmatic response to the demands of Palestinian nationalism and a reevaluation of Zionism as an ideology.

The first vehicle for such change is the solution of the Palestinian refugee problem. The 1967 War shifted the responsibility from other Arab states to Israel. As a result of the territorial conquests, Israel now had the wherewithal to effect a solution almost unilaterally. Avnery proposes a three-step plan. The first step requires that Israel offer repatriation to all those Palestinians who have lost their land as a result of Israeli-Arab conflict, some 100,000 refugees, in his estimate. The second stipulates that those choosing not to return would be compensated for their losses.

> The repatriates would be settled and provided with new means of livelihood in the cities and villages, much as Jewish immigrants are. . . . Compensation to those relinquishing the right to return would be in hard currency and would cover abandoned property as well as loss of livelihood, education and so forth.

The third and most important step in Avnery's proposal is the creation of a Palestinian state on the West Bank and the Gaza Strip, as mentioned above. A federal pact would link the two nations, similar to the agreements joining the participants of NATO or the Warsaw Pact. Military affairs would thereby be coordinated and foreign armies excluded, in order to allow the region to diffuse with little outside intervention. Such a program would carry international guarantees, to be enforced by the UN. Other forms of interference might be similarly circumvented through parallel economic and political accords.

The capital of the new republic of Palestine would be Jerusalem, which would also remain the capital of the state of Israel. Thus the city would be open to citizens of both states, yet retaining some independent municipal control of its own. This would comprise "a solution—the only practical one I believe—to an issue charged with emotions, both religious and nationalist, which make retreat for either side impossible." In this way, the two futre states would amalgamate their resources and coalesce their respective forces in the quest for peace.[17]

While Avnery realizes that his proposals may seem radical at first blush, sufficiently large segments of the Israeli populace are disenchanted with the present governmental direction and susceptible to fresh alternatives for change. A peace movement is already evident and has included many distinguished political and intellectual leaders, indeed even within the government itself. It lies with these activists to demonstrate that "important elements in the Arab World are ready to deal with them and work out with them a practical way to peace."[18]

In very practical terms, Avnery has participated in attempts to unify the peace factions of which he speaks and to create an electoral front to offer voters a realistic alternative. He has made overtures to the non-Soviet Communist Party, Maki, as well as to student and academic groups such as Siach—the new Israeli Left—and Techelet-Adom—the Blue-Red Faction. At times, this had led to sharp personal conflicts, such as the conflict between Avnery and the late Moshe Sneh, secretary of Maki. It was Avnery's contention that he could not join in a political alliance with one who had justified the Doctors' Plot and the Slansky trials of Stalinist Russia, as had Sneh. Consequently, such union was impossible.

Sneh's death in 1972 reopened the possibility of a united peace front composed almost exclusively of left-wing elements within the Israeli political arena. Though Avnery has emphatically denied that there is anything characteristically leftist about this thought, the content of his coalitions have perforce implied otherwise. On the eve of the 1973 elections, and before the October War, negotiations were reopened with Meir Peil and Shmuel Mikunis, leaders of Moked, the result of a coalition of Maki and the more moderate Tchelet-Adom group.

Subsequently, hopes for a united front were dashed when personality conflicts between Avnery and Peil developed, allegedly over who would head the party list. Further, Moked suffered an internal rift over the question of unilateral withdrawal from occupied territories. The more moderate faction later joined with the Black Panthers, while the radical Moked group, led by long-time leftist leader Esther Wilenska, left the party and joined with Avnery to form Meri—the Israeli Radical Party. The negotiations went poorly for Avnery. The 1973 election, in the wake of the October War, saw him unable to win even one seat in the Knesset while Peil, leader of Moked, was seated in the Knesset for the next term.[19]

Aside from such political machinations, Avnery has also been known to utilize the forces of confrontation in order to better publicize his position. As a member of the Knesset, for example, he destroyed his identification card from the rostrum to protest debates over personal status (see Chapter 3). The issue of the religious establishment, one of particular interest to him, also led him to protest physically and he has been ejected from the Halls of Knesset because of his unruly behavior.

In addition to his long-range designs, Avnery has also called for sweeping changes in the form and structure of Israeli politics. The parties, most powerful as political institutions, are the first to require internal change. Avnery would sever the link between a party and any commercial enterprise—effectively destroying them as independent economic institutions. A freer competition for votes and a freer atmosphere for voter choice would be effectuated as constituents became gradually less dependent upon the parties for their livelihood and well being.

Further, the supremacy of partisan politics has been reflected by the confused state of parliamentary affairs. "Our Parliament is a fiction," Avnery claims. It appears at once unfettered, yet without a will or direction of its own. It too, therefore, is shaped and molded only by the parties which, in coalition, form its leadership.

That is why it adopts laws that could never pass the American Supreme Court. My solution is to see to the writing of a formal constitution which would serve as a context for political action and thus secure personal and civil freedoms.[20]

Avnery has also called for the separation of the executive from the legislative functions in the Knesset. At present, that body is weakened by its collective cabinet, whose members stand for election not as individuals but as obscure names on party lists, another example of partisan strength. Avnery would have cabinet leaders stand for election as individuals, with platforms of their own.

Such tactical maneuvering is by no means sufficient, but only transitional in nature, leading toward a major realignment of political forces. Change here will ignore historical ties and vested interests in order to offer the voter a clear and honest choice.

> Salvation can only come from new bodies, outside the present establishment, and I welcome warmly every pioneering effort in that direction. New coalitions from left to right may result in new values. I foresee the creation of two political forces, one right-wing/nationalist and the second liberal/socialist, which might be the foundation of a new political system.[21]

Such thinking conforms to Avnery's essential confidence in the nature of the Israeli populace in contradistinction to his jaundiced view of its leadership. He displays a similar optimism in his prescriptions for the Arabs of the West Bank. While immediate recognition of a Palestinian state is not acceptable to Israel at the present time, Avnery has called for greater freedom for the communal and political leadership of the occupied areas. Rather than being a license for terrorism, this would allow a more realistic picture of both Israelis and Arabs to emerge. In Avnery's words:

> There is no doubt that it would help . . . and in the end serve Israel's real interests, if the prohibition against legitimate political activity in the occupied territories were finally lifted. If West Bank and Gaza residents could freely express themselves, form political associations, debate and discuss their future, then realism would prevail over dreams, and it would be possible to move toward peace.[22]

ON BALANCE

In many ways, Avnery represents one of the most interesting and durable of Israel's ideologists of dissent. He is at once consistent yet difficult to characterize, idealistic yet highly practical. The tenor of his writing appears to be frivolous and unrealistic, yet his aims are serious and intended to be understood as such. It is perhaps this very enigmatic nature and inscrutability that makes him popular and creatively flexible as a political figure.

Avnery's two great desires appear to be development of a lasting peace in the Middle East and the separation of religious Judaism from its established status in Israel. In a sense, the one is predicated upon the other. It is Avnery's contention that peace can only come when Israel is prepared to join with its neighbors as a full resident of the Middle East. This depends upon its political secularization—the separation of religion and state. That few—if any—Arab states have taken a similar step toward such total secularization seems not to concern him.

In addition, Avnery is somewhat less virulently anti-Zionist than other Israeli dissenters. It is his contention that Zionism is already dead and awaits only the proper recognition for it to be laid to its final rest. One cannot oppose something that no longer exists, he claims. Rather, what must be done is convince those of the Israeli leadership that establishing power on the basis of calls to a dead ideology is counterproductive and unwise. Short of success there, such leaders must be simply separated from their offices.

The key to the peace that Avnery seeks lies in unilateral Israeli action—a unilateral decision to secularize and mute its ties with Jewry throughout the world and a decision to establish a Palestinian state on the West Bank and in Gaza. Such a move would knock the wind from the sails of the Arab cause and whittle away at the constituency that terrorists now serve.

Internally, Avnery has called for structural change in order to make a more conducive environment for regional peace. He has participated in negotiations with peace movements of other types within Israel, although some of these seem to have gone awry because of the clash of personalities. He has also moved for the restructuring of the Israeli party system and its ties to various commercial enterprises. Further, it is his claim that the partisan domination of the Parliament is a natural result of the link between the legislative and executive powers, something that he would sever.

It is perhaps a tribute to Avnery that he enjoys a measure of popularity beyond what might be expected given the extreme nature of his thinking and the flamboyancy of his life style. His magazine has a wide readership, particularly among the young. There are, indeed, many in positions of influence who respond to his thrusts positively, yet cannot admit to their sentiments. While the core of his ideology is doubless unacceptable to the vast majority of Israelis, much of what he has supported is now common thought among "doves" within the Israeli establishment. It is his claim that the change is in the Israeli polity, not in Uri Avnery, who is arguing the same line he did in the 1950s.

NOTES

1. Avnery's magnum opus, for example, is called *The War of the Seventh Day* in Hebrew but called *Israel Without Zionists* in its English edition. The following historical discusion of Avnery's development and the creation of *Haolam Hazeh* as a political force is based upon Uri Avnery, *Israel Without Zionists* (New York: Macmillan, 1968), pp. 3–34; Rael Isaac, *Israel Divided: Ideological Politics in the Jewish State* (Baltimore: Johns Hopkins University Press, 1976); Aaron Becher, "A Fringe Group Whose Voice Has No Correlation to Its Power," *Yediot Achronot* (June 9, 1972).

2. On the Black Panthers, see Chapter 10.

3. Interview with Avnery, July 1976.

4. Avnery, *Israel Without Zionists*, Chap. 2 and pp. 200–04.

5. Uri Avnery, "Reflections on Mr. Hammami," *New Outlook* (January 1976), p. 52. See also Uri Avnery, "The Coming War," *Haolam Hazeh* (April 2, 1975), p. 15, and Uri Avnery, "Gaza: Dayan's Torment," *Haolam Hazeh* (July 1971), p. 12.

6. See Avnery's proposal for the separation of religion and state, presented in the Knesset on May 31, 1966, *Divrei HaKnesset* (6th Knesset, 63rd sess.), p. 1576. Also, see Ervin Birnbaum, *The Politics of Compromise: State and Religion in Israel* (Rutherford, N.J.: Fairleigh Dickinson University, 1970), pp. 280–88; also see interview of Avnery in Yoel Marcus, "Meet Uri Avnery: Peace, Pornography and Politics," *Israel Magazine* (June 1971), p. 62.

7. Uri Avnery, "The Third Year of the Six Days' War," in *Reflections on the Middle East Crisis*, ed. Herbert Mason (Paris: Mouton, 1970), p. 62.

8. See transcript of a press conference held at the Israel Newsman's Club—reprinted in *Haolam Hazeh* (July 14, 1976), p. 38.

9. Interview with Avnery, op. cit.

10. Uri Avnery, "The New Leaders," *New Outlook* (July-August 1976), pp. 20–22.

11. Uri Avnery, "Unofficial and Unrepresentative: Transcript of an Interview at the Hague," *New Middle East* (September 1969), pp. 23–28; see also Avnery, *Israel Without Zionism*, pp. 198–99.

12. Uri Avnery, "Jerusalem is Not Saigon," *New Outlook* (May-June 1975), p. 26; Uri Avnery, "One Word: Palestine," *Haolam Hazeh* (December 30, 1969), pp. 12–13; and Uri Avnery, "Playing with Fire," *Haolam Hazeh* (July 23, 1975), pp. 8–9, 16.

13. Interview with Avnery, op. cit.

14. See Avnery's lettter to the editor of the Jerusalem *Post*, October 8, 1973. For a good description of the present position of peace activists in Israel, see Isaac, *Israel Divided*, Chap. 4.

15. Uri Avnery, "The Palestinian Option," in *The Palestinians: People, History, Politics*, ed. Michael Curtis et al. (New Brunswick, N.J.: Transaction, 1975), pp. 191, 193. See also Uri Avnery, "Go Believe the Arabs!" *Haolam Hazeh* (April 30, 1975), p. 13.

16. Interview with Avnery, op. cit.

17. Avnery, *Israel Without Zionists*, p. 200. Though such thinking has pervaded much of Avnery's writing, he has also questioned its viability. See, for example, Avnery, "Unofficial and Unrepresentative," p. 26.

18. Among those believed to be supporters of the Israeli peace movement are such eminent political figures as Abba Eban, Lova Eliav, Yitzhak Ben-Aharon and the late Avraham Ofer; see Uri Avnery, "Fighting for the Peace: The Silent Minority," *New Middle East* (March-April, 1972), pp. 21–22. See also Erich Isaac and Rael Isaac, "Israel's Dissenting Intellectuals," *Conservative Judaism* (Spring 1972).

19. See "Disunity Hits Hopes for a United Left," Jerusalem *Post* (July 30, 1973), and "Fringe Parties Fight for Votes," Jerusalem *Post* (December 30, 1973).

20. Interview with Avnery, op. cit.; see also Uri Avnery, "Behind Closed Doors," *Haolam Hazeh* (July 7, 1976), p. 11.

21. Transcript of press conference held at the Israel Newsman's Club—reprinted in *Haolam Hazeh* (July 14, 1976), p. 38.

22. Avnery, "The New Leaders," p. 22.

5

RAKAH: THE NEW COMMUNIST LIST

A formal Communist Party, responsive to Moscow, has been part of the Palestine-Israel political spectrum since 1919, though it remained illegal under British jurisdiction until 1941. Calling itself the Socialist Workers Party (Mifleget Poalim Sotzialistim), it drew its membership from left-wing members of the Poale Zion movement, early pioneers who had become alienated from Zionism and from young people who were attracted by its underground status. In order to gain full Comintern recognition, the party officially disclaimed Zionism, Jewish immigration to Palestine, and the revival of the Hebrew language—even as far as changing its name to the Yiddish, Palestinishe Kommunistishe Partei (Palestine Communist Party—PCP). Comintern recognition came in 1924.

The Party was filled with internal strife and external conflict from its very inception. Officially a non-Zionist movement, it militated against Jewish settlement in Palestine and encouraged emigration to the Soviet Jewish settlement of Birobijan in Siberia, to which some of the Party's members left in the late twenties and early thirties.[1] In addition, the Party—under orders from Moscow—defended Arab rioting in 1929 and took the Arab position on land disputes throughout the period. As a result of these activities, the PCP was expelled from the Histadrut and was able to muster only 2.5 percent of the 1925 vote and 1 percent of the 1931 vote to the elected Jewish Assembly (Asefat Hanivharim).[2]

Internally, the Party was always split between its largely Jewish leadership and the need to attract a largely Arab constituency. In an attempt to "Arabize," a campaign to send non-Jewish members to Moscow for training was undertaken and one such, Ridwan Al-Hilu, was appointed Party secretary in 1934. Yet attempts to unify Arab peasants under the banner of international communism were equally unsuccessful because of lingering feudal relationships and traditions in Arab society as well as purely national upheavals within the Arab world in the late 1930s.[3]

In effect, the Party was split between its Jewish and Arab cadres, though its attempts at proselytism were singularly unsuccessful among the masses of both communities. The Party attempted to walk this ideological tightrope while still maintaining its anti-Zionist stance and its loyalty to the Soviet Union. In 1941, after the Nazi abrogation of its nonaggression pact with the USSR, the PCP joined the Allied war effort and was awarded legal status by the British.

It was soon afterward that the Party suffered its first major schism. By 1943, as a result of illegal immigration in the face of the British White Paper of 1939, large numbers of Jewish migrants had reached Palestine and the Party's Jewish leaders wished to redirect their efforts and attempt to activate these new settlers. After considerable inner dissension, a split resulted along largely ethnic lines, with the Arab faction assuming a nationalist stance as the Arab League of National Liberation. The Jewish faction, in turn, split between traditional and nationalist elements. The latter, the Communist Educational Association, established contacts with various Zionist and Jewish terrorist groups, and Jewish Communists were re-admitted to the Histadrut.[4]

With the founding of the state of Israel through Soviet support, the various factions of the Party were united as the Israel Communist Party (ICP or Maki—its Hebrew acronym). The ICP expressed loyalty to the state though maintaining its anti-Zionist posture and defending the rights of Arab refugees to repatriation and compensation. The ICP gained one of its most creative spokesmen, Moshe Sneh, as a result of a rift within the Marxist-Zionist Party, Mapam, in 1955. Sneh, a former General Zionist and commander of the famed Zionist military branch, the Haganah, had split with Mapam over its break with the Soviet Union in the wake of the anti-Semitic Doctors' Plot and the Slansky trials of 1952. Sneh was subsequently to become the secretary of Maki and editor of its official organ, Kol Ha'am.[5]

The Party continued its precarious existence during the next seventeen years, attempting to convince the toiling masses of Israel that their only salvation was through identification with the Soviet Union. A Communist kibbutz, Yad Hannah Senesh, was established in 1955 and Maki gained a modicum of Jewish respectability. Its main activities were within the Arab community of Israel, however, where the ICP represented the sole alternative to the Zionist parties. Consequently, it was able to elect a parliamentary delegation ranging between three and six members, the height being reached in the 1955 Knesset.[6]

The festering wounds within the Party were brought to the fore in 1965. On the eve of the national elections, Maki split with the Soviet Union over the proper socialist appraisal of various Arab regimes and suffered an internal split as a result. The bulk of its Jewish membership, led by Sneh and Shmuel Mikunis, remained loyal to the Party and sided with it against the USSR, while its largely Arab wing, led by Tawfiq Tubi and Meir Wilner, created the New Communist List (Rakah being its Hebrew acronym).

For most Israeli Arabs, Rakah was now a more suitable alternative to the Zionist line. Its leadership and ideological nature was more characteristically Arab and it was more clearly anti-Zionist than was Maki. Rakah polled more than twice the votes of Maki and placed three Knesset members to Maki's one. The Soviet Union, for its part, remained temporarily neutral and invited delegations of both parties to its Twenty-Third Party Conress. This dual recognition was short-lived, however.

In the wake of the 1967 War, the rift between Maki and Rakah expanded. Maki generally supported the Israeli war effort and justified Israel's position in terms of self-defense. It criticized the USSR for taking the Arab side and seriously impeding the cause of peace. Rakah, rather, argued the Soviet line, defined Israel as the aggressor and demanded immediate evacuation of all territories taken as a result of the war. Both the Soviet Union and Israel's Arabs disavowed Maki and each lent their support to Rakah, resulting in an electoral increase of some 50 percent in the 1969 election and an additional 37 percent in 1973.

Rakah has consequently become the most radical element in the Israeli Parliament, in the sense that it is the only party that unabashedly attempts to represent Palestinian nationalism and assumes a staunchly anti-Zionist pose. It has continued to walk an ideological tightrope between the needs of its largely Arab constituency and its loyalties to the Soviet line. It has also come to be seen, both by Arab voters and Israeli leadership, as a party of protest and dissent within the official structure of the Knesset, and though it maintains the name Rakah in Hebrew publications, it calls itself the Israel Communist Party (ICP) abroad.*

---

*In 1973, Maki joined with a group of non-Communist students and intellectuals known as Tchelet-Adom (Blue-Red), led by former military strategist Meir Peil. The new coalition

WORLD VIEW

Perhaps the two most important elements in Rakah's perception of the political universe are its ideological ties to the Soviet Union and its very practical ties to the demands of Israel's Arab minority. Though the Party has attracted a small number of Jewish voters, this has generally constituted only about a fifth of its constituency. Much of Rakah's success, therefore, depends upon its ability to synthesize these two influences in its program and in the mind of the Arab voter.

In general, such an ideological marriage has not been an easy one to consummate. Traditional Marxism has always been suspicious of nationalist movements, often considering them generally reactionary and contrary to the goals of international socialism. To the Arab community of Israel, however, a national state and the liberation of the Palestinians as a people is of the utmost importance and political programs are often evaluated in that context.

Further, Arab village life and peasant traditions do not lend themselves to theories of collectivization and communal labor. Communist attacks on individual ownership and private property run contrary to centuries of sustenance farming and near feudalism. Consequently, these ideas are extended a cool reception at best. Equally, Arab traditions are closely related to religious beliefs and customs that frame much of village life and are hostile to Communist advances. It is no accident that most of Israel's Arab Communist leaders have come from the better educated Christian, rather than Muslim, families.[7]

It can also be understood that Rakah's close ties to the Soviet Union mean that its position will be influenced by the USSR and its relationship with Arab regimes. Here the problem is two-fold. When the Soviet Union increases its influence with Arab states that are Israel's avowed foes, then the Party must temper its support with an eye to questions of loyalty to the Jewish state. When the USSR suffers a retreat or seems to be pressuring Arab states, then the Party is put in the position of apologist to Israel's Arab minority.

---

changed its name to Moked (the Focus) and played down its Communist affiliations. It should also be noted that another non-Zionist, Uri Avnery, won a Knesset seat in 1965 and again in 1969. Though he supported some form of Palestinian statehood, he represented the Jewish antiestablishment perspective and his election was more a function of his personal notoriety as a journalist than the result of a developed party structure.

As a result, Rakah has attempted to avoid those issues that might prove ideologically inconvenient. It has rather concentrated its attack upon the relationship between Israel's Zionist leadership and the alleged forces of imperialism among the Western nations, notably the United States, West Germany, Great Britain and South Africa. The claim is that the tension between Israel and its Arab neighbors is a direct result of collusion with these capitalist states and their manipulative attempts to prevent the advancement of progressive forces in the Middle East.

It is here that the motivation of Israeli expansionism may be seen. In the words of one leading Rakah member,

> the expansionist Israeli policy is given support by precisely those forces in the capitalist world who aspire to sabotage the detente in international tension, to prevent the victory of the principles of peaceful coexistence in international relations between states with different social regimes, and to turn back the wheel of history to the epoch of the cold war.[8]

In this sense, the Zionist leadership in Israel has forged a partnership wih the forces of Western imperialism. The West hopes to maintain a good position vis-à-vis Arab oil interests, while preventing Communist penetration in the region. It therefore uses Israel as a "whip" with which to suppress movements of social change among the Arab states. By continuing to arm Israel, the United States is able to hold a beachhead in the Middle East by proxy.

The Israeli government is perfectly happy to play this role in return for the considerable help—military and economic aid and outright grants, such as donations and reparation payments—that has been forthcoming. While little of this money ever reaches the toiling masses, Rakah claims, it does serve to allow the appearance of affluence and to artificially buoy the economy. It is therefore to the interest of the Israeli leadership to place a wedge between the United States and the Soviet Union, issue warnings of Soviet penetration and its peril, and

> to stoke up political and military tensions in the region, because every complication favors their expansionist plans and provides them with an excuse to sidestep a settlement of the Palestinian problem.[9]

Yet far more troubling than the suppression of radical movements by Western imperialism is the gross injustice suffered by Israel's Arab minority. Entitled to the same national and civil rights as the Jewish population, the Israeli government has allegedly stripped this community of even the most fundamental rights of ownership and liberty. Specious arrests, land expropriations, and curfews are just some of the tactics employed not only by occupationary forces on the West Bank but also by civil authorities within Israel proper.

Rakah has strained to portray itself as the sole political organization within Israel that represents the national and individual rights of its Arab minority. Thus the Party, early in its history, expressed the view that Palestinians, wherever they reside, constitute one nation with clear territorial rights in the region. Styling itself "the vanguard of the just struggle of the Arab People in Israel," Rakah has demanded the elimination of government blacklists, confiscation of property and the whole array of "cruel acts of oppression in the occupied territories [which include the] murder of pupils and unarmed men and women"[10]

Such brutality is one more consequence of the close relationship between Israel and the United States. Since its leaders perceive their strength to be based upon their utility as the representatives of the West in the region, it is necessary for the Israeli government to appear resolute in their dealings with the Arab World. Lifting noxious restrictions from the Arab community might allow dissident elements to gain a foothold and be construed as weakness in Israeli resolve. It is therefore necessary to deny rights and annex property in the name of self-defense.

The problems that result from the close relationship between Israel and the West are held in bold contrast, by ICP leaders, with the peaceful motivation of the Soviet Union. While the United States is alleged to have no reason for regional involvement beyond the concerns of its own oil lobby, the USSR is held to have a legitimate interest in that which concerns its southern flank. Further, its overt empathy with the people of the Third World, as expressed by the Twentieth Party Conference of the Soviet Communist Party, make it the natural intermediary for serious peace negotiations.

Yet, does it not seem that an identification with the Soviet Union, given its close relationship with the Arab world, runs counter to Israel's best interests—even in Rakah's estimation? Quite the contrary, argues Rakah secretary Meir Wilner:

> Peace and tranquility in the Middle East are the goals of the Soviet policy in the area. The Soviet Union is interested in creating conditions for the development of relations with all states in the Middle East. There is not, nor can there be, any prejudices against any of these

states, including Israel, if the latter drops its policy of aggression. . . .
The Soviet government stresses in a clear and unequivocal manner that
it is interested in normalization and developing relations with Israel if
she will step unto the path of peace. And peace is the foremost national
interest of the Israeli people.[11]

Economically, indeed the relationship between Israel and the United
States has been disastrous, in Rakah's estimation. The Zionist government
has incurred a debt of some $18 billion, about half of which is interest.
Living under the constant fear that their creditors will demand payment,
Israel's leaders have become little more than wards of the United States
and its imperialist allies. Such a result has been perceived even among
American Jews and progressive elements in Israel.

We ought never to forget that American Jews are

Americans first and foremost. If the United States were to call in its
debt there is little that they could do, or would do to save her. Israel
would choke.[12]

Equally,

Even in Israel itself, the sober-minded are aware of the limitations of
the Zionist lobby in the United States. The U.S. stake in a militarily
strong Israel, too, has its limits. Some Israeli observers hold that if the
U.S. ruling circles grow weary and arrive at the conclusion that Israel's
policy is contrary to their interest, U.S. support will cease to be as
unconditional as it is now. Facts intimating "weariness" keep coming
to light.[13]

As a result of the government's economic bondage and the bankruptcy
perceived in its policies, Rakah senses considerable unrest within Israeli
society. Ready for change, the Israeli working class has demonstrated its
alienation by means of strikes, protest rallies, and a general economic
slowdown. The time is ripe for a united front of laborers, Palestinian Arabs,
and progressive forces to eradicate the weaknesses of Israeli capitalism
and aggression.[14]

VALUES AND GOALS

Just as Rakah views the world through the prism of Soviet Marxism, so
too does this powerful influence affect the content of its prescriptions for

the future. In effect, its values and goals are clear outgrowths of its evaluation of the state of affairs in the region. Further, the leadership of Rakah believes—as do all good Communists—that history will bear them out. Indeed, the mounting international pressure on Israel to make territorial concessions and the growing popularity of the party among Israel's Arabs is taken as the beginnings of that very vindication.

Clearly, they argue, it is the Soviet path that will lead to a lasting and secure peace throughout the region. Was not the USSR first among the community of nations to extend de jure recognition to the fledgling state of Israel some three days after its birth, in May of 1948? Was it not the British who stood in the way of independence to begin with? Is not West German aid blood money from those who were responsible for the destruction of European Jewry? It is only the short-sighted nature of the Israeli leadership and its aggressive tendencies that prevent it from realizing these facts and the Soviet lead toward peace.

Consequently, to be loyal to the Soviet Union is quite in keeping with Israel's better interests. Part of the program for peace calls for full Arab recognition of the rights of the Jewish people to a state in the Middle East. Such a requirement, however, can only be fulfilled by means of international guarantees, and it is therefore necessary that it be carried out under the auspices of the UN, particularly in keeping with its Resolution 242. This resolution, in Rakah's view, requires that Israel rescind its claim to all territories taken in the June 1967 War.[15]

It must be understood, therefore, that to Rakah there is no contradiction between being a "good Israeli" and being a Communist. Indeed, its Jewish members of Knesset will often preface their remarks by recalling their Jewish and pioneering credentials[16] Nonetheless, an essential part of the Party's program deals with the "legitimate rights" of the Palestinian people resident under Israeli jurisdiction. Those living in Israel prior to 1967 were always subject to discrimination, a reprehensible practice in itself. However, those in territories taken in 1967 represent an especially acute case.

Rakah has indicated, unconditionally, that the recognition of this problem and its immediate resolution by means of Palestinian self-determination is prerequisite to the normalization of relations between Israel and its Arab neighbors, and to the curbing of terrorism. Thus:

> today peace is possible only if three elements exist: total Israeli withdrawal from the areas she has been occupying since 1967; Israeli acceptance of the right of self-determination of the Palestine Arab Nation, including a state of its own; Arab acceptance of the right of the Jews to live in a state of their own.[17]

In addition, Rakah has called for a comprehensiuve program of repatriation for those Arabs who have been displaced by one or another of the wars that have plagued the region in the past three decades.

Until these rights are recognized, however, the ICP will continue to sympathize with most radical and nationalist elements within the Palestinian camp. At base, it has always been the Party's contention that the Arab-Israeli confrontation reflects the collision of two equally legitimate national entities. The denial of these rights by one of the two parties quite naturally leads to a justifiable militancy in protest from the other. In particular, this militancy is the correct response to a military occupation, which no nation can tolerate.

As a result, incidents of Palestinian terror in the occupied areas are often reported warmly in the Party press. In particular, the actions of the Palestinian Liberation Organization (PLO) are supported as being representative of this malaise. Even mild rebukes of terrorism, usually that which takes place within Israel's pre-1967 borders, are prefaced with long justifications and denunciations of Israeli policy and alleged intransigence, and followed by lengthy reports of Israeli raids across the borders of neighboring states.[18]

The Israeli who is truly concerned with the effects of such terror would do well, then, to look toward his own government for balm. Only significant changes in both the actions and stated policies of the Israeli leadership—generally in consort with the prescriptions of the Soviet Union—will bring peace and stability to the region. Palestinian militancy and terrorism is only an expression of the anguish and frustration in reaction to Israeli aggression, no matter how lamentable it may be.

The proper path for the responsible Israeli is protest. Thus:

> those who condemn events such as the tragedies at Kiryat Shmoneh in April 1974 and Maalot in May 1974 and aspire to insure a life of peace and tranquility for the citizens of Israel, must raise their voices against the government's policy which ignores the rights of the Palestine Arab People and permits vengeful raids against their refugee camps.[19]

Thus the goals of Israeli and Palestinian nationalism require major changes within the state of Israel. These changes, aside from being political and diplomatic, are also economic and ideological. A shift from its capitalist underpinnings is a first step toward sharing the country's meager resources with the toiling masses. As of now, major concessions are being made to capital investors, in order to boost the lagging economy and foster closer relations with foreign states. Such investors are exempted from many duties, offered bonuses, for exports, and allowed to take profits out of the country. Yet the fiscal crisis continues and unemployment is on the constant increase. Clearly the reasoning is faulty.

The cause for economic failure and foreign estrangement, in Rakah's view, is not the lack of capital investment—which should be curbed and not allowed to expand—but the government's general economic, social, and political policies. Thus it is the Israeli propensity for expansion and aggression that has caused its rift from the nations of the world and required that it overextend itself economically. This results in stronger trade relations with the United States and Western Europe, established industrial powers. Such relations with developed countries "only cause Israel to face conditions of competition that are unbearable for the Israeli economy."[20]

Finally, the acceptance of a Jewish presence in the Middle East is also predicated upon a major ideological upheaval within the state. Aside from the recognition of the Palestinian nation, Israeli leaders must lose their commitments to Zionism, the theoretical framework which rationalizes the ties to the imperialist bloc. Rather than representing a course for Jewish independence, Zionism has created a dangerous stratification within the Jewish people and separated them from their natural allies: Arab neighbors and the USSR.

In this sense, the battle against an imperialist, bourgeois Zionism is a Jewish nationalist imperative.

> Rather than prevent anti-semitism as it claimed, Zionism has caused hatred of Jews. Rather than unite Jews, it has brought them dissension. Therefore, the struggle against the ideology and practicality of Zionism is an act of Israeli patriotism. It is a struggle for the true national interests of the Israeli People, for the interests of the Jewish laborers all over, for the cause of peace, national independence, democracy and socialism.[21]

STRATEGIES FOR SOCIAL CHANGE

Rakah's tactical prescriptions are at once long range and immediate. Its dogma requires that Israel withdraw immediately from the occupied territories and repatriate Arab refugees. Nevertheless, the Party must stand for election and therefore utilize many of the same political forms that characterize electoral politics elsewhere. Its primary objective here is to win as many Arab voters without estranging itself from its limited Jewish constituency. This is generally attempted by assuming the most radical line possible without threatening its own legitimacy within the Israeli political system and with an eye to the needs of the Jewish laborer.

The Party has been able to muster much of its vote for lack of an alternative. It is clear that its success among younger Arabs implies little more than a protest for those who feel that they have nothing to gain by voting for the more traditional Zionist parties. The older and more established Arab voters, however, have generally made peace with the Israeli state and are more likely to choose one of the list of Arab candidates affiliated to the Labor Alignment. Many have voted for the National Religious Party, despite its loyalties to traditional Judaism, because of the hold it has on the Ministries of Welfare, Reglions, and the Interior. This in return for the patronage and largess that is left to the discretion of the respective officials.[22]

It is not surprising, then, to find that Rakah has largely concentrated its efforts on the Arab youth and young Arab educators who are less well established within the communities. As with traditional groups elsewhere, the young and the better educated are most attuned to appeals of change and dissent. In addition, teachers in the local Arab school systems are in a particularly ambiguous position. This because they are at once employees of the Israeli state—and presumably loyal to it—yet responsive to the calls for unity and nationalism from their students and unemployed peers. As a result they are especially vulnerable to Rakah's line.[23]

It is no surprise, therefore, to find an active Young Communist League of Israel (YCLI) as one of Rakah's most prized affilites. The group has been actively organizing both Arab and Jewish youth of progressive tendencies in several larger cities and throughout the occupied ares. It is the work of the league to

> educate for peaceful coexistence of the two peoples—and thereby act against the poison and hatred infused into the youth by the Israeli authorities. The fundamental problem of the Y.C.L.I. is how to move and convince the numerous young people who live in despair, that there exists a path to peace. The problem is how to infuse into them a feeling of confidence into a brighter perspective instead of hatred.[24]

Aside from the usual activities designed to gain membership and expand the influence of the Party per se, the league has involved itself in areas that are of particular interest to students in Israel, Arab and Jewish alike. In particular, the YCLI has called for a reduction of study fees in secondary schools and universities and mobilization in defense of the rights of working youth. This is parallel with the expected calls for the release of "administrative detainees" and the alleged expropriation of Arab lands.

Not unlike minority Communist Parties elsewhere, Rakah has also called for the creation of a united front with cognate groups who may disagree on tactical, ideological, or personal grounds In particular, the Party has attempted to rally the "forces of peace," as it calls them, and it is not unusual to find the names of Nahum Goldmann (venerable former head of the World Jewish Congress) and various "doves" within the Zionist establishment cited in its literature. This is seen as an indication that dissenting elements are

> becoming visible in Israeli society, although so far they are not dom-inant; more and more the rallying against the annexationist war mad-ness and against the facist danger is coming to the fore. The Communist Party fulfills an important role in consolidating, encouraging and rally-ing these same forces.[25]

The Party has utilized this same tactic in the creation of so-called democratic fronts, i.e., broad-based alliances with non-Communist elements among Arab leaders in the occupied territories. In so doing, Rakah has had to face the task of activating Arab villagers to participate in Israeli politics (that is, for example, to vote, to rally) and then to convince them that the Rakah-dominated front was its sole electoral alternative. Despite these difficulties, Arab voters have often lent stunning support to Rakah's electoral efforts. In Nazareth, for example, the Democratic Front polled 67.3 percent of the municipal vote and captured the mayoralty in the December 1975 local elections.

It may be noted that Rakah's success in gaining the vote of West Bank Arabs has not actually been a function of its ideology or program. In the case of Nazareth, in particular, much of the vote was a reaction to the corruption and inefficiency of the various administrations, dating to the pre-1967 period. In addition, the sensibilities of the residents of Nazareth were considerably ruffled when the minister of labor threatened to cut government support were the Communist list elected. Such a statement at the eve of the election played directly into the Party's desire to be viewed as an avenue of protest and independence.[26]

There is also some indication that Rakah has become sensitive to the wedge that much of its pro-Palestinian line has created between it and Jewish Israelis. While this has not led to significant ideological changes, there is at least one instance in which it has led to a shift within the Party's hierarchy. In early 1972, one of its parliamentary delegation, Emil Habibi, a Christian Arab of Nazareth, resigned his seat and was replaced by Avraham Levenbraun, a Jewish resident of Tel Aviv.

The Party's leadership denies emphatically that there is anything significant in Habibi's resignation beyond his own ill health and sincere desire to return to a quiet village life. It must be more than coincidence, however, that the change came on the heels of an Israeli crackdown on Arab nationalism within its borders and a visit from a Soviet Party delegation. In addition, the Party has seen fit to send Jewish leaders for its representations to peace conferences that have been held in Helsinki, Rome, and Bologna. It would be auspicious for all concerned were Rakah to gain Jewish Israeli adherents without losing its influence with Arab voters. In general, however, the attempt has not been successful.[27]

In addition, the party has strengthened its links with Communist Parties elsewhere. In particular, Rakah delegations have visited several East European countries of late and a Soviet delegation of journalists and academics arrived in Israel for an extensive tour during the spring of 1976. Equally important, in an unprecedented show of unanimity, the Jordanian Communist Party—illegal in that country—joined in a common resolution with the ICP condemning the Israeli occupation and calling for the creation of a Palestinian state on the West Bank. As a consequence, Rakah leadership has also been evident in various left-wing Israeli circles and the Party has called for a greater voice in parliamentary affairs and three seats within the cabinet. Such demands are clearly unrealistic and probably not meant to be taken seriously.[28]

Although the Party's official stance decries violence, its presence has been felt in several of Rakah's activities. Most notable among these was the Arab general strike held on March 31, 1976. Called Land Day, this protest was held in reaction to alleged expulsions and expropriations of Arab land. Rioting and looting were widespread on the West Bank and in Arab sections of the Galilee. In confrontations with security and defense forces, several deaths and dozens of serious injuries were sustained. The actions of Arab villagers and the reactions of Israeli authorities were roundly criticized from all corners.[29]

Yet, perhaps more may be learned of Rakah's tactics by even a cursory glance at its preparations for the strike. Considerable evidence indicates that the bulk of the Arab population and much of its leadership was not in favor of a violent strike. Rakah forces and their sympathizers within the villages canvassed for support and militantly rallied for the strike. Terror and beatings were common and moderate leaders were often jailed for their own protection while public statements and circulars were used to discredit such leadership. Even in the face of such brutality, Arab leaders in Taiba, Daliat Al-Carmet, Gush Halav, and Haifa staunchly opposed the strike.[30]

Characteristically, Rakah condemned the Israeli forces and government authorities for the strike and blamed them fully for the deaths that occurred. Thus:

> land seizures are an outspoken expression of a policy of racist nationalist oppression. The Central Committee condemns the sanguinary attack ordered by the government against the Arab population with the aim to suppress the just and legitimate strike. It was a premeditated murderous onslaught aimed at "teaching them a lesson" by way of a strong-arm policy in order to teach them—the Arab population—not to resist the robbing of their land, not to dare to demand equal rights in their homeland.[31]

SUMMARY

Rakah's influence within the policy-making bodies of Israeli politics is slight. It is by its nature antiestablishment and serves its constituency best as a form of protest. Those Jewish Israelis who support it have long since soured on the idea of operating within the more legitimate forms of authority—even those to the left in such parties as Mapam—and in most instances have declared themselves anti-Zionist. The prospect of the ICP having a serious impact upon the form and structure of Israeli policy, therefore, is not even slight.

Indeed, it may even be an exaggeration to call the Party "Communist" even given the heterogeneity that characterizes much of the communist world. Aside from largely rhetorical pronouncements about economic oppression and the evils of capitalism, there is little that is comprehensively Marxist about the Party's program. Rather, it is fair to claim that the Party is much more a pro-Soviet grouping. Stabs at such things as the "capitalist bloc" are often thinly veiled attacks on the United States and have little to do with traditional Marxism.

In addition, though the Party's platform is replete with declarations of altruistic nationalism, its relationship with similar parties throughout the Arab world, or any other group there, has been slight and inconsistent. The most recent venture of this type, a joint declaration with the Jordanian Communist Party, may represent a shift in this situation, however. This could be a significant event, therefore, in the Party's development.

It may be speculated that Rakah does have some value for the Soviet Union, however. The Party is useful as a prop to overcome what appears to be an anti-Jewish strain within Soviet domestic policy. Demands by Jewish activists for emigration rights and cultural and religious freedom have put the USSR in a bad diplomatic light and have even threatened to influence attempts at detente with the United States. The existence of an Israeli Communist Party with strong loyalties to the Soviet Union may mitigate some of these effects. This may have contributed to the alleged Soviet suggestion that Rakah increase the visibility of its Jewish leadership in 1972 and could imply similar moves in the future.

It may also be that Rakah serves as a whip for Soviet relations with Arab states. There appears to be a relationship between the attention paid by the Soviet press to Rakah and the warmth of Soviet friendship with given Arab countries. Praise of the Israeli Communists often implies indirect criticism for Arab policy. As a tool of diplomacy, foreign policy, and perhaps intelligence, the Party is therefore worthy of Soviet support and encouragement.

Much more significant than its relations with the USSR is Rakah's success in establishing itself as the legitimate spokesman for the demands of the Israeli Arab minority. Indeed, it has become the major example of joint Jewish-Arab cooperation within the Israeli political system. In many ways, the Party has struck a responsive chord in this large minority community that alignment-affiliated Arabs or official Arab policy have never reached. This may have severe implications for the future of this Arab community within the context of Israeli life.

For many years, the Israeli government has depended upon Arab specialists who have counseled the use of force and a hard line toward Arab demands for civil freedoms and a patronizing policy in economic and welfare terms. This, it has been argued, is the language that Arabs understand best. For the older generation, some of this reasoning may be correct. A strong reaction has been engendered, however, among younger Arab leaders, for whom such a policy may no longer be viable. The popularity of Rakah with them can be seen as a signal of this shift. Indeed, the very fact that they have turned to so radical a means of protest—without regard for the substance of their demands—seems to indicate the near bankruptcy of the government's program and the need for change.

There is also reason to believe that much of the Arab leadership would be willing to display a more moderate posture but for the bullying and occasional brutality of Rakah supporters. The absence of an acceptable alternative, one that might allow a modicum of respectability (perhaps even national pride and cultural independence), yet remain within the general purview of Israeli legitimacy, is all the more lamentable as a result. This might allow a natural integration of at least creative parts of the Arab community within the Israeli society, the very society that helped educate and modernize it.

Such an organizational form, therefore, might serve the needs of both the Arab community and the Israeli government while militating against the ills of radicalization which result from an increase in Rakah's influence. Until an alternative emerges, however, it may be expected that the Party will continue to gain popularity among Israel's younger Arabs and could eventually serve as a threat to the stability of this already fragile Middle-Eastern polity.

NOTES

1. For an analysis of the motivation for and development of the Soviet-Jewish colony of Birobidjan, see David J. Schnall, "Territoriality and the Jews, 1924–1936: A Case Study of Soviet Minority Group Policies," *The Helderberg Review* (Spring 1972), pp. 49–59.

2. Moshe Burstein, *Self-Government of the Jews in Palestine since 1900* (Tel Aviv, 1934), pp. 111–19.

3. Moshe Czudnowski and Jacob Landau, *The Israeli Communist Party and the Elections for the Fifth Knesset* (Stanford, Calif.: Hoover Institute, 1965), pp. 6–10.

4. David J. Schnall, "Notes on the Political Thought of Dr. Moshe Sneh," *Middle East Journal* (Summer 1973), pp. 345–46.

5. Ibid., pp. 342–45.

6. For a good general review of the Party's history to this point, see Walter Laquer, *Communism and Nationalism in the Middle East* (New York: Praeger, 1957), pp. 73–119.

7. Martin Slann, "Ideology and Ethnicity in Israel's Two Communist Parties: The Conflict Between Maki and Rakah," *Studies in Comparative Communism* (Winter 1974), pp. 362–63. The seminal work dealing with Arab life in Israel is the somewhat dated study by Jacob Landau, *The Arabs in Israel: A Political Study* (London: Oxford University Press, 1969).

8. David Khenin, "Israel After the October War," *World Marxist Review* (February 1974), p. 98.

9. Emil Touma, "Limits of Partnership in U.S.-Israeli Relations," *World Marxist Review* (June 1975), p. 93.

10. Central Committee, "Nine Years after the June 1967 War and What Now?" *Information Bulletin of the Communist Party of Israel* (henceforth *IBCPI*) (June 1976), pp. 5–7. See also Landau, *Arabs in Israel*, pp. 88–89, 226–27.

11. *Zu Haderekh* (Rakah Hebrew language publication) (May 12, 1976). See also Emil Touma, "The Soviet Union and the Palestine Question," *IBCPI* (May 1976), pp. 49–66.

12. Personal interview with member of Knesset Rakah M. K. Avraham Levenbraun (July 1976).

13. Touma, "Limits of Partnership," p. 94.

14. "The Government Must Reject Nationalism, Occupation, and War," *Arakhim: Problems of Peace and Socialism* (February 1975), pp. 16–18. See also the interview of Rakah Secretary General Meir Wilner in *New Times* (June 1973), pp. 10–11.

15. See "A Just and Stable Peace Can Be Attained: Statement of the Political Bureau of the Communist Party of Israel," *Zu Haderekh* (March 3, 1976). There is evidence that the Party sees this as merely a transitory phase on the road to a full implementation of the UN Partition Plan of 1947. In such a case, Israel would stand to lose far more territory and Jerusalem would fall to international jurisdiction, well within Arab borders. See Clinton Bailey, "The Communist Party and the Arabs in Israel," *Midstream* (May 1970), p. 53.

16. See, for example, the parliamentary confrontation between Meir Wilner and Matityahu Drobless of the Likud Party, as reported in the Jerusalem *Post* (April 4, 1976). Also, see the interview of Wilner in William Brannigan, "The Communist Parties of Israel," *The Nation* (October 25, 1970), p. 400.

17. Tawfiq Ziyyad, cited in Moshe Kohn, "Red Mayor for Nazareth," *Jerusalem Post Magazine* (December 19, 1975).

18. Instances of this ideological stance are numerous. See, for example, "Report of the Central Committee to the Seventeenth Congress," *IBCPI*, Seventeenth Congress Material (July 1972), pp. 31–46, 60–64. Also, see *Al-Ittihad* (Rakah daily Arabic publication, October 3, 1969) and *Zu Haderekh* (January 8, 1975). It should be noted that though the ICP has stated its support for Jewish rights to a national home in Palestine, it has not always been definite about the legitimacy of these rights as compared to those of the Palestinian Arabs. During the period of its split from Maki, for example, the pro-Arab wing, which was to become Rakah, argued that those who define the Mideast conflict in terms of two competing nationalisms were "playing into the hands of the imperialists." *Kol Ha'am* (May 19, 1965).

19. David Khenin, "For a Policy of Reason," *World Marxist Review* (February 1975), p. 18. See also "Statement on the Attack on the Savoy Hotel in Tel Aviv," *IBCPI* (February-March 1975), p. 16.

20. Avraham Levenbraun, "Law for the Encoruagement of Capital Investments Increases Burden on Wage Earners," *IBCPI* (June 1976), pp. 22–23.

21. Meir Wilner, "The Ideological and Practical Struggle with Zionism," *Arakhim: Problems of Peace and Socialism* (October 1975), p. 15.

22. Subhi Abu-Ghoush, "The Politics of an Arab Village in Israel" (Ph.D. diss.), cited in Martin Slann, op. cit., p. 368. See also Jacob Landau, "The Israeli Arabs in the Elections to the Fourth Knesset," *International Review of Social History* (Spring 1962), pp. 1–32.

23. Landau, *The Arabs in Israel*, pp. 88–93, 141. See also Jacob Landau, "A Note on the Leadership of Israeli Arabs," in *Political Institutions and Processes in Israel*, ed. Moshe Lissak and Emanuel Guttmann (Jerusalem: Hebrew University Press, 1971), pp. 383–94.

24. "Report of the National Conference of the Young Communist League of Israel," *IBCPI* (March 1976), p. 65.

25. Meir Wilner, "The Charter of Independence Put to the Test of Time," *IBCPI* (May 1976), p. 12.

26. Jerusalem *Post* (December 11, 1975); see also Matityahu Peled, "The Cure for Nazareth," *New Outlook* (January 1976), pp. 35–38.

27. Moshe Meisels, "Rakah Attempts to Sharpen its 'Jewish Profile'," *Ma-ariv* (February 25, 1972). See also the transcript of Jerusalem Radio, domestic service (June 21, 1972).

28. For reports of such actions, see the Jerusalem *Post* (May 2, 1976; May 5, 1976; and July 29, 1976).

29. Yosef Goell, "Shattered Illusions," *Jerusalem Post Magazine* (April 2, 1976).

30. See the Jerusalem *Post* for the week of March 25, 1976. See also the Jerusalem *Post* (April 9, 1976; April 16, 1976; and May 25, 1976).

31. "Resolution of the Central Committee. Communist Party of Israel, on the Day of the Land," *IBCPI* (April 1976), p. 4.

6

MATZPEN: THE ISRAELI
SOCIALIST ORGANIZATION

Organized communism in Israel has had a tense history, filled with internal conflict and stress. As noted elsewhere, this is a function of its attempts at loyalty to the Soviet Union and legitimacy in Israel as well as the demands of its Jewish leadership and its largely Arab consituency.[1] The Israel Socialist Organization (ISO) is the offshoot of an ideological rift within the Communist Party of Israel and in many ways reflects not only the instabilities of the latter but also the influence of youth-oriented movements of the left throughout the world.

The earliest rumblings of discontent within the party leading to the schism, were already discernible in 1960–61.[2] A small group of the Party's younger members were becoming restless with the dogmatic and somewhat heavy-handed ways of the Party's leadership. Topheavy with administrative cadres, walking an ideological tightrope between the Zionist and Arab positions, the party was allegedly losing the revolutionary fire which had made it attractive to these younger adherents. Turning from a commitment to Marxism, the Party was now umbilically linked to the Moscow line and to retain its legitimacy spoke out only on those domestic issues that were viewed as safe.

The ties to Moscow were becoming particularly irksome to these dissenters. It was their opinion that the USSR had also lost much of its revolutionary nature and was becoming one more established, bureaucratic, national state. Private interests seemed to be taking precedence over revolutionary zeal and Marxist principle losing to good diplomatic relations. This view was punctuated by the Soviet resolution to open relations with the capitalist world under the banner of peaceful coexistence, a concept which these young Communists found repugnant.

This disaffected group remained quite small at first, numbering no more than about a dozen party members. To discuss their unhappiness, several coffee houses and parlor cliques emerged. From these, the dissidents formed small groups, cells or "groupuscles" as they came to be called. Two parallel lines developed but differences were far more a matter of personalities and location than ideology or tactics. Lines of communication were opened with non-Communist leftists and dissenters such as Uri Avnery and Natan Yellin-Mor, whose Semitic Union was still in its active stages of development.[3]

Though such contacts were generally unsatisfying, their development inspired a desire for independence from the ICP and the aspiration to form a revolutionary organization more attuned to the minds of the young radicals. Sensing an inherent dislike for the directions of the Israel Communist Party, they were unable to link themselves to an issue or ideology that offered greater play for their frustrations. In the final analysis, the Party was doing the responsible, socialist thing by following the lead of the Soviet Union, no matter how inherently incorrect it seemed.

The year 1962 was momentous in this regard. On the heels of the revolution in Cuba and the confrontation between the United States and the USSR over missiles there, a sharp rift appeared to be developing between the Soviet Union and Communist China. Further, the break seemed to reflect many of the same issues that troubled these groupuscles within the Israel Communist Party. In each instance, the Maoist line was closer to the radical revolutionary desires of the Israeli dissidents and pulled the divergent elements in both Haifa and Tel Aviv together and toward a united break.

The leadership of the new group was a variegated lot. Some, such as Haim Hanegbi and Oded Pilavsky, came by their radicalism through Zionist-Socialist youth movements. Others were attracted through contacts they made in the armed forces, as was former sailor Akiva Orr. Still others floated into the organization almost by accident, through discussions at coffee houses and private apartments—as did Ari Bober. Moshe Machover, an expatriate mathematician lecturing at the University of London, represents the intellectual element within the group. In addition, its radical ideology held an attraction for newer immigrants, particularly a contingent from South America.

In symbolic defiance of the legitimate political system, these exiles from the ICP refused to call themselves a party or, by implication, to stand for election. Rather, they adopted the title Israel Socialist Organization, underlining the more fluid and radical nature of their formation, and chose the popular title Matzpen (the compass), for their publications. It is by the latter name that the group became known.

Perhaps most significant in its early development was a particularly fruitful contact made with a Christian Arab writer from Haifa, Jabbara Nikola. An intellectual and somewhat charismatic leader of a group of radical Arab Israelis, Nikola had long since broken with formal socialist parties but still maintained close contact with the Fourth Trotskyist International, then convened in Paris. Though much older than the members of the new organization, Nikola sensed a commonal tie between them and invited the Matzpen leadership to open negotiations toward merger.

The fledgling ISO was flattered by Nikola's offer. First, the latter's influence and credentials were not insignificant. Second, it gave the new organization an ideological father in Trotsky and a prophet in Nikola. Practically speaking, Matzpen could double its membership in one fell swoop and lay claim to internationalism by becoming a genuinely binational organization. After numerous meetings and painstaking ideological debate over matters theoretical, international, and tactical, a merger was struck and Matzpen adopted an internationalist Trotskyist plank into its radical platform.

It is interesting to note that the development of the Israel Socialist Organization is not unlike similar trends seen throughout Europe in the early sixties and in the United States somewhat later. In particular, parallels may be drawn with New Left groups that were formed as splinters from organized Communist parties in France and Germany in the wake of the Algerian Revolution. Interestingly, one of the major figures of these European movements, Danny Cohn-Bendit, also figures in the development of Matzpen. A friend of Haim Hanegbi, Cohn-Bendit was invited to speak at a kibbutz where his remarks caused a near riot. He was also partially responsible for the splintering of Matzpen, of which more below.

Prior to 1967, the ISO said little that was of particular relevance to most Israelis. Still imbued with much of its own pioneering and socialist ideology and surrounded by hostile neighbors who appeared to be in league with the forces of international communism, the Israeli polity had little use for one more faction of radical extremists. Matzpen support remained minuscule and it gained attention only as a curiosity or a negative influence in both the foreign and domestic press.

The June 1967 War changed the position of Israel in the minds of New Left and Third World movements. Largely indifferent or mildly positive in the past, these now came to see Israel as an extension of Western imperialism in the Middle East. Always uneasy with the close relationship between Israel and the United States, New Left theorists now equated

American aggression in the Far East with Israel's alleged expansionism. Seeking a voice and cognate spirit within, Matzpen found itself vaulted into the forefront and lionized by those who supported the New Left throughout the world. It was largely under the auspices of such elements that Ari Bober in 1970 was invited to tour the United States and present his radical position.[4]

Presently, four independent strains of thought have emerged as a result of internal fractionalizing within Matzpen. Some of these rifts are attributable to ideological differences and the desire for dogmatic purity above all. Others are more a result of conflicts of personality and perceptions of potential constituency demands and support. Still others may be a reflection of internal strains and dissatisfactions inherent in a small, decentralized, radical youth movement.

The Tel Aviv faction, led by Hanegbi and Pilavski, is closest to the original both in terms of membership and orientation. The Jerusalem branch, led by Bober, remains closest to the Trotskyist line and emphasizes the export of revolution. This faction has attempted to open communications with similar movements of radical revolution abroad and has published a collection of English language ISO works. Most of the authors are either members of the Jerusalem branch or expatriots with similar sympathies.

A third faction is composed largely of emigrants from South America. Calling itself the Struggle faction, this group has predicated its proposed method of revolution upon the canvassing of laborers in Israel. In many ways it has emphasized these needs over those of internationalism and has therefore been accused of syndicalism. Finally, the Revolutionary Communist Alliance represents the most militant elements of Matzpen. Under the aforementioned influence of Danny Cohn-Bendit, this faction has allegedly participated in several militant protests and has maintained contact with agents of Arab powers.[5]

WORLD VIEW

Militantly anti-Zionist, the Israel Socialist Organization is, in many ways, the most radical of all organizations of dissent in Israel. Its membership is an ethnic mixture of native Israelis, Christian Arabs, and newer immigrants from Europe and the Western Hemisphere. In addition, Israeli migrants abroad have created a subgroup which serves as spokesman and publicist for the ISO line. Based in London, this wing of the organization is known as the Israel Revolutionary Action Committee Abroad (ISRACA) and is directed by Moshe Machover, now a lecturer at the University of London.

Committed as it is to Marxist doctrine and the economic interpretation of history, Matzpen has involved itself not only in the study and analysis of topical issues in contemporary Israel, but has also dwelled at length on the foundations of Zionist history, the early Jewish settlement of Palestine and the movement for independence. The major thrust of the analysis is aimed at the fundamental injustices perceived in the Israeli treatment of Palestinians under Jewish jurisdiction. The ISO has also attacked governmental policy regarding the occupied territories and discrimination against Oriental Jews, i.e., those who emigrated from Arab or non-Western nations.

As a consequence, Zionism is their ideological villain in the Middle East conflict. An expansionist doctrine, Zionism allegedly exists first to foster the interests of the Israeli state and second its European Jewish entrepreneurs. The dominant Zionist forces have allied themselves with Western imperialists and have served as their bulwark and lackeys in the battle against revolutionary change in the Middle East.

Yet there is a clear recognition that Israeli society is by no means a classic case of capitalism, but is peculiar and unique in many ways. Historically, it is claimed, Jewish settlement of Palestine was based on an unusual form of colonization, not unlike that which resulted in white dominated minority governments in Rhodesia and South Africa. Rather than being the reflection of a direct policy of any given nation state, it was the result of Zionist agitation and the policy of an exclusionary ideology. In this sense, Israel has been superimposed upon a Third World native culture with which it has little in common. This is termed a settler society.[6]

Therefore, the mass of Israeli society has been imbued with a pioneering ideology and mentality which makes class consciousness difficult. It is eternally pitted against the indigenous population of Palestine, its Arab residents. The cause for this unfortunate malaise is to be found in political Zionism:

> as long as Zionism is politically and ideologically dominant . . . and forms the accepted framework of politics, there is no chance whatsoever of the Israeli working-class becoming a revolutionary class. . . . Israeli workers nearly always put their national loyalties before their class loyalties.

A function of this development is the impact of ethnic considerations upon Israeli social and economic life. The Oriental Jew is subject to discrimination and oppression at the hands of the authorities. Yet, these immigrants from the Arab world tend to blame their culture—which they have been convinced is inferior—rather than Israeli capitalism for their plight. Further, like the feelings of poor American whites toward blacks, their status at the bottom rung of the socioeconomic ladder makes them the more rabidly anti-Arab.[7]

Economically, the case of Israel is equally unique. It is constantly in need of funds to support its enormous military establishment and defend its position in the Arab world. Most of its economic enterprises and agricultural cooperatives operate at a loss and are fraught with corruption. The nation must therefore depend upon aid and support from "imperialist" nations abroad. Indeed, thanks to the support it does receive, most notably from the United States, the Israeli standard of living is kept artificially high, relative to the other countries in the region.

Paradoxically, Israel has been able to maintain an independent international position in the face of this aid, Matzpen argues. The key to this puzzle lies in the nature of the "unilateral capital transfers" which have been forthcoming from Western nations. Such transfers include large donations from Western Jewish communities and reparation payments from West Germany. Unlike other forms of foreign aid or investments, these funds reach Israel "without being subject to conditions governing returns of capital or payments of dividends." In Matzpen's estimation, some 70 percent of the inflow of funds from foreign sources has been of this type and the otherwise sagging Israeli economy is thereby buoyed. Despite its economic dependence, Israel's leadership has avoided direct exploitation.

This massive inflow of free capital has neither reached the Israeli masses nor has it made its way to the bulk of the bourgeoisie. Rather, it has come to the hands of the chief instruments of Zionist oppression, the Jewish Agency, the bureaucracy of the Labor Party, and the Histadrut— Israel's mammoth labor union. Funds collected abroad are then filtered into the Israeli economy according to the perceived priorities of Zionist leaders. The diverse strains of Israeli society have been unified under the banner of Zionism, as interpreted by these state institutions.

These bureaucracies are largely independent and face little opposition from within.

> This has proved successful since not only is the Israeli working-class organizationally and economically under the complete control of the Labor bureaucracy but so too is the Israeli bourgoisie. Historically, the bureaucracy has shaped most of the institutions, values, and practices of Israeli society without any successful opposition from within, and

subject only to the external constraints imposed by imperialism and the resistance of the Arabs.[8]

The policies of the Zionist leadership are largely implemented by the massive trade union enterprise, the Histadrut. As both the central labor force and one of Israel's largest employers, the body has allegedly monopolized the economic life of all workers and professionals while representing no one but itself and the Labor Party. The organization established its position by moving into the forefront of "agricultural colonization and in winning places of work for Jewish laborers by evicting Arab peasants and workers." Today it has no rival.

Rather than being a true trade union, however, Matzpen claims that the Histadrut actually inhibits the cause of its members. Thus:

> A trade union should be based upon the needs of the workers. But the Histadrut was created only to organize Jewish labor for the Zionist cause. Even capitalist societies have trade unions, but not in Israel. Here, there is no independent labor organization. The Histadrut is a labor union in the same sense as the unions in the U.S.S.R. Its purpose is actually anti-labor: to allow the Zionist forces to organize among the workers.[9]

Such domination on the part of ossified unresponsive national institutions places the Israeli laborer and his Arab counterpart in an unenviable position.

Finally, the position of the ISO has also included the qualified equation of Zionism with racism and national oppression. By its nature, Zionism has demanded that the state of Israel be Jewish and being Jewish confers upon one special rights and privileges. These include immediate citizenship, aid for returning migrants, and special exemptions for new arrivals. Arabs, be they long-standing citizens or new immigrants, are neither offered these aids nor are they socially accepted. In fact, they are subject to suspicion and treated with caution and harshness. Their land may be delegated for expropriation and their jobs can be sacrificed for the needs of Jewish workers, often by administrative fiat.

In this sense, Israel's Arabs are neither allowed to pass unobtrusively into Jewish society, should they so desire, nor are they permitted to express a national identity of their own. Yet the Zionist form of racism, as with much else in Israel, is unique.

> The Zionist leaders and their followers do not necessarily hold racist views. Many of them do not consider the Jews to be a superior people

and the Arabs an inferior mob. Zionist racism is basically a practical
one, that stems from the fact that Zionist settlement could be implemented only at the expense of the Palestinian Arabs' rights. The Zionist
enterprise . . . is one of settling Jews on Arab land, of transforming an
Arab country into a Jewish one.

As a consequence, the transformation of which is spoken here, naturally
leads to this form of discrimination and racism toward the Arab native. In
Matzpen's estimation, Zionism and racism are necessary concomitants
one with the other, though not necessarily intentional ones. The elimination of racism, therefore, requires the elimination of Zionism.[10]

VALUES AND GOALS

In the estimation of Matzpen many of these oppressions and injustices
could be easily eliminated. Since they are largely attributable to the structures of political Zionism, the first necessity is the elimination of Zionism as
a political and ideological force in the Middle East. With this would naturally come the restructuring of Israeli society along more democratic lines, a
break with the forces of imperialism, as well as with the world Jewish
community. This first major goal has been euphemistically called the
process of "de-Zionization."
Interestingly the ISO has given this process priority over the classic
Marxist requirements of class struggle, perhaps a concession to the unique
nature of Israeli capitalism. Precisely because Zionism as an ideology has
done so much to shape the character of Israel and the Mideast conflict,
Matzpen

gives primacy to the anti-Zionist struggle and subordinates all other
issues, such as the economic struggle of the working-class, to this
struggle. It considers the overthrow of Zionism as the first task con-
fronting revolutionaries in Israel. . . . It supports anti-imperialist
struggles and the Palestinian struggle against Israeli domination.[11]

The Palestinian struggle is not given unequivocal support, however.
Rather, it is justified only to the extent that its end is to weaken the
influence of Zionism. While the ISO affirms the "right of oppressed people
to fight against oppression by any means they see fit," the major Palestinian organizations appear to ignore the realities of history and the
socialist imperative in the Middle East. No movement can succeed, in
Matzpen's estimation, if it subordinates all other goals to one that is purely
national and above the class struggle.

In addition, Matzpen takes exception to one more principle which they perceive to motivate Palestinian militance. The movement seems not to accept the idea

> that the victorious revolution in the region . . . will grant the right of self-determination to the non-Arab national entities living inside the Arab World, including the Israeli people.

What will replace Zionism in a successful revolution cannot be as chauvinistic as was its precursor. Otherwise the revolution will have been for naught.[12]

In this sense the "de-Zionization" of Israel is only a first step toward a grand socialist revolution which is prescribed for the whole region. In fact, the potential for such change is estimated to be greater in Arab lands which are not subject to Western support, than in Israel. It is expected that the spontaneous eruptions in Arab lands will precipitate change within Israel and encourage the Israeli masses to overthrow the oppressive forces of Zionism and join with their laboring allies elsewhere. Such a movement will be the result of internal strains rather than an import from other socialist lands.

Clearly, the goals of Mtzpen call not only for political changes but for changes in the fabric of life in the Middle East. Nothing short of classic socialism can liberate "the immense energies latent in the masses and channel them to actuate social and economic progress." A Zionist survival in Israel is alleged to be based upon its service as an imperialist bulwark against revolutionary change. Should such eruptions occur and Israel prove ineffective, the West would soon remove the artificial prop on which Israel's Zionist leaders depend.[13]

Matzpen is most specific, however, in its prescriptions for that which should take place within the geographic entity now termed Israel. In its ultimate formulation, the call is made for the dismantling of the forms and structures of the Zionist state.

> In order to create a socialist program in Israel, it is necessary to eliminate this institution known as the State of Israel. There can be no Zionist enterprise without a direct contact with the forces of the imperialist plan. If one wants change he must work to shatter the State.

In its stead would be

> a government based upon socialist principles and part of a vast Socialist union, rather than a national state. In such a form, there would be no

difference between a Jew or an Arab. It would be a state without the institutional trappings of Zionism.[14]

In its essence, Matzpen's program delineates four points prerequisite for the creation of an acceptable secular democratic state of Israel. These points are of a transitional nature in that they begin with those elements most immediate to the needs of the masses—as Matzpen perceives them—and move gradually toward grand designs for radical change and revolution.

The first requires the elimination of the hatred Histadrut, that institution which in the guise of a trade union actually operates in opposition to the needs of the workers. The Histadrut would be replaced by a militant trade organization elected at the lowest level and led by committees of workers. Rather than represent the Zionist state, such a union will struggle for the benefits of laborers to whom it will be responsive, and uncover the alleged fraud in the Histadrut mode of operation. By this means, workers will become radicalized and accustomed to militant action.

A second crucial requirement for the transformation of the Zionist state is the total separation of religion and state. Considered "an elementary demand long ago achieved in most capitalist democracies," such a move will have broad appeal "because of the oppressive intervention of the reactionary religious establishment in the everyday life of every Israeli." It is this link to the Jewish religion that creates the demand for a Jewish state and stands in the way of normalizing relations with the peoples and nations of the region. The attempt to join all the world's Jews in one

> political grouping and to join all their classes and philosophies is not only a theoretical absurdity but also a practical impossibility. It is an attempt which creates a confrontation between Jews and the world's progressive forces.

A third requirement—which is in fact part and parcel of the process of secularization—is the elimination of the law of return. According to present Israeli legislation, any Jew—upon showing proper identification—can claim Israeli citizenship almost upon entering the state. This privilege is denied non-Jewish immigrants who must wait several years and undergo a naturalization process similar to that of other nations. Initiated in the wake of the Nazi atrocities and the very real possibility that many might have been saved but for a friendly power to take them in, the law was meant to insure that there would be no more illegal immigrants and stateless persons.

As one prime example of the privileges enjoyed by Jews exclusively, the law of return must be struck down, the ISO argues. Aside from equalizing the status of all Israelis before the law, its elimination will also go far in solving a fundamental problem which faces even Jewish Israeli society: the definition of Jew. Extending, as it does, various benefits, this status has become a troublesome legal and practical issue instigating difficulties over intermarriages, civil liberties, and inheritance procedures. Its demise will be a boon to all concerned.

Finally, "de-Zionization" demands the severing of all relations with the forces of imperialism. Such a break implies not only those ties with the official governments of capitalist powers but also informal ties with Jewish communities throughout the world. In many ways this is inherent in the secularization of the state and its elimination of those laws that confer unequal benefits to its citizens. Similarly, it is implied in the concerted effort to become one with the region and its peoples.

> The rupture of these ties will eliminate the other basic antagonism between the Israeli Jews and the Arab nation, the antagonism resulting from the counter-revolutionary services the Zionist state offers imperialism.[15]

In sum, Matzpen's prescriptions include an ideological change in Israel which would allow radical modifications in the nature of Middle Eastern life. A mass socialist revolution is demanded within the Arab world—yet one which would still consider the unique needs of non-Arab minorities. Under such new regimes differences between peoples, whether national, religious, or racial, would gradually become of little import.

STRATEGIES FOR SOCIAL CHANGE

As with other movements of long-range dissent, Matzpen's proposals for change are at once specific and vague. Their direction seems aimed at the radicalization and politicization of the Israeli working class. In simple terms, this means breaking the laborers from their close ties with centrist political parties and the Histadrut. Since these latter institutions hold sway over pensions, health and retirement funds, and various other workers' benefits, the task is no simple matter.

As mentioned above, the ISO foresees a new labor structure replacing the much-despised Histadrut. Essentially, this will be a decentralized trade union based upon committees elected at lower levels. It is expected that such committees will coalesce into a radical force with similar committees replacing other institutions. Along with like minded political organizations elsewhere, these groups will become the foundation for a revolutionary front to battle for socialist change throughout the region.

Though Matzpen is rarely specific about the issue of violence, it is clear that the sort of radical change being discussed is not likely to come in a peaceful manner. Some of this is implied in the following statement:

> There is no national liberation without expelling imperialism and its allies in the area, i.e., without a socialist revolution. The way to accomplish this is through the establishment of an all-Middle East proletarian party which would fight imperialism, Zionism and Arab reaction for the socialist revolution.[16]

Matzpen has not made clear what is meant by "the establishment of an all-Middle East proletarian party." Precisely how such a party should be formed, what structure it would take, with whom it would ally—both inside and outside the region—and what relationship it might have with similar revolutionary forces elsewhere, are all issues that remain vague and imprecise. It is clear, however, that the ISO views itself as the vanguard of the laboring classes and the first faint stirrings of such a revolutionary force. It is therefore incumbent upon it to fulfill its historic mission and galvanize others toward its goal.

Through the genesis of the movement—in the form of the Israel Socialist Organization—the initial cadres of the party are being formed. More than simply a peace front which is even supported by elements within the Israeli establishment, the party is presently gaining valuable practical and theoretical experience. By mastering the means of persuasion—moral, economic, and physical—important foundation work has already begun.

One of the newer means of persuasion has led the ISO to compete with other left-wing elements for the support of Israel's youth. The leadership has all but despaired of winning support among the nation's older generation and has emphasized the importance of the adolescent and young adult population—perhaps a reflection of the movement's history as a youthful dissenting faction from the Israel Communist Pary and Israel's contingent in the New Left.

Matzpen has organized "Hafarperet"—the mole—a youth wing aimed at attracting converts from both upper and lower class homes. The group has encouraged its members to refuse the Israel Army oath of allegiance as well as military service in the occupied areas. In addition, Hafarperet represented the ISO in protest actions on the campus of the

Hebrew University and joined with other left-wing elements in East Jerusalem rallies to show solidarity with West Bank Arabs on Land Day, March 31, 1976.[17]

In addition, there is some evidence that the constant barrage of radical protest rhetoric has led several members (and former members) of the ISO to the movement's logical extreme. The most militant faction of the organization—known variously as the Revolutionary Communist Alliance or the Red Front—has invited representatives of revolutionary movements in Europe and the United States to speak at various Matzpen programs. As mentioned above, the kibbutz appearance of Danny Cohn-Bendit caused a near riot.

Further, though Matzpen literature has never set a specific timetable for its proposals nor overtly called for acts of sedition, the Red Front has indicated the need to militantly "upset the superiority of Israeli Defense Forces as a stage in the path to the revolution and the liquidation of the Zionist State." In a sensational case which shocked the Israeli population, Matzpen leader and former kibbutnik Ehud Adiv was implicated in a treason charge. He, Dan Vered, and four other former ISO members were arrested for allegedly spying for the Syrian Secret Service.[18]

Parallel to such activism, Matzpen has also been involved in the establishment of a foreign-based wing, the Israel Revolutionary Action Committee Abroad (ISRACA) whose function it has been to organize anti-Zionist forces in several European cities. As such, the ISO represents an unprecedented attempt on the part of an Israeli group to bring the anti-Zionist position before the world. Various seminar programs, study centers, and position papers have been presented in this effort and alliances have been forged with like minded Arab and European student organizations.

Most notable in this tactic is the coalition of anti-Zionist forces forged by Matzpen under the auspices of the Bertrand Russell Peace Foundation in London. Dating to spring 1967, this group has consistently issued anti-Israel statements that have been printed in the London *Times*, as well as in other local media, and have been carried in numerous European publications and wire services. Although Matzpen's influence in Israeli politics is generally conceded to be small, it was largely in response to such activism abroad that the Israeli government attempted to pass a law curtailing the scope of political action taken by Israeli citizens outside the country.[19]

Perhaps the most concise statement of its radical tactics comes from Matzpen itself:

> We appeal to students and youth to reject completely the propaganda
> for annexation of the territories and to organize protests in universities

and schools against the growing fascist propaganda, against the liquidation of democratic rights under the cover of security requirements,
against the persecution of the Arab population in Israel and against
anti-Arab incitement. ... Demonstrations, meetings, pickets,
petitions, letters to the press—all these means should be used to
struggle for withdrawal.[20]

It is within this context that Matzpen has called upon revolutionary elements both within and without Israel to "wage an eternal war imposed by
destiny."[21]

A SUMMARY PERSPECTIVE

Matzpen, the Israel Socialist Organization, is at once a unique and a
common political phenomenon. It is unique within the Israeli political
spectrum in that it represents a youth-based radical socialist movement
whose very raison d'être is anti-Zionist. Socialist organizations abound in
Israeli political history and each has had its youth wing. However, these
have all been marked with a greater or lesser tinge of Zionist philosophy,
whether politically, culturally, or religiously based. Non-Zionist movements, though few, have generally not been avowedly Marxist Trotskyist
as has the ISO. Equally, the bitter and extreme nature of Matzpen's dissent
is something largely unknown to Israeli politics no matter what the source.
Its existence has often elicited shock and disbelief.

At the same time, when one broadens the perspective to include
European and American political systems, the existence of organizations
like the ISO is not surprising and indeed a commonplace. It may well be a
tribute to the consensus—based upon the structures and institutions—of
Israeli society, that so few such extreme movements exist, and those that
do, carry relatively little impact. The decade of the sixties witnessed the
eruption of ideological movements throughout the Western world. In the
general category of the New Left, these organizations attracted campus
youth, were armed with revolutionary prescriptions for change, and often
included violence as a tactic for their realization.

In many ways, Matzpen resembles New Left organizations elsewhere.
In its origin, the movement was an offshoot of the Israel Communist Party,
whose idological underpinnings were considered too bureaucratic and far
from the ideal of international revolution. An identity with the Soviet
Union, it seems, could be as heavy handed and unsatisfactory as a link with
the forces of capitalism. The result of the melding of several ideological

positions, the ISO comes by its Trotskyism from without—through alliances with older radical elements. Its ties to the New Left were underlined by a close relationship with some of its leading international figures.

Following patterns established by such groups, Matzpen has also been wracked with fissures which severely limit its effectiveness. Either because of the demands for ideological purity above all, or because of organizational differences, or because of the very simple conflicts of personalities, at least four different currents of thought are attributable to the movement. These range from a form of economic syndicalism to a militant attempt to undermine the security of the Israeli state. Members of the latter faction have been implicated in espionage circles collaborating with Arab forces.

This internal problem has also been reflected in Matzpen's relationship with other movements of the Israeli left. Whether non-Zionist or more moderate, such groups and the ISO have not been able to find a common cause. Interestingly, the Zionist Left and its offshoots in the so-called peace movement have been the objects of much of Matzpen's sharpest criticism. Because the ISO does not stand for election, however, it has seen fit to endorse the electoral list of Rakah, the Arab-directed, Soviet-oriented Israel Communist Party.

In terms of its contribution to the content of Israeli politics, there is little doubt that Matzpan's impact is minimal. This will continue at least until it is prepared to join with more moderate, even Zionist, groups who have pressed for peace in return for territorial cessions. In this light, the ISO would have to limit the extent of its radicalism and soften the lines that it has espoused since its formation. In addition, it might well have to dispense with its foreign wing—the Israel Revolutionary Action Committee Abroad. Since this group, and the publicity it receives, is Matzpen's most creative aspect, it is unlikely that such a development will take place.

At present, therefore, the organization serves largely for its shock value. It upsets and embarrasses Israeli leaders—as well as the public—that such a group exists and indeed that its leadership includes scions of some of Israel's oldest families. Equally, the operation of anti-Zionist groups working in collaboration with Arab organizations abroad, outside the framework of Israeli control, yet led and manned by expatriate Israelis, is a disturbing consequence of Matzpen's growth. The disturbance is multiplied by the steady stream of migrants from Israel to Western nations, individuals who may serve as converts to Matzpen's cause—an event that has yet to occur on any large scale.

NOTES

1. See my "Notes on the Political Thought of Dr. Moshe Sneh," *Middle East Journal* (Summer 1973), pp. 342–52; see also my "Dialectic Zionism," *Judaism* (Summer 1973), pp. 334–41. The point is also discussed in my "Organized Communism in Israel," *Midstream* (August-September 1978), pp. 26–36.

2. The ensuing discussion of the genesis of the ISO is based upon these sources: Nira Yuval-Davis, "Leftists in Israel: Matzpen—The Israel Socialist Organization" (Master's thesis, Hebrew University, 1973); Raphael Bankler, "The Story of Matzpen's Development," *Al Hamishmar* (December 15, 1972); Aaron Becher, "A Fringe Group Whose Voice Has No Correlation to Its Power," *Yediot Achronot* (June 9, 1972); Helen Epstein, "New Arrivals on the Israeli Left," *Midstream* (October 1970), pp. 13–14; Peretz Merhav, "The Strategy of the Israeli Left," *New Outlook* (September-October 1970), pp. 40–44.

3. For an analysis of Avnery's thought, see my "Native Anti-Zionism: Ideologies of Radical Dissent in Israel," *Middle East Journal* (Spring 1977), pp. 157–74. See also Chapter 3 above.

4. Ehud Shprinzak, *The Blossoming of the Politics of Delegitimacy in Israel*, Eshkol Institute for Economic, Social, and Political Research, Special Publication no. 8 (Jerusalem: Hebrew University, 1973), pp. 45–46. See also Ehud Sprinzak, "Democracy and Illegitimacy: A Study of the American and the French Student Protest Movements" (Ph.D. diss., Yale University, 1972).

5. Bankler, op. cit.

6. Moshe Machover, "Zionism, National Oppression and Racism," *Matzpen* (March 1976), pp. 7–8.

7. Haim Hanegbi, Moshe Machover, and Akiva Orr, "The Class Nature of Israeli Society," *New Left Review* (January-February 1971), p. 6.

8. The analysis was offered in an interview with a former member of Matzpen's Jerusalem branch, Marius Shattner. See also Moshe Machover and Akiva Orr, "The Nature of Israel," in *The Other Israel: The Radical Case against Zionism*, ed. Ari Bober (New York: Macmillan, 1972), p. 98.

9. Personal interview with Haim Hanegbi, August 1976.

10. Machover, "Zionism, National Oppression," pp. 6–7.

11. Hanegbi, Machover, and Orr, "The Class Nature," p. 25. See also "Zionism Against Jews" and "Anti-Zionism," *Matzpen* (March 1976), pp. 8–9. As noted above, it is precisely the precedence given economic over political issues that has allegedly led the "Struggle" faction toward the sins of syndicalism.

12. Akiva Orr and Moshe Machover, "The Zionist Left and the Palestinian Resistance," in *The Other Israel: The Radical Case against Zionism*, ed. Ari Bober (New York: Macmillan, 1972), p. 186. See also Carl Gersham, "Matzpen and Its Sponsors," *Commentary* (August 1970), pp. 52–53; and Akiva Orr, "On the Right to Self-Determination," *Matzpen* (May 1976), pp. 10–11.

13. Interview with Hanegbi. See also A. Fairjohn and Moshe Machover, "The Fourth Round," *Matzpen* (April 1974), pp. 4–7; and "General Declaration of the Israel Socialist Organization" (March 22, 1968).

14. Interview with Hanegbi. Somewhat contradictorily, Matzpen has also argued that while differences between Jews and Arabs should be eliminated, there should be no forcible coercion employed in a decision to maintain a Jewish state, even after the socialist revolution. "As long as they [Israeli Jews] refuse to join the socialist union, we will support their right to a

separate state, but we will not agree to a Jewish State in the Zionist sense of the word"
(Machover, "Zionism, National Oppression," p. 7). Perhaps these apparent contradictions
are attributable to the several streams of thought within the ISO.

15. Matzpen's program for "de-Zionization" has been presented many times and in
many forms. Perhaps its most concise and original elaboration is to be found in the following:
Ari Bober, "Conclusions," in *The Other Israel: The Radical Case against Zionism*, ed. Ari
Bober (New York: Macmillan, 1972), pp. 1915204, and Israel Socialist Organization, "Fifteen
Basic Principles," *Matzpen* (September 1972), p. 2.

16. "Peaceful Coexistence and Its Consequences in the Area," *Matzpen Position
Paper*—reprinted in Bober, *The Other Israel*, p. 254. See also Becher, op. cit., for a historical
analysis of this thesis.

17. See the Jerusalem *Post* (December 14, 1972 and December 19, 1973). Also, see "A
Letter to the Central Committee of the Israel Communist Party—Rakah," *Special Matzpen
Publication* (March 31, 1976).

18. Jerusalem *Post* (December 11, 1972 and December 12, 1972).

19. Shprinzak, "The Blossoming of the Politics," pp. 47–50.

20. "Down with the Occupation," *I.S.O.: A Collection of Political Statements* (n.d.), p.
11.

21. See also Hanegbi, Machover, and Orr, "The Class Nature," pp. 11–12.

7

MOKED: THE FOCUS

As detailed above, the original Israel Communist Party (Maki) was the source for other dissenting elements in Israeli politics. Matzpen, the largely youth oriented and Trotskyist wing, broke with Maki in 1962. Rakah, which was created out of the rift of 1965, remained loyal to the Soviet line and attracted the bulk of the party's Arab voters and supporters. In much of its recent literature, Rakah refers to itself as the Israel Communist Party.

The most direct descendant of Maki, however, is the Moked (Focus) alignment.[1] Composed of Maki members who remained within the party after its break with the Soviet Union, it was formed in alliance with left-wing student and academic groups on the eve of the 1973 election. The primary component of these was Tchelet-Adom (Blue-Red faction), a socialist organization of peace activists led by Meir Peil. Though Maki maintained an independent existence after this election, its viability as such showed immediate strain. A complete unification under Moked was imminent.

Part of this weakness may be attributed to Maki's loss of its most powerful and creative members, Moshe Sneh and Shmuel Mikunis. The former, who died in 1972, was among the engineers of Maki policy for almost two decades and had served as editor of its organ, *Kol Ha'am* (Voice of the People), and as Party secretary. Mikunis, former general secretary of the Party and its sole representative to the 1965 Knesset, resigned in protest of "the decisions, deeds, and defaults of Maki" in 1974. His resignation was the culmination of a rightward shift of Party policy, which had its roots in the break with the USSR and the 1967 War.

Sneh was in many ways a most enigmatic and inscrutable individual. His youth—following graduation from medical school—was spent within the mainstream of the Zionist movement. He served as chairman of the Central Committee of the Polish Zionist Organization and editor of *Opinia* and *Hajut*, Jewish publications in prewar Poland. Arriving in Palestine in 1940, he rose to the post of director of the Haganah, organizing illegal immigration operations and armed resistance to British policies until 1946. Sneh also served on the Executive Committee of the Jewish Agency and as political director of its Paris-based European office until 1947.

It is then that his political estrangement from Zionism began. Resigning his positions within the Jewish Agency, Sneh joined Mapam, the socialist-Zionist Party, which he represented in the Knesset until 1953. He left Mapam when the party broke with the USSR over the anti-Semitic overtones of the Doctors' Plot in Moscow and the Slansky trials in Prague. Creating the Left Socialist Party, Sneh merged his group with the Israel Comunist Party in 1954. Attracting a member of such status and distinction was a particular accomplishment for Maki. He quickly rose to prominence within the Party and was elected to Knesset on its list the following year.

For the next ten years, the Party walked an ideological tightrope, not unlike the present condition of Rakah described elsewhere. Its leadership was composed primarily of Jewish members who did not wish to endanger the legitimacy of the Party within a Jewish state. Indeed, Israel had the only legal Communist Party in the Middle East until Lebanon allowed Communist political activism in 1971. Yet the bulk of the Party's constituency was Arab and its ideological loyalties were to the Soviet Union. It was expedient, therefore, to underplay international issues, especially in light of the growing friendship between the USSR and the Arab world. Instead, domestic issues were emphasized, on which Maki held a predictably Marxist view—in opposition to reliance upon capitalist foreign aid and in favor of the nationalization of industry.

The break with the USSR and the internal rupture of the Party in 1965 was particularly damaging to the Sneh-Mikunis wing that remained to lead Maki. Much of the Arab support upon which it had come to depend was now transferred to the new party, Rakah. In addition, its claim to bi-nationalism was compromised as Maki's leading Arab members left the Party. Included here were Tawfiq Tubi, Tawfiq Ziyyad and Emil Habibi, all of whom gained prominence in the years following as members of Rakah.

The final nail in the coffin of Maki-USSR relations was driven in the wake of the 1967 war. In contradistinction to Soviet support for the Arab position, Maki argued that the 1967 War was a function of Arab annihilation-bent policies supported and abetted by the Soviet Union. For the

Israeli people, the Six Day War was one of defense for their actual physical existence and for the actual sovereignty of the State of Israel. For the USSR to support Arab militancy was a moral and tactical blunder of the highest order.

The estrangement of the Party from virtually all that it had established during the first two decades of the state left its leaders in a dilemma. Strategically unable to return to its support of the Soviet Union, Maki was bereft of an ideological source. Equally, the Arab vote upon which it had previously depended sought Rakah as a more suitable electoral alternative. It would be impossible for Maki to regain their confidence without identifying itself with the Rakah position and calling into question the legitimacy of its own existence. The dilemma was underlined by Maki's inability to win more than one seat in the 1965 and 1969 Knesset elections.

Consequently, the Party's leadership undertook a noticeable shift in policy after 1967. In an attempt to attract the non-Communist left, Maki declared its identification with Jewish nationalism and its military and security demands. Sneh, in his final political testament, negated his prior rejection of Zionism as having no justification, neither theoretically nor practically from any serious point of view. Similarly, Mikunis declared that Maki would be the shield of Israel's existence, independence, security and future. With the occasional exception of the Romanian Communist Party, relations with the Communist bloc were broken.

By no means was this development universally acceptable to the Party's membership. Many could not support Rakah's militant pro-Arabism, yet opposed perceived Israeli intransigence and held strong Communist loyalties. Declarations of support for Isaeli policy were distasteful to them. In particular, they suspected that overtures toward Mapam, New Left, and student groups would inevitably lead to the negotiation of ideological purity.

The climax of this political quest was the coalition with Tchelet-Adom in July 1973. The group was composed of students and academics, many of whom had been weaned within the youth and kibbutz movements of left-wing Zionism. Their sentiments were largely independent-socialist, with a few outwardly identifying themselves as Communist, given all that the term implies. The leading members of the group had distinguished themselves in many fields of endeavor, including the military.

Notable among these is party leader Meir Peil. A popular soldier and military tactician, Peil served in the Haganah and the Israeli Defense Force for 28 years. He was commander of the Central Officers' School and one of the architects of Israeli military strategy until his retirement with the rank of colonel in 1971. Allegedly released to complete his academic training,

Peil claims that he was eased from his position within the army for his left-leaning political sympathies and his open feud with then Defense Minister Moshe Dayan.

Peil enrolled at Tel Aviv University, where he wrote an award-winning doctoral thesis on the emergence of the Israel Defense Force from the various prestate military formations. He later joined the faculty of that university and won national recognition for his writing in the area of military and political history and the relationship between armed action and battlefield ethics. In 1973, following the alliance of Maki with Tchelet-Adom, the name Moked was chosen for the new electoral list and the party increased its voter support by 41 percent over the 1969 election. Nevertheless, it was awarded only one parliamentary seat which went to Peil as leader of the Moked list.

It should be noted that a significant portion of Maki's membership opposed the alliance with Moked and the "rightward deviation" which they perceived inherent in it. Rallying behind veteran Maki leader Esther Wilenska, the group called itself the Israel Communist Opposition. As early as Spring 1972, it condemned the more moderate tendencies of Maki leadership and called for an alliance with radical elements outside the Party. To that end, Wilenska participated in a Left Forum serving as an umbrella for dissidents of all stripe. Negotiations were opened with Siach (Israeli New Left), Brit Hasmol (the Left-Wing Alliance), and Uri Avnery.

Thus once more the Party faced an internal rupture over ideological matters. Unlike its previous experiences, there were no ethnic overtones in this debate. It was rather a matter of moderation versus radicalism, with dashes of ideological purity and personality conflicts. The alliance with Peil precipitated Wilenska's exit from Maki. Although he served as second on the 1973 Moked list, Shmuel Mikunis, party veteran and ideologue, followed suit in late 1974, justifying the conclusion that, despite its chronological links and historical roots, Moked represents a new political genesis much apart both ideologically and tactically from Maki, its Communist forebearer.

WORLD VIEW

In many senses, Moked differs ideologically from other left-wing subjects of this study. While Rakah, Matzpen, and Haolam Hazeh have indicated their extreme opposition to Zionism and distrust of its institutions, Moked strikes a more moderate, conciliatory note. Much of its leadership is loyal to the Zionist imperative and visualizes radical change within the context of the present society. To them, ingathering the exiles is still a meaningful political goal.

The view is personified in Meir Peil, who describes himself as a "Zionist-Communist" who long ago left the "Soviet Church." Not unlike evolutionary and Fabian circles elsewhere, this thinking is influenced by traditionally Jewish considerations, framing the movements's perceptions of social and political reality.

> Zionism is the national liberation movement of the Jewish People. We must concentrate as many Jews as possible in Israel to establish an independent modern nation living in an independent Jewish State. It is not sufficient to concentrate Jews, however. We must establish a nation based on productive Jewish labor, to create an egalitarian state, i.e., a socialist state. This is the union of the Zionist and socialist dream.

In this sense, Moked does not negate the value of the "galut," communities of Jews in the Diaspora. Unlike some Zionist theorists, it sees the Israeli state as the vanguard of the Jewish people—its visionary leadership fulfilling an age-old dream. While Jews elsewhere are invited to join, it is recognized that not all are prepared or able to serve in an advance guard. For them, Israel will be a source of pride and refuge, should it be needed.

As an entity which represents the aspirations of millions outside its borders, Israel has very special moral and ethical obligations. It cannot be a state like any other, with essentially secular and material purposes. It must fulfill the special role imposed upon it by its relationship to Judaism and the Jews of the Diaspora. An independent state is not sufficient; Israel must be "a spiritual, moral and humanistic center of Jewish culture and philosophy." The obligation also imposes a unique ethic for political and military affairs. It is here that the movement approximates the thinking of Asher Zvi Ginsberg (Ahad Ha'am).[2]

The clearest manifestation of this moral dilemma regards the problem of Palestinian nationalism. While always careful to express its support for the security and defense of the state of Israel, Moked considers official treatment of this issue as inappropriate both in principle and tactic.

> The land of Israel is the dual birthplace of two people: the Jewish Nation and the Arab Palestinian Nation. . . . The rights of the Palestinian Nation to an independent territory, as yet unknown, is based upon the desire to live in peaceful coexistence with the State of Israel. . . . Every policy of annexation and denial of one people over another— such as those of the Land of Israel Movement or the Popular Front for the Liberation of Palestine—is a grave threat to both people and should be opposed in every way possible.[3]

Further, it is a grievous error to believe that the problem of Palestinian nationalism will dissipate. Its intensity increases with every military or terrorist action, no matter who is the victor. The Palestinian interest perceives itself to have been abandoned by its Arab patrons and disregarded in any disengagement agreements with Israel. Its leadership will do all in its power, both in Israel and in the Arab world, to undermine these accords, placing yet greater pressure upon Israel to act in retaliation.

Ironically, Israel's present intransigence is playing into the hands of the Palestinian extremists. Holding some two million Arabs in its jurisdiction unintentionally creates a second nation, with unequal status and a social position based upon deprivation and discrimination. Unwittingly, Israel is underwriting a Palestinaian national renaissance.

> Anyone who had trouble understanding the phenomenon will easily comprehend it by moving among the country's construction workers. He will find that most of them are Arabs from the West Bank, Gaza and Israel, all in the same boat and speaking the same language, their work supervised by Jewish foremen. Such work groups [are] an expression of a mini-renaissance of the Palestinian national movement under Israeli government sponsorship. . . . [This] constitutes a time-bomb which will one day reveal itself in another variation in the long line of national conflicts.[4]

In addition to the ethical considerations involved, it is claimed that present Israeli policy is based upon a series of misapprehensions and mistaken premises. The first is a paranoid belief that the world stands against Israel in principle leaving it as the sole arbiter of its fate. The result is an upsurge in right-wing annexationist sentiment which is strategically unsound and politically irrational. Rather than lead to peace and security it merely deepens the mistrust and hatred of both sides.

Further, this collective paranoia becomes a self-fulfilling prophecy leading to disregard for the requirements of international order. As Israel's mistrust expands and its resolve hardens, it becomes more isolated from the nations of the world, realizing the loneliness it presupposes.

> We cannot accept the assumption . . . that the resolutions of the United Nations Assembly are not important. No state, even a great power can risk isolation and hostility in the world arena. This is bad in times of peace as well as in times of war. The accumulation of resolutions which condemn Israel endangers our relations with the peoples of the world and assists those who oppose our very existence.[5]

There are serious military fallacies in the present government policy as well, Moked asserts. Security is much more a function of political than battlefield considerations. While it is essential that Israel's borders be defensible—leaving the definition of that term open—military action is not dependent upon "strategic depth" alone. The territorial distance between Israeli centers of population and those of enemy forces are no longer determining factors in modern warfare.

Support for this argument is summoned from Israel's strategic position prior to its past two wars. In June 1967, Israel lacked depth and had militarily improper borders. Yet its support from allies and its political freedom allowed it to strike a preemptive blow exhibiting great mobility and creativity. Without the support of these allies, Israel's freedom was severely limited in October 1973, making a preemptive strike impossible and forcing Israel into a position of re-action to attack rather than initiate. This fatefully deferred the creativity of its attack. Thus the strategic depth of conquered territories may well have been a military debility.[6]

Conversely, Israel had little to fear from either the Palestinians or the Arab states. It is far superior militarily, and will continue in that position for a long time to come.

> It must be emphasized that Israel has nothing to worry about militarily at any time in the forseeable future, even if there would be serious outbreaks of violence on the part of the Palestinian public and the Palestinian guerilla movements. . . . If this activity reaches very serious dimensions there will be no alternative but to mobilize most of the I.D.F. and to clean up the area in a thorough manner. . . . The result of such an action—it would not take long—would be disaster for the Palestinians. . . . This is the immense difference between Israel and Vietnam.

Consequently, to hold the territories for purposes of security is either a strategic mistake or an apology for annexation.[7]

Internally, the occupation and Israel's isolation from the world has moved the masses to the right, in the direction of hawkishness and imperialism. The event is reflected in the growing popularity of annexationism within the Labor Alignment and the Likud. It is also apparent in the movement of the National Religious Party and its youth faction, Gush Emunim.

In addition, the lack of leadership has resulted in an economy marked by rampant inflation and fiscal irresponsibility. Rising costs, decreasing government subsidies, and an expanding military budget all contribute to an industrial stagnation that hits the laborer hardest, it is argued. The reactionary policies of the Labor government discriminated against the poor and Oriental workers, and pushed them toward the right wing.

Nevertheless, the government appears to be blind to these developments and continues on its self-destructive path. Its economic program lays the main burden upon that part of the popultion that is least able to afford it. The wealthy continue to accumulate profit and smuggle capital with impunity. Since they often deal in foreign currency, the sequence of devaluations actually benefit them while "the meager ones who make up the overwhelming majority of the people, are the main victims of the speedy inflation."[8]

Yet the movement is somewhat ambivalent about the willingness of the laboring masses to unite and oppose the oppressive policies of their masters. The proletariat seems to have developed a trade union mentality with strong right-wing biases.

> The working class of a generation ago was far more enlightened— "maskil." They were workers by choice. . . . To my father, to be a worker was an ideal and with such people one could talk ideology. Today's worker is simpler and so are his needs. He wants a bit more security and a few more lira. . . . [Therefore] to rebuild the Histadrut will bring even worse results because capitalist, right-wing workers will come to power. George Meany is waiting around the corner.[9]

VALUES AND GOALS

The tactical, moral, and military estimations presented above lead Moked to several conclusions, in the form of goals for the immediate future. The first is the need for negotiations with any responsible representatives of the Palestinians, including the PLO. In addition, Israel must be prepared to enter into similar accords with various combatants among the Arab states: Egypt, Syria, and Jordan. Agreement with the latter is particularly vital and complex because of the stakes it has in the Palestinian question as well.

Since merely holding territories does not necessarily lead to peace and security, one must be prepared to consider the value of these territories as bargaining cards. The government must declare its willingness to discuss return of these territories in exchange for their demilitarization, along with various military and political guarantees.

While the willingness to return all conquered areas should be asserted from the outset, these do not have to be relinquished at once. A justifiable suspicion exists between all parties concerned and its elimination and replacement by mutual trust will doubtless be a long and protracted process. Consequently, there is no reason why land could not be returned to the Arab states gradually, based upon fixed military and political contracts.[10]

The crux of the peace issue, however, is not the battle with established Arab regimes but the problem of Palestinian nationalism. For reasons of self-interest, if not morality, Israel should help in the establishment of a Palestinian state, in return for recognition. Such a state would be the result of popular self-determination and might enter into a federation with Israel or Jordan or both, should it so desire. Its boundaries would include Judea and Samaria on the West Bank, the Gaza Strip, and a portion of East Jerusalem responsible to an umbrella municipality that includes its Jewish sector. It is also proposed that Israel allow a free port on the Mediterranean.

Contrary to the accepted belief, such a state would be relatively stable and not serve as a jumping-off point for terrorist activity in Israel. The Israeli military deterrent, it is asserted, would insure the sincerity of these negotiations, as well as territorial integrity growing from any decisions made. Further,

> Whatever Palestinian entity is established, their interests in survival and existence will overcome any desire to sponsor terrorist activities toward Israel. Even being indifferent to such actions would be contrary to their best interests and endanger the very existence of their regime. . . . Israel is sufficiently strong to take this chance.

In any event, the Arab world will not stand still for a unilateral Israeli annexation but will initiate another round of warfare. Even if Israel wins, her victory would be cut short by the big powers again, leaving her political position unacceptably indecisive and inviting still more war.

True to its spirit of gradualism, however, Moked has called for stringent limitations on the armed and police powers of the new Palestinian entity, paralleling restrictions imposed by the four powers (U.S., USSR, UK, and France) on Austria prior to 1955. In addition, arrangements for inspection will be made either bilaterally or under the auspices of the UN. Mutual diplomatic recognition would also be underwritten by political and economic accords and the extradition of terrorists and criminals on both sides.[11]

In fact, rather than being a dangerous gamble, allowing the establishment of a Palestinian national entity would have multiple benefits for Israeli domestic affairs. Aside from the lasting peace that it would bring, such accords would also stem the tide of two dangerous political trends. These are the increase in right-wing chauvinism and the gradual acceptance of the role of conqueror and colonist among the Israeli populace. Both tendencies run counter to the classic designs of either Zionism or socialism upon which the country was founded.

Rather than learn the lesson of the 1973 War, that is, that territories are valuable only as bargaining cards and do not offer security in themselves, these elements have hardened their demands and attempt to force the Israeli government to follow suit. For the protection of a peace initiative as well as the values of democracy and freedom within Israel, such ideological influences must be repulsed.

> An active struggle against the escalation of chauvinism which lurks in the near future is not to be considered only as an obligation to be undertaken by those who favor a political peace initiative vis-à-vis the Arab world, but also as an urgent duty for those who are concerned about the democratic regime that exists in Israel. . . . The current leaders of what was once Labor Israel are trying to secure the remnants of their power by reconciling themselves with or even joining the wave of extreme nationalism. The only domestic groups which can stem the tide of the depressing development of chauvinism . . . are those dovish groups which call for a peace initiative and those honest socialist groups.

Short of this, it is claimed, a peace will be imposed from without and Israel will become a garrison state with no contemporary value as a nation or a center for Jewish culture. It will be "the Prussia of the Middle East."[12]

Equally abhorrent is the brutality and fanaticism that follow in the wake of national discrimination against the Palestinian people. As the nation complies with the role of conqueror and the military continues to control an unwilling minority (which presently constitutes some 40 percent of the Israeli population), the idea of violent suppression becomes desirable and preferred. This seriously endangers the moral fiber of the military. Further, unlike many other states, the Israel Defense Force is a citizen army within which some 80 percent of the Israeli male population serve until the age of fifty. Consequently, that which damages the morality of the army actually affects the character of the entire nation.

It is incumbent upon the military to adopt a policy of the "purity of arms" in which justice and propriety take precedent over strategic pragmatism.

> Even if our Arab enemies still are at a historical stage in their development where "an eye for an eye" is an inherent part of their culture and

they have little concern for "purity of arms" this still does not justify our acting the way they do. We don't operate the way they do in almost any other field . . . there is no reason whatsoever for us to begin learning from them their primitive criteria of murder and crude retribution. If we have transgressed in such matters, from time to time, we must have the courage of being ashamed of it. We must free ourselves of such acts rather than sanctify them.

Aside from the moral imperatives of "arms purity"—a factor which would compel its institution in any event—there are important tactical and political gains to be made as well. Strict battlefield morality does not impair the effectiveness of a fighting force, but rather convinces combatants of the justice of the cause and the legitimacy of the leadership. Additionally, it is a principle which may well serve Zionism in various international tribunals. [13]

Finally, all this makes an effective and viable electoral alternative necessary within Israel. The Labor Alignment has displayed its weakness and the ease with which it may follow the chauvinistic demands of its opposition to the Right. Without despairing of change within already established institutions, the Left must rally support so that the ruling alignment may shift its direction comfortably.

In order that this take place, Moked proposes

a true combination of class loyalty and national responsibility to Israel's security and peace; a sincere effort to obtain peace without fostering any illusions and without blurring any nationalistic manifestations . . . devotion to the idea of socialism, but firmly disowning the path of the Soviet leadership. [14]

STRATEGIES FOR SOCIAL CHANGE

Despite its critical evaluation of Israel's social and political state, Moked offers tactical prescriptions that are practical and moderate. Above all, it appears to be concerned with the image of the left as being unloyal and in some way detrimental to the state's welfare. The movement strains to display the military accomplishments of its leading members and declares its primary concern for Israel, Zionism, and Jewish well being everywhere.

To that end, it sends delegates to international conferences of socialists and Communists, representing the interests of the state. Moked claims to have defeated anti-Israel resolutions at numerous international conferences, over and above the objections of third world nations and its colleagues in the Israeli Left, Rakah. It has also led the Party to join the

World Jewish Congress and participate in international programs of Jewish culture and thought. The trend has been sorely attacked, however, from Maki's more radical left wing—many of whom have left the Party in the past three years.[15]

The internal strains have operated counter to one other of Moked's pronounced tactics. It is the desire of the movement to unite the Left—from Mapam to Rakah—in a grand coalition, offering an alternative of peace and socialism to the Israeli public. Various attempts have been made to join forces with the multiple factions of the Black Panthers, Uri Avnery and the Radical Party, and the Israel New Left. The scheme fell on bad times, however, when differences over socialist fervor came to the fore. In addition, it appears that personality conflicts developed between Avnery and Peil as to who would lead the new alignment's electoral list.[16]

More recently, new cooperative ventures have been undertaken by Moked leadership. One in particular became a national scandal. In October 1976, four distinguished Israelis met with representatives of the Palestine Liberation Organization in Paris. Included among them were Meir Peil, Uri Avnery, peace activist and retired army quartermaster Mati Peled, and Ya'acov Arnon, chairman of the board of the Israel Electric Corporation. Criticized by Premier Rabin and Justice Minister Zadok, the meetings were considered criminal and pressure was applied to have the attorney general seek an indictment under a new law forbidding contact with foreign agents.

In addition, Moked has declared its willingness to act as an agent in rallying socialist and peace elements within the ruling alignment. Overtures have been made toward Lova Eliav and Yitzhak Ben-Aharon, leading establishment doves. Contact has also been made with Breira, a dissenting group of American Jews led by peace activists in the New York area and at several large campuses throughout the United States.[17]

Internally, Moked has called for sweeping economic and social changes in the makeup of Israeli institutions and political life. The first is a separation of religion and state with modifications designed to accommodate for the unique needs of Israeli society.

> We see some aspects wherein Israeli law should yield and adapt itself to the needs of the religious community. Israel should respect equally civil and religious procedures in marriage and divorce. The choice then should be left to the individual. . . . There must be an alternative for civil marriage as well as the validity of reform or conservative rabbinic practice. . . . We will, of course, respect religious educational systems and support them but it is not the State's job to elect or nominate rabbis.[18]

Allowing the practice of liberal Jewish rabbis is a particularly sore point within Israel's strictly Orthodox religious establishment.

Especially irksome is the lopsided allocation of resources and wealth, aided and abetted by the political system. Corruption is rampant and the implementation of policy is specifically designed to favor the wealthy. The movement has called for effective price and profit controls to limit the real economic gains of the rich and allow the wages of the poor to absorb inflationary trends. In addition, Mopked has demanded that the government reallocate resources and priorities, so as to develop poor urban areas and immigrant settlement towns, as well as employment programs and educational facilities.

In most specific terms, Moked has called upon the government to introduce a detailed program of redistribution. This would require that it

a. impose a special tax on excess profits from the war and from orders placed by security forces;

b. suspend the distribution of dividends above a 6 percent profit in enterprises, banks, and companies;

c. raise the rates of companies' taxes considerably;

d. impose a tax on capital profits derived from land, stock market, and capital shares and bonds transactions;

e. suspend the privileges and bonuses awarded in accordance with the Law for the Encouragement of Capital Investment;

f. restrict the hidden subsidies amounting to hundreds of millions of Israeli pounds annually, given by the government in the form of cheap loans from development budgets at 6 to 9 percent interest. These loans have become an important source of easy profit-making at a time of galloping inflation.[19]

To call for the elimination of Israeli institutions, however, is both unrealistic and counterproductive, the movement argues. A viable alternative for the Israeli people depends upon the credibility and respectability that the programs of Moked gain publicly. Supporting insurrection will never bring such viability. Further, merely placing the ownership of the means of production in the hands of labor's representatives is insufficient if such people operate by capitalist principles. Replacing them with more decentralized institutions might result in greater capitalist and right-wing influence, reflecting the biases of many laborers today.

This appears to be Moked's strongest argument for working within the present system. Nevertheless, it does not preclude the use of actions that are extraparliamentary in nature. However, such strategies would never be utilized to the detriment of the security and welfare of the state.

For us the parliament and institutions of the State are but one sphere of political struggle. We also fight in the streets through demonstrations, strikes and rallies. Should we break the law, we are prepared to suffer the consequences. . . . We still believe, however, that there is yet a chance to change the political and economic policies of Israel, by changing the leadership. In one more generation this may no longer be possible and violence will be necessary.[20]

SUMMARY AND COMMENTS

Moked is the direct descendant of the original Israel Communist Party, Maki. Though it has also given birth to several other factions and political parties, Maki remained as a political institution until it formally joined with a group of students and peace activists to create a new coalition under the leadership of Meir Peil. The group presented an electoral list in the 1973 elections and succeeded in placing only its first candidate, Peil, in the Knesset. Several overtures have been made to other socialist and dissenting groups, although conflicts of ideology and personality have generally prevented firm commitments from being made.

Ideological prescripts of the movement are somewhat unique by comparison to others presently under discussion. Moked claims an allegiance to socialism, Zionism, and political and military morality. Its socialism is independent of any international stance, especially that of the Soviet or Maoist camps. Evolutionary rather than revolutionary in nature, its ideology harkens to early laborist thought in Palestine as well as to the writings of the Fabians in Britain.

The movement further affirms the inherent compatibility of Zionism and socialism. The former represents Jewish national liberation and is still a viable and meaningful construct. It is only because Zionism has been compromised by short-sighted understandings of military and diplomatic security that Israel has been driven along the road of capitalist expansion. A return to the essential ideals and the simplicity of the kibbutz would do much to return the spirit and idealism for which the country was once noted.

Most important, by both socialist and Zionist standards, Israel must be peculiarly Jewish. The elements that shape its domestic and foreign policies must bear the mark of Jewish culture, humanism, and ethics. Not unlike the writings of Ah'ad Haam at the turn of the century, Moked argues that Israel must be a showplace of culture, in which new social and political forms are developed and used. Short of this, the state of Israel fails to fulfill its very special mission.

Commitments to these three ideological forces are reflected clearly in all aspects of Moked thought. Its world view belies a considered disappointment with the development of Israeli policy. Content to be isolated from the community of nations, the Israeli leadership has posited a "go it alone" stance. It views the entire world as its enemy and is unwilling to consider negotiations with the forces of Palestinian nationalism, who also represent a legitimate force in the region.

Rather than defeating this movement, present Israeli policy is underwriting a Palestinian rebirth, by allowing Arab workers and villagers to develop a self-conscious identity as a second nation, lacking in full freedom or national status. Further, there appears to be a dangerous emergence of religious-romantic fanaticism, demanding annexation of conquered areas and suppression of any conciliatory dissent. This is the harbinger of a damaging fascism or irredentism and must be squelched before it is allowed to spread.

It is prescribed that a full peace movement be allowed to help create a Palestinian state, détente with the Arabs, and the disestablishment of religion. Short of this, the Israeli population will become accustomed to its new role of conqueror and may develop mental and cultural forms to accommodate. Attributable largely to Peil is the parallel concept of "arms purity," whereby morality on the battlefield is of the essence, lest Israel's citizen army breed a population of brutal spartans who idealize the front and evaluate standards by their crudest military importance. Only the restructuring of peace priorities can prevent this danger.

Yet, despite its dissatisfaction with the present Israeli cultural and political institutions, Moked appears bent on working within the system. Though demonstrations and occasional violence may be condoned, there is little hope for a successful massive revolution, nor is the movement nihilistic enough to believe that revolution would necessarily bring positive change. Rather, it is necessary to reorganize the various parties and, particularly, the Histadrut, to allow greater participation and more socialist venture. Changing the tax structure and allowing for the rise of a new and more pragmatic leadership may avert what might otherwise be the inevitable: a revolution or the development of fascism in Israel.

NOTES

1. The following historical discussion of the development of Maki and its fusion into Moked was culled from the following: Walter Laquer, *Communism and Nationalism in the Middle East* (New York: Praeger, 1957), pp. 73–119; Moshe Czudnowski and Jacob Landau, *The Israeli Communist Party and the Elections for the Fifth Knesset, 1961* (Stanford, Calif.:

Hoover Institute, 1965); David J. Schnall, "Notes on the Political Thought of Dr. Moshe Sneh," *Middle East Journal* (Summer 1973), pp. 342–52; David J. Schnall, "Dialectic Zionism," *Judaism* (Summer 1973), pp. 334–41; Martin Slann, "Ideology and Ethnicity in Israel's Two Communist Parties: The Conflict Between Maki and Rakah," *Studies in Comparative Communism* (Winter 1974), pp. 359–74.

2. Personal interview with Meir Peil, August 1976, on Ahad Ha'am, see Arthur Hertzberg, ed., *The Zionist Idea* (New York: Atheneum, 1975), pp. 249–77.

3. "Fourth Section in the Moked Program," *Ba-Moked* (May 25, 1976).

4. Meir Peil, "The State of Israel and the Palestinian National Movement," *New Outlook* (November 1976), pp. 32–33.

5. Berl Balti, "The P.L.O., Moscow, and the Geneva Conference," *Israel at Peace: Kol Ha'am* (January 1975), p. 1.

6. Meir Peil, "Political and Military Reflections in the Wake of the War of October, 1973," *New Outlook* (December 1973–January 1974), pp. 4–17.

7. Meir Peil, "The Dynamics of Power: Morality in Armed Conflict after the Six Day War," in *Modern Jewish Ethics: Theory and Practice*, ed. Marvin Fox (Columbus: Ohio State University Press, 1975), pp. 198–99. See also Meir Peil, "Military Aspects of the Partial Agreemnt," *New Outlook* (July–August 1975), pp. 11–14.

8. "Report of the Fifteenth Session of the Central Committee of Maki" (June 1, 1974), cited in *Israel at Peace; Kol Ha'am* (March 1974), p. 3. See also Raoul Teitelbaum, "The Fat and the Meager," *Israel at Peace: Kol Ha'am* (January 1975), pp. 10–11.

9. Peil interview.

10. Peil, "Political and Military Reflections," pp. 10–11.

11. Peil interview. See also Peil, "The State of Israel," pp. 31–32.

12. Meir Peil, "The Real Threat to Israel," *New Outlook* (January 1976), pp. 11–12.

13. Peil, "The Dynamics of Power," p. 193. See also the "Report of the First General Conference of Moked," *Ba-Moked* (July 16, 1976); and Meir Peil, "The Moral Use of Arms," *New Outlook* (February 1973), pp. 30–41.

14. "The Central Committee of Maki on the Resignation of Shmuel Mikunis," *Israel at Peace: Kol Ha'am* (January 1975), p. 9. See also, Berl Balti, "For an Alternative Left Policy," *Israel at Peace: Kol Ha'am* (March 1974), pp. 4–5. For a contrasting view, see Esther Wilenska, "How the Crisis Within Maki Came Into Being," in *What Happened in Maki* (Tel Aviv. Israeli Communist Opposition, 1973).

15. See "A Step in the Right Direction" and "Der. Berman Foiled Adoption of Anti-Israel Resolution in Paris," *Israel at Peace: Kol Ha'am* (March 1974), pp. 1, 6.

16. Jerusalem *Post* (July 27, 1973 and October 8, 1973). It should be noted that Peil and Avnery did join together in the 1977 election behind Lova Eliav, to form Sheli. See pp. 300–301.

17. Jerusalem *Post* (October 26, 1976, November 9, 1976, and November 16, 1976). Also, "For the Unity and Development of the Left in Israel," *Ba-Moked* (August 2, 1976).

18. Peil interview.

19. Proposal submitted by Moked delegation to the Twelfth Congress of the Labor Federation of Israel (Histadrut); see *Israel at Peace: Kol Ha'am* (January 1975), pp. 10–11.

20. Peil interview. See also Ya'acov Litai, "On the Path of 'Moked'," *Ba-Moked* (July 16, 1976).

III

THE ETHNIC
AND RELIGIOUS
COMMUNITIES

8

NATORE KARTA:
RELIGIOUS ANTI-ZIONISM

Natore Karta, an ultrareligious and militantly anti-Zionist movement, is centered in the Meah Shearim section of Jerusalem. The name, meaning guardians of the city, is taken from a talmudic reference to the sages and religious scholars of a municipality as its guardians. Natore Karta views itself as all that stands between the Jews of Jerusalem and destruction, for only they are true to the age-old teachings of Torah and rabbinic lore.

To understand the basis of its anti-Zionism, one must examine the relationship between Jewish orthodoxy and the Zionist movement during the early and mid-twentieth century.[1] To some religious leaders it was a holy task to help rebuild the Jewish commonwealth and see that Jewish tradiion had salient input toward that end. The Mizrahi and National Religious movements are the outgrowth of that theological position and have moved into the sociopolitical mainstream as a result.

By no means was this a universal attitude, however. Notably among Hassidic communities in Eastern Europe and leaders of Agudat Israel (a strictly Orthodox Jewish organization, founded in 1912) in Germany and Poland, considerable ambivalence was expressed toward a Jewish national movement. Though faithful Jews had prayed for a return to Zion for eighteen hundred years, this was always seen as divine prerogative, to be accompanied by the coming of the Messiah. The prospect of a self-initiated restoration had little precedent in Jewish history and conjured visions of the Sabbatean and mystical aberrations of the Middle Ages.

The low level of religious observance among most Zionist leaders seemed to confirm these fears. Surely the messianic return would be carried out by those true to ritual observance. The attempts of these secularists and nonbelievers was no more than a sinful usurpation which would alienate the faithful from their spiritual sources. Consequently, many religious sages of pre-World War II Europe opposed the "Zionist heresy" and warned that rather than salvation, the movement would bring only abomination and destruction.

Among the devout Jews of Jersualem as well, such feeling was not uncommon—particularly in the wake of the Balfour Declaration of 1917, in which the British government indicated its interests in a Jewish national homeland in Palestine. Opposition was especially to be found within the Edah Haredit (Jerusalem's organized religious community). An Ashkenazic body led by Rabbi Moshe Diskin of Brisk, Lithuania, and by Rabbi Joseph Sonnenfeld, the group was largely composed of East European emigrants to the Holy Land. It operated ritual food facilities, synagogues, and charitable agencies under the direction of a rabbinic council and court of arbitration.

With the rise of Nazism in Germany, this community was joined by many German and Polish refugees of Agudat Israel sentiment and anti-Zionist feeling was thereby strengthened. Nevertheless, an otherwise imminent clash was deferred to pursue a common foe. Attempts to rescue Jews from the war's horrors allowed common ground for cooperation between Zionist forces and these religious elements. Also, within Agudist ranks there were many who were increasingly open to Zionist ideology, if not its covert supporters.

This was underscored by the founding of Kibbutz Hafetz Hayyim by a wing of Agudah in 1944. The event signaled an internecine struggle between the anti-Zionist elements within the Edah Haredit and Agudat Israel and the larger body of Agudat Israel, which seemed to be making peace with the idea of a Jewish state. The anti-Zionists joined with their opposite numbers among various Hungarian and Romanian immigrants of Hassidic background. The name Natore Karta was first prominently displayed in a 1942 campaign, though this alliance of forces appears to date to protest actions of the late thirties. The group was successful in gaining control of the Rabbinic Council of the Edah Haredit in 1945 and a permanent rupture with Agudat Israel was accomplished in 1949. It was then that the latter organized itself into a political party that was later to be the coalition partner in an early Israeli government.

Two other personalities have had particular influence upon the ideology of Natore Karta, one the spiritual and theological, while the other is the practical and strategic. Rabbi Joel Teitelbaum is successor to the Hungarian-Romanian Hassidic dynasty of Satmar and Muncacz and fifth in descent from the founder of the movement. Rabbi Teitelbaum grudgingly utilized Zionist forces to save himself from the Nazi onslaught and escaped to the Holy Land after the war.

He subsequently left Israel and settled with his followers in the Williamsburg section of Brooklyn. There he formulated a complex theology based upon classical sources in opposition to the Zionist movement. Rabbi Teitelbaum was accepted as spiritual leader of Natore Karta in 1953. He periodically visits Jersusalem, generally on the eve of elections, to warn his adherents against participation, and is careful not to ride in any conveyance bearing Israeli insignia.

The local leader of Natore Karta, until his death in 1974, was Rabbi Amram Blau. In contrast to Rabbi Teitelbaum, Rabbi Blau's authority was generally tactical rather than theological, to the extent that the two can be clearly differentiated. Scion of one of Jerusalem's older families, Blau rose to prominence as an Agudah youth leader in the 1940s. His militance had been noted by religious leaders Aaron Katzenellenbogen and Rabbi J. H. Duschinsky, heir to the positions of Rabbis Diskin and Sonnenfeld.

By then, Blau already had impressive credentials as a religious zealot and rabid anti-Zionist. As early as 1923, he had joined a holy war against the Zionists, choosing with personal vengence the then Chief Rabbi Abraham Kook as a central target. He vigorously opposed participation in the Jewish national council, voting in municipal elections, and the opening of a welfare office in Meah Shearim. This last matter put him at odds with Agudah leaders, who were willing to accept Zionist funds while opposing its philosophy. His militant protest of a Saturday soccer match which violated the observance of the Sabbath resulted in arrest and jail for Blau in 1930.

Blau prided himself on his good relations with local Arabs prior to the accession of Zionism. In 1921 he purchased five hundred dunams of land outside Jerusalem and was subsequently elected to the local municipal council. Though he refused to visit the area—or any other under Zionist occuption—he maintained communications with Moslem leaders in Jordan and East Jerusalem until his death. It was his firm belief that Zionist aspirations stood between Arab-Jewish cooperation in the Middle East.

WORLD VIEW

Natore Karta claims to be the legitimate spiritual and ideological carrier of the European Jewish tradition. Its perspective clearly reflects this claim and appears to be a function of its understanding of the relationship between Jewry, the gentile world, and God. For two thousand years, the Jewish people have lived under gentile rule as a punishment for their sins. Such rule, harsh though it may be, is God's will and to rebel against it is, by implication, rebellion against the Lord.

Further, pretenses toward independence are also seen as manifestations against the ruling nations at whose suffrance the Jewish community exists. Rather than bringing redemption, they only prolong the agony.

> The salvation and security of the Jewish People in the diaspora depends upon the good will and patience of the gentile nations. It is our task to accept our travails and mistreatment with love and to await God's Redemption, rather than to oppose them. Standing against the nations with force and arms brings only sorrow and death to our people.[2]

The attempt at Jewish independence without divine intervention is considered heretical, therefore; only with the coming of the Messiah will a "Torah nationalism" emerge. Any initiative is usurpation and deserves the most vigorous form of punishment. The role of the Jew is to remain passive and satisfied with his lot under non-Jewish rule.

Such a posture is supported by the most important of all sources, the source of precedent. Through the millenia of their exile, the Jewish people realized that their well being depended on this interlocking relationship with the gentile and the Lord and consequently, no matter what other sins they committed, the sin of national usurpation was not among them. Such a development is the product of the modern era only.

Zionism, therefore, is the worst usurpation and affront to the simple passivity of traditional Judaism. Recent tragedies that have befallen the Jewish people are attributable to this rebellion against the Lord. In the view of Natore Karta, nazism was a direct result of unwarranted Zionist agitation and nationalist demands. Equally, both nazism and Zionism are derivatives of the same source: European nationalism. The one movement has little more Jewish content than the other.[3]

Further, the movement claims a tacit conformity of actions between the early Zionists and the Nazis—though this may not have been intentional. Natore Karta points to cooperation between the Jews of Palestine and the Nazi party over deportations and the transfer of funds from Germany to various Jewish institutions in the Holy Land. Though the cash belonged to deported Jews, it remained in the hands of the Zionists.

Equally, when opportunities arose to save German Jews, the Zionists naturally chose to aid those who either had funds or were involved in Jewish national movements in Europe. The oppositionists—generally to be found among the more traditionally religious elements—were ignored. This gives lie to the Zionist claim to represent all Jews in their enterprise.

Even later, the movement asserts, many Jews might have been saved from the death camps but for Zionist political ambitions and aspirations. Joel Brand's attempt to negotiate with Adolf Eichmann for the safety of Hungarian Jewry in 1944 continues to be a Natore Karta cause célèbre. Other less sensational but equally damaging episodes are also prominently detailed in their literature.[4]

Similarly, conflict with and military or terrorist losses to the Arab world are attributed to the sins of Zionism. Were it not for the intervention of Zionist aims and their intransigence in the creation of a state, Britain would have doubless permitted unlimited emigration to Palestine, both during and after World War II. Furthermore, there need never have been a 1948 War. Military actions since might have been avoided, if the naturally expansive and aggressive nature of Zionism had been replaced by the pacifistic and retiring traditions of torah Judaism. Any war undertaken without the direction and authority of Jewish religious leadership is little short of murder.

Very special criticism is reserved for those religious elements that have supported the Jewish state and participated in its governance. Found within the Agudah and National Religious Parties, these rabbis and religious leaders are traitors to their tradition. Aware of the restrictions imposed by Jewish law and theology which forbid national initiative, these collaborators have sold their consciences in return for the financial support of the Zionist state. Thus their claim to authority has been besmirched.

Further, accepting Zionist funds also implies accepting Zionist influence; those religious institutions who have allowed the first will ultimately allow the second. Their own guilt makes them justify their sins with externals such as buildings and facilities. It also forces them to turn upon those who remain true to tradition, Natore Karta.

> The Natore Karta, the orthodox Jews whose minds are not confused, refuse to accept money from Zionist sources at a time when the "saviours" of Torah and the builders of buildings, have put up their edifices with Zionist assistance and support. . . . Money is accompanied by influence and the fact is that all these great builders, who seek with all their might to hate the Natore Karta, have incorporated in their buildings the influence of Zionism. This influence bores holes in the walls and through them Zionism creeps into the building and causes the Zionist heresy to seep into the very teaching given within the walls. When one gives way to the current, one tends to be swept away by the stream.[5]

There is also a tactical base to the movement's opposition to Zionist nationalism. The ultimate goal of the Zionist movement is the ingathering of the exiles, i.e., a total immigration of all Jews to the state of Israel. Unless carried out under the direction of the Messiah, such a move would be tragic folly. Rather than strengthen the Jewish people, it would make them more vulnerable because of the ease with which the forces of evil could then locate them. To the contrary, Jews are at their most secure when they are dispersed among the nations and left to deal with their gentile rulers on an individual basis. It is then that the Jewish genius for survival and success is most manifest.

The more sensitive elements within Natore Karta claim a victory of sorts. They assert that Zionism has died even among the established Israeli leadership. It is now merely the "child's play of old European Jews who enjoy vying for the spoils of political office." It is in this sense a passing phase—as are all movements of iniquity, by comparison to the eternal value of Judaism—and already in its death throes. Even the representatives of the Zionist cause, Natore Karta asserts, realize that without a religious base and context there is no hope for a territorial and political structure.

Finally, aside from the physical and theological horrors of the Zionist heresy stands a spiritual one aimed at the heart of Jewish life. No longer the ethical "people of the book," Zionism has made Jews like all the other peoples. A geopolitical force is identified with the state. Pacifism and transcendentalism have always been basic to Jewish thought, but it is to the Eastern faiths that the world now turns for inspiration.

In this sense, the Zionists have robbed Judaism of its very essence, married it to European nationalism or socialism and betrayed the centuries-old yearnings of a people.

> As soon as one delves into the essence of Judaism, one senses the bankruptcy of Zionism. The latter has lost the love of Zion that characterized Halevi, the Jews of Yemen, the medieval mystics. . . . A state and a culture are mutually exclusive, the one dependent upon the many, the other upon quality. The strength of Judaism has always been its rejection of numbers and physical strength for the moral perfection of the few. Zionism has taken Jews and made gentiles of them.[6]

VALUES AND GOALS

The values of Natore Karta are simple and monolithic. It is Zionist ideology which antagonizes the entire world, brings destruction to the Jewish people and discourages divine favor. The apparent victories of the

Jewish state are manifestations of the devil, carried out to test and confound the Jewish nation. Consequently, it is the task of the faithful to do all in their power to separate themselves from this evil enterprise, limit its influence, and pray for its destruction.

This perspective is supported by numerous classical Jewish texts and rabbinic writings. The most cogently and frequently used is a homiletic tale recorded in the Babylonian Talmud. It is told that with the destruction of the second Holy Temple in Jerusalem (ca. 70 C.E.), the Lord enforced a unique bargain with the Jewish people in return for their well being. He demanded that they swear (a) not to return en masse to their Holy Land, (b) to be loyal to the lands and governments of their dispersion, and (c) not to attempt to hasten the Redemption. To Natore Karta these are taken to be fundamentals of Jewish living and basic to the survival of the nation.[7]

This almost fatalistic acceptance of mistreatment by the gentile world is also reflected in any approaches to it, even outside the context of that which is largely political. A show of strength or any unusual display of public activity is unwise for it only allows the non-Jewish world an unnecessary opportunity to talk about us. The less they remember and discuss us, the better will be our fortunes. Further, if ever necessary, one should not confront the gentile world contentiously, but rather softly and humbly.[8]

Within this vein, the ideology of Natore Karta glorifies the tragedies and suppressions of the past. Only through such difficulties is moral and spiritual fiber developed and strengthened. It is not the role of the Jew, they assert, to be a military hero. If one must choose a model, one should look not to the futile partisans of the Warsaw Ghetto uprising but rather to the pacifists who gave their lives willingly for the glory of God. Only their deaths had meaning. The very children of those European Jews who were steeped in the love of torah and morality have, in Israel, become spartan secularists who profane daily the memory of their martyred forebearers.

It is in the Diaspora that Judaism fulfills its purpose and realizes its vitality.

> Jews have known how to overcome their position of weakness in the "galut." They are not attuned to a position of power. Strength can only come to them through a Torah perspective. Jews knew how to use their apparent weakness as a tool for success and influence. They stood between good and bad . . . a role they can never play in their own state. Trouble and tragedy are not necessarily bad. One learns from his pain and suffering. This had strengthened the Jew, made him flexible yet tenacious.[9]

Rather than hope for salvation through the conduits of improper initiative and usurpation, Natore Karta has called for believing Jews to return to the faith of their people and trust in divine redemption. The very irreligious nature of the Zionist enterprise is ample confirmation of its heresy, for it is inconceivable that the Lord would bring His redemption through secular agents. Rather than bring Jews back to their tradition, these have given the nation a sense of ungodly independence and bravado. Walking the streets of Tel Aviv or Jerusalem impresses one with the influence of Western culture, materialism, and decadence. Little of the holiness and purity that is Judaism is evident.

In its most radical and optimistic formulations, the movement has called for the dismantling of the Israeli state and its reversion to either Arabic or international jurisdiction. Improvement within its present governmental context is impossible. Firstly, the very idea of a Jewish commonwealth is an aberration prior to the messianic succession. Secondly, the present social and political system is fundamentally defective and one cannot build upon a weak foundation. The eternal and enduring values of Judaism must form the basis of a Jewish state and these are not the stuff of Israeli politics.

Further, the policy of dissolution is most in accord with divine will. Only through the elimination of this false and deceptive structure—and the false security it affords—will the messianic era be introduced. Thus, almost paradoxically, the renunciation of statehood and the improper human overreaching that it represents is intended to allow for the accession of another statehood, more in tune with the demands of piety and observance. For the interim, the Jewish population can depend upon the UN for its well being. In any event, their danger from Arab attack was only the result of Zionist ambition.[10]

Until such time as this dissolution occurs, the faithful must separate themselves completely from this damning influence and crush any attempts at incursion into their lives. Further, they must actively protest the most flagrant forms of its desecration. In its quest for simple morality and propriety, Natore Karta performs a holy but lonely task, other religious elements have sold their organizational souls in return for the support of the Zionist establishment.

There is but one alternative:

> to be ever alert for their influence which spreads like a flame, to flee from them and all that is theirs. Neither should one walk with them nor connect himself to them, but rather, a wall of hatred should be implanted between us, the better to shut out their impact, lest they move us in their direction, God forbid.[11]

Even the use of Zionist funds for apparently holy purposes is rejected, therefore, lest there be overt or implicit strings attached.

In a more active sense, Natore Karta has taken it upon itself to protest transgressions of religious law and to put both moral and political pressure upon governmental and religious authorities to support their position. Zionist administrations are responsible for the desecration of the Sabbath, they assert, as well as violations of standards of public decency and morality. In a more subtle sense, they are also the cause of the general influence of secularism and decadence in all aspects of daily life. Both through active protest and exemplary personal behavior such manifestations must be destroyed or "the Holy Land will spew you forth from its midst."

A particular form of desecration that has been opposed by Natore Karta is the conscription of females into the armed forces. By Israeli law, all women are to be drafted unless their degree of religious obsevance prohibits participation. Traditionally, for reasons of modesty and chastity, it was considered unseemly for a woman to serve in the military. The law, Natore Karta asserts, is only an excuse for harassing religious elements in Israel and reflects the inherently evil nature of the Zionist authorities.

Because the nature of the law deals with the degree of religious adherence,

> they must test how religious the girl is. Needless to say, they bother each individual girl endlessly, until they discover something wrong she has comitted and they say, "If you are like that then you can go to the army as well." . . . You think that they need the girls for military service? No! They want to destroy Judaism and in order to do so they will see to it that they take as many as possible.[12]

Finally, Natore Karta fervently awaits the coming of the Messiah and with it the divine Redemption. Jews as a people are wholly bound to the Torah and its commandments, they argue. It was by divine decree that Jews were exiled and only thus can they be returned. In days past, the Jewish people understood this and only attempted to penetrate more fully the "treasures of holiness" that were their tradition. It is the Jewish goal to follow that supernatural plan outlined in the torah.

Clearly, nationalism and political agitation are not part of this plan.

> Statehood may mean happiness to any other people—but we Jews have been destined for a higher and an essentially different purpose. . . . It is manifestly absurd to believe that we have been waiting for two thousand years, with so much anguish, with such high hopes and such

heartfelt prayers merely in order to finish up playing the same role in the world as an Albania or Honduras.

Only by returning to his tradition and abandoning this foolish and vain national arrogance can the Jew fulfill the "higher and essentially different purpose" which destiny demands.[13]

STRATEGIES FOR SOCIAL CHANGE

Declarations of pacifism and reticence to the contrary, Natore Karta has been among the most active of ideological movements. Its tactics reflect the two-fold desire to demur from any Zionist collaboration and to protest the usurpations and indecencies perceived to be in the very nature of Jewish nationalism. The task has led them to Arab leaders, British and American officials, gentile religious leaders and the councils of the UN.

In a passive sense, the movement prohibits even the most innocent forms of participation in everyday secular life. This includes the use of municipal facilities and social benefits. Natore Karta members have resigned from any form of citizenship, paying no taxes, refusing to vote, and of course, to serve in the military. Many refrain from the use of water, gas, and electric supplies, pasting stamps on envelopes upside down in the event that necessity requires the use of postal services.

The movement has actively protested those more flagrant forms of desecration, particularly as they come closest to their life styles. The routing of public transportation close to their homes and its tendency to operate too soon after the end of the Sabbath has been a constant issue. Similarly, the performance of autopsies in state hospitals and the opening of a public swimming pool and sports arena in Jerusalem have also caused tension sometimes ending in violent conflict with police.

The bitter hatred of Zionism and the Jewish state has led the movement in directions that might well be considered treasonous. Prior to the establishment of the state, for example, a Natore Karta delegation pleaded for an extension of the British Mandate before the United Nations Special Commission on Palestine. During the 1948 War of Liberation, members of the sect refused to participate in battle. They sealed their thoroughfares during the bitter siege of Jerusalem and maintained contact with the Arab forces. Unsatisfied with the war's outcome, they again petitioned the UN for the internationalization of Jerusalem.[14]

More recently, spokesmen for the movement have revived this desire for a pluralist, secular state. Arguing that the concept of a self-initiated

Jewish state is by its nature contrary to Judaism, the movement has decided that it would do best with either a secular or Arab-dominated state under UN supervision. It has requested, therefore, special refugee status for "Jews who wish to disassociate themselves from the Zionist blasphemy."[15]

Internally, the movement has disseminated its views by means of several publications entitled "Hahoma" (the wall) and "Homotenu" (our wall). Its line is taught at the various schools and yeshivot within the Meah Shearim section of Jerusalem. Unity is maintained through subtle sanctions. Those disagreeing, for example, are subject to dismissal from the yeshiva. Aside from the embarrassment and social ostracism that would follow, such dismissal would also mean the discontinuance of financial support given to all yeshiva students.[16]

In its most radical form, youth elements within Natore Karta have even supported Palestinian terror in the hope that it may bring the fall of the Jewish state. It is the position that Jews and Arabs lived in harmony prior to the accession of Zionism and its elimination, violent or otherwise, would bring about friendly relations. In a letter sent by the movement's former secretary to both Yassar Arafat and Gerald Ford, it was declared that

> Natore Karta welcomes the state proposed by the Palestine Liberation Organization in which Arabs and Jews would live together under a government which would insure the blossoming of Judaism just as it did under Moslem rule in Spain.

Though later denied by the movement's counsil, the communiqué also declared Natore Karta's willingness to serve as Jewish adviser to a Palestinian government in exile.[17]

On occasion, Natore Karta has asked world leaders to intervene with the Israeli government on the movement's behalf. In addition to Gerald Ford, messages have been sent to Pope Paul VI, Kurt Waldheim, and Richard Nixon. When a scandal was raised over government attempts to enforce health standards in a Meah Shearim slaughterhouse, formal protest was lodged with the UN under Libyan sponsorship.[18]

Through its supporters in New York, the movement has sought to bring its ideology before the American people and to explain that there is a fundamental difference between Judaism and the Zionist line. The following is from an advertisement in the New York *Times*:

> Those who have suffered or may suffer through Zionist military or political activities should not blame the Jewish People for deeds com-

mitted by the Zionists—who have all turned their backs on Jewish tradition. Zionist politicians and their fellow-travelers do not speak for the Jewish People. Indeed the Zionist conspiracy against Jewish tradition and Jewish law makes Zionism and all its activities and entities the arch-enemy of the Jewish People today.[19]

By the same token, Natore Karta has also attempted to show its solidarity and support with the most extreme of Palestinian elements under Israeli jurisdiction. In 1973, Rabbi Amram Blau invited the editor of *Al-Sa'ab*, a radical Arab newspaper in East Jerusalem, to interview him. Blau indicated that thousands of Natore Karta members in Israel, Europe, and America opposed the Zionist state and supported the Palestinian cause. The interview was published along with a picture of the sign that hung over Blau's door declaring "Here lives a Jew—not a Zionist."[20]

Finally, in almost enigmatic fashion, Rabbi Blau prohibited visiting any of the sites that had been taken by Zionist military conquest. These included some of Judaism's holiest places: the Tomb of the Patriarchs in Hebron, the Tomb of Rachel in Bethlehem, and the Western Wall in East Jerusalem—as well as some of Blau's own property, north of Jerusalem. Indeed, with few exceptions, he would not leave Jerusalem at all.

One of these exceptions, however, caused a considerable scandal. In 1965, Rabbi Blau decided to remarry and chose the converted daughter of French Catholics as his new bride. Aside from the twenty-five year difference in their ages, the match was considered unseemly because of her background and Rabbi Blau was called upon to recant his proposal by the Rabbinic Council of the Edah Haredit. Ever the iconoclast, Blau refused and was married in Tel Aviv; the sect would not permit the ceremony to take place in the Holy City. It was a tribute to Blau's charisma and flexibility that, despite the controversy, he was able to maintain leadership of the movement until his death in 1974.[21]

IN SUM

Unlike other movements of social change, the roots of Natore Karta are founded in the sources of classical Judaism. It seeks justification in the body of religious law and the authority of rabbinic decision. Mystical elements are grounded in this context as well: the relationship between God, His people and their land. The movement acts upon the conviction with the belief that such will bring divine favor and in this sense there are many similarities with Gush Emunim, another contemporary Israeli protest group.

Born of East European orthodoxy, Natore Karta views the national enterprise as usurpation and rebellion against divine prerogative. Having taken an oath to abstain from national initiative, Zionism represents a dangerous renege. Directed by nonbelievers, the Zionist movement has accomplished nothing but to infuse the nation with Western secularism, materialism and self-doubt. Rather than bring salvation as promised, it has only moved the people further from their religious beliefs and heritage.

In its attempts to bring these issues to the fore, the movement has enlisted the aid of supporters in many parts of the world, particularly among the Satmar Hassidic sect in Brooklyn. The two groups, in fact, share a spiritual leader in Rabbi Joel Teitelbaum. Through these international connections, Natore Karta has presented its ideology to world leaders and used the UN as a forum for its views. This, too, makes it unique by Israeli standards of dissent.

The ideological formulations of Natore Karta may be viewed in still another light. Rather than defend a century of Zionist development as a political force, the movement looks toward two thousand years of Jewish dispersion and indeed glorifies this experience. The values of simple faith, pacifism, and dependence upon divine initiative form the core of this belief. The Jewish people have agreed to abstain from national agitation and rebellion against their rulers. Those who abrogate this agreement with the Lord bring terror and destruction. The gentile world is still in its ascendancy and Jews would do best to closet themselves in the safety of corporate ghettos and await Divine Redemption at the hands of the Messiah. Approaches to the non-Jew should be made delicately and humbly; shows of bravado are unwise and characteristically un-Jewish.

Ironically, in evaluating this manifestation of anti-Zionism, the Israeli Government has been most patient and understanding. Indeed, its posture toward Natore Karta appears to be one of condescending amusement. The movement harkens to a religious simplicity and innocence which many government leaders can understand from their own past and with which they can almost identify.

As a cultural oddity, Natore Karta recalls a life style that was brutally uprooted and destroyed, but which once flourished in Eastern Europe. Despite their militant anti-Zionism, therefore, its adherents have been left to themselves despite their opposition to taxation, conscription, or municipal participation. Confrontations have occurred only when the movement has wandered outside its residential boundaries to protest some form of religious profanation.

NOTES

1. The historical development of Natore Karta ideology in this chapter is based upon the following sources: Walter Laquer, *The History of Zionism* (New York: Holt, Rinehart and Winston, 1972), pp. 407–16; Emile Marmorstein, *Heaven at Bay* (London: Oxford University Press, 1969), pp. 71–90; S. Clement Leslie, *The Rift in Israel* (New York: Schocken, 1971), pp. 57–71; Haim Pikrash, "One Hundred Years of Meah Shearim," *Hatzofeh* (April 12, 1974); Moshe Sheshar, "The Value of the State within the Religious Community," *Hatzofeh* (September 16, 1974).

2. Natore Karta, *An Insight toward Independence*, Pamphlet (Jerusalem, 1970), p. 34.

3. *Mishmeret Homotenu* (Natore Karta periodical) (May 17, 1962).

4. Yerahmiel Domb, "The Millions That Could Have Been Saved," *The Jewish Guardian* (May 30, 1976), pp. 9–13; see also Natore Karta, *An Insight toward Independence*, pp. 37–38. For an objective presentation of these events, see Raul Hilberg, *The Destruction of European Jewry, 1933–1945* (Chicago: Quadrangle Books, 1971) or Nora Levin, *The Holocaust* (New York: Thomas Y. Crowell, 1968).

5. Yerahmiel Domb, "Neturei Karta," in *Zionism Reconsidered*, ed. Michael Selzer (New York: Macmillan, 1970), p. 34.

6. Personal interview with retired Natore Karta spokesman, Rabbi Label Weissfisch, August 1976.

7. The talmudic source is Ketubot 111a.

8. Natore Karta, *An Insight toward Independence*, p. 36.

9. Interview with Weissfisch. See also Amram Blau, *Kingship Shall Revert to Apostasy* (Jerusalem: Hamakor, 1970), pp. 53–57.

10. See Norman Lamm, "The Ideology of Neturei Karta: According to the Satmerer Version," *Tradition* (Fall 1971), p. 50.

11. Natore Karta, *A Clarification*, pamphlet (Jerusalem, 1960), p. 2.

12. Rabbi Moshe Sternbuch, "The Position of Religion in Eretz Israel Today," *The Jewish Guardian* (May 30, 1976), p. 7. See also the Jerusalem *Post* (November 23, 1976).

13. Yerahmiel Domb, *The Transformation* (London: Tomchei Natore Karta, 1958), p. 46; see also Herbert Weiner, "The Case for Natore Karta," *The Jewish Digest* (March 1964), pp. 59–64.

14. *Yediot Achronot* (July 7, 1974), and *Ma-ariv* (July 14, 1974). See also Emile Marmorstein, "Religious Opposition to Nationalism in the Middle East," *International Affairs* (July 1952), pp. 344–59.

15. Jerusalem *Post* (August 28, 1973; June 11, 1974; and January 15, 1976).

16. David Hasenson, Rachel Nitzan, and Aaron Rahmut, "Natore Karta: An Extremist Group" (Senior thesis, Hebrew University, 1974), p. 24.

17. Jerusalem *Post* (February 18, 1975, and June 4, 1975).

18. Jerusalem *Post* (May 19, 1976).

19. New York *Times* (March 12, 1971).

20. *Ma-ariv* (December 30, 1973).

21. Menahem Michaelson, "Rabbi Amran Blau: The Eternal Rebel," *Yediot Achronot* (July 7, 1974); see also Gila Berkowitz, "Madam Rabbanit," *Israel Magazine* (December 1972), pp. 71–75.

9

GUSH EMUNIM: MESSIANISM AND DISSENT

Gush Emunim (the Bloc of the Faithful) is composed largely of religious students and followers of Rabbi Zvi Yehuda Kook, interpreter and exegete of his late father, Rabbi Abraham Kook, chief rabbi of Israel. Centered at the school that bears his father's name, the movement has become one of the most popular of all dissident groups in Israel's brief history.

Unlike other subjects of this study, Gush does not reject Zionism or the institutions of the Israeli state. On the contrary, its ideological positions are prototypically Zionist and nationalist. Its complaint is that the state has veered from the self-confident and determined past that marked its earlier success. Instead, it has been overtaken by a lack of resolution and self-doubt. Defined in both secular and religious terms, willingness to sacrifice territorial integrity for vague promises of peace is both blunder and moral sin. The consequent policies supported by the movement are annexationist bordering on irredentism. Gush Emunim is the single instance of right-wing radicalism here under discussion.

In many ways, the movement derives its ideology from two parallel sources: the first religious, the second secular nationalist.[1] As has been noted, among the early leaders of the Zionist movement were a variety of rabbis who united to form the Mizrahi Party at the turn of the century. These religious pioneers stood apart from other Zionists for their belief that the reestablishment of the Jewish commonwealth was a divine principle which would herald the messianic era. They also stood apart from other religious sages in their willingness to work with secularists and freethinkers in the founding and settling of the state.

Mizrahi, later to become the National Religious Party (NRP) in coalition with splinter elements, easily entered the mainstream of Israeli life with the founding of the state. It served in virtually all of the state's cabinets, took over several ministries, and in essence became the backbone of the religious establishment. In addition, it sponsored agricultural communes operated by strict religious principle and founded institutions of Jewish learning under state subsidy.

With its participation in the political establishment and the experience of statehood, the National Religious Party saw its primary goal as bringing as many aspects of daily life under religious control as possible. These included such questions as personal status, marriage and divorce, and dietary laws for state-run institutions. In return for this hegemony, the party was docile in matters of foreign affairs, military security and domestic economics, bowing to the will of its senior coalition partner, the Labor Alignment.

By the same token, however, a generation of religious Zionists were being raised within the youth movement of the NRP and its religious schools. The political machinations and compromises of their elders notwithstanding, these students were much imbued with the spirit of activism and a fierce love for the land. Religion and nationalism were united in a singular sense of purpose and the result was a maximilist territorial politic unbridled by the moderating effects of practical political participation.

The nature of the growing generational conflict within the NRP is best exemplified by the very incident that brought the issue to a head. On the eve of Israel Independence Day, 1967, Rabbi Zvi Yehuda Kook addressed his students. He recalled the sins of the nation in abandoning Hebron and Bethlehem to Arab jurisdiction. Retrospectively, seen in the light of the victories some four weeks later, his words appeared prophetic and nurtured an annexationist spirit with an emphasis upon settlement.

A parallel source in the foundation of the movement was the renewal of a pioneering spirit among more secular elements after the 1967 War. Organized as the Land of Israel Movement, it drew its support from several disaffected sectors of the Israeli polity. These included members of the political establishment from both the Right and the Left, members of kubbutzim (notably those of the Kibbutz Hameuchad group, a constituent of the Labor Alignment), nationalist poets and literary figures, and demobilized soldiers.

Two elements appeared to unite this disparate and rather motley lot. In the first instance, most were either alienated from the ideological centers within which they were nurtured or disenchanted with the lack of sincerity and spirit. Though it began as an exciting experiment in national and social rejuvenation, Israeli society had turned somewhat mundane and bureaucratic, leaving some of the most creative and spirited of its younger generation cold and unsatisfied.

In addition, particularly for the elders within the group, there still existed strong sentiments that the land of Israel should never have been partitioned in 1948. Though secular rather than religious, the belief was spiritual (or even mystical) in its character. The people of Israel were meant to live on a complete territory, they claimed, and creating artificial divisions would never bring a stable peace. Some reached the same point but from leftist sentiments, that is, the desire for an undivided and truly binational state, harkening back to the ideology of the early Shomer Hatzair, Marxist youth movement.

Whatever their motivation, members of the Land of Israel Movement were elated by the results of the 1967 War. It was now within the province of the Israeli government to create the "Greater Israel" of which they dreamed and unilaterally fulfill the destiny of the Jewish people. By simple annexation and settlement, Israel could become a secure and stable entity with its own claims to binationalism and a de facto solution to the Palestinian problem.

While the disgruntled youth of the NRP remained organizationally linked to the party, many stalked out individually to join the Land of Israel people in their very practical plans for settlement on the conquered territories. In particular, early communities were founded at Kiryat Arba, a new Jewish quarter near Hebron, in the Etzion region, and in the Golan. Almost by way of response, the Labor government considered a plan by Deputy Premier Yigal Allon for settlement "beyond the Green Line," i.e., pre-1967 borders. Though proposed during the summer of 1967, the plan was never fully activated and may have been little more than a ploy to encourage Arab negotiations.

The participation of representatives of the Labor Alignment in Land of Israel activities proved to be a source of embarrassment for many within the government. Nevertheless, the movement gained little popularity beyond its own immediate circle and fared poorly as an electoral list in 1969. Its impact on ideology was considerable, however, in that it made the ground fertile for Gush Emunim, at least in part a spiritual progenitor.[2]

The pioneering cause languished during the next several years, to be rejuvenated by the 1973 War. Though by most accounts Israel did not lose—indeed in many senses it may be said to have won—it failed to gain the elegant and decisive victory to which it had become accustomed. The nation was left in a state of demoralization, recrimination, and self-doubt.

These feelings, reflected in harsh accusations and forced resignations in the war's wake, were openly apparent during the election which followed.

Though still but a faction within the NRP, the settlement activists seemed to exhibit a spiritual appeal sorely lacking during those gray times. To the bulk of the party faithful, however, the ideology was an anomaly and of little use in the hard world of protracted coalition negotiations following the 1973 election. Clearly, limitation within the NRP was no asset to these dissidents.

Further, the appeal of religious settlement transcended party lines. Perhaps even as a surprise to the dissidents themselves, secular Israelis and those little interested in formal politics were attracted to the Rabbi Kook Yeshiva and the cause of pioneerism. An independent organization was imperative.

The formal founding of the movement may be dated to February 1974, when a conference of yeshiva students, members of the armed forces, and activists was held at Kfar Etzion. The significance of the site, built to replace a town wiped out in 1948, founded and established by children and friends of those who perished—was not lost on those in attendance. Here the movement adopted its name, a loose organizational structure, and severed its links with the NRP. It soon undertook fund raising activities and parlor meetings, recruited members from sympathetic religious schools and youth movements and directed its message to all who would listen.

WORLD VIEW

At the risk of oversimplifying, it is fair to say that the ideology of Gush Emunim is derived from a devout marriage of religious Judaism and classical, nonsocialist Zionism. Much of the source for this thinking is rooted in the work of Rabbi Abraham Kook, as interpreted by his son Rabbi Zvi Yehuda Kook, and propagated at the educational institutions that have developed around him. The center of this activity is Yeshivat Mercaz Harav Kook, an institution of higher Jewish learning and research in Jerusalem.

The result of this ideological union is a world view that is both optimistic and affirmative, yet critical and denigratory. The feeling is reflected in a strong attachment to the land of Israel and an emphasis on its centrality in the religious life of the Jew.

> Kedusha, holiness, is a concrete reality, not just a set of legal concepts. Every piece of our land is holy—a present from God. There must be a

link between this "kedusha" and that of the Torah and the People. This is the beginning of the Redemption, the time to join these forms of "kedusha." It is the time to confront historic questions in prepration tor this Redemption.

The tie to the land is linked to a feeling of impending change. This is the momentous Redemption for which Jews have prayed during the past twenty centuries. It is the belief of Gush Emunim that the time is at hand.[3]

The right of the Jewish people to their land is incontestable and not subject to negotiation. Though confirmed by international bodies, the essence of the claim dates to the covenant between God and Abraham, in Biblical times. Further, this right is nontransferable; sections of the land may belong to individuals but the land in its entirety belongs to the Jewish people and their future generations. The site of ancient kingdoms and the Holy Temple, an inherent spiritual connection exists between the people and their home.

The line of reasoning follows closely Rabbi Kook's declaration that the founding of the state of Israel represents the beginning of the messianic era. Success in reclaiming the land and attracting Jews from the lands of their exile are seen as confirmation.

> The true Redemption, which is to be manifested in the complete re-settlement in the Land and the revival of Israel in it, is thus seen to be a continuation of renewed settlement in the Land accompanied by the ingathering of the captive exiles within its boundaries. This appears as the peak of the actual fulfillment of our inheriting the Land, of its being in our possession and not "in that of any other of the nations nor in a state of desolation," of the rule of our own government in it, and of the adherence of our group behavior to its real holiness.[4]

In addition to these mystical visions of messianic Redemption stands a practical critique of the moral stance and determination of the Israeli leadership. The government has abandoned those very qualities upon which the nation was based. In their stead stands a crass materialism and lack of self-confidence. Though difficulty and hardship have been no strangers to Jewish or Israeli history, there was always a basic faith in the propriety of the cause. Such faith must be renewed.

Further, the movement senses a belief in the abstract value of a peace that seems determined not to come, dramatic missions and good will to the contrary. Returning territories and expecting security in return may be the most irrational, mystical, even suicidal action of all. It is borne of ignorance—in the first instance, ignorance of Jewish history and in the second instance, a misunderstanding of what motivates the Arab world. Indeed, from the beginning, Jews have been asked to make territorial concessions: the British White Paper of 1938, the UN partition of 1948, and the return of the Sinai in 1956.

Nevertheless, such concessions have done little to pacify Arab demands or to prevent the continuation of their murderous terrorism. The wanton slaughter of Jewish civilians, both before and after 1948, the Gush claim, had little to do with territorial aspirations. "There is no doubt that the Arab's basic desire is to expel the people of Israel from her Land."[5]

Such thinking has obviously led to sentiments of right-wing expansionism. The position is underscored by a religious sense of history and the importance of inhabiting the land as part of this destiny. Living in the land of Israel is equivalent to fulfilling all other religious requirements. To this end even war may have a holy purpose, particularly the war of 1967. It was then that sites of religious and historical importance were returned to Jewish jurisdiction, such as Hebron, the Tomb of Rachel, the Tomb of Joseph, and the Western Wall.

Most particularly, the reunification of Jerusalem is taken to symbolize the rejoining of the people with its heritage under the auspices of a divine commonwealth. To return any of this land would be heresy. The travail of the 1973 War, the significance of its occurrence on Yom Kippur, which was also on a Saturday—Sabbath—that year, and other military, economic, or diplomatic setbacks stand as confirmation. It is the way of the Almighty to offer trials to the faithful, trials which will cleanse and purify, before the advent of the Messiah and the age of peace and tranquility. Thus:

> This gradual process that marks the advance of Israel's Redemption in all its aspects, practical and spiritual, also includes within itself all the reverses and failures, all the hindrances and complications that attend every stage of the process . . . various faults, and weaknesses, obscurities and corruptions, will occur and come into prominence. These necessitate increased correction and strengthening, added exaltation and betterment, "the excellence of dignity and the excellence of power" in the direction of perfection and raising of standards.[6]

Furthermore, government opposition, especially that of the Labor Alignment, is alleged to be far more partisan than it is either moral or strategic. It irks the leadership that Gush Emunim has begun a series of settlements outside the traditional hegemony of party, government, or Histadrut. The resulting independence from credits, grants, and subsidies (as well as the control they imply) is more than can be tolerated. With it, of course, comes ideological independence as well.

The critique of Israeli life is reflected in social terms. Societal problems are attributed to a perceived indifference to "productive labor," that is, an orientation toward earning the highest wage for the least work. Alienated from the land, both conceptually and spiritually, the nation is left adrift. It has developed a ubiquitous and abundant bureaucracy and a reputation as an "international schnorer" (freeloader).

The sum of such thinking is an extremely hard line vis-à-vis Palestinian nationalism. The complexion of the land must remain Jewish; while Arab residents may have rights therein, they can never have the "rights of Israel." Living as a minority, they may own land, but they can "never own the Land." There is no Palestinian problem, Gush leaders assert. It is merely a question of how Arabs may live peacefully in a Jewish state. Put cogently:

> They have to know that there is no such thing as Arab territory in the land of Israel. It is a victory of Arab propaganda that people speak of Samaria as Arab territory.[7]

This, Gush argues, is really not a new ideological formulation at all. It is very much in the mainstream of classical Zionism. That it sounds radical and romantic today is a reflection of how far the state of Israel has moved from its original moorings. More serious even than the indifference to religious obligation has been the inability of the leadership to provide a clear territorial policy or force a meaningful and secure peace. This alone supports the movement's dissent.

Finally, the Gush is most sensitive to the claim that it is little more than a front for the National Religious Party and that its thinking is more partisanship than theology. It has continually attempted to divorce itself from the NRP and seriously considered offering an independent electoral list in the 1977 election. The issue, it claims, is not one of political maneuvering but of the spiritual existence of the state.

> These religious parties are no longer spiritual. They are like merchants in the marketplace. We are open to any Jew—religious or not. We are not a partisan movement. We are a political pressure group and a spiritual movement in essence.[8]

VALUES AND GOALS

Gush Emunim has presented a specific set of goals to overcome the problems it perceives. The first and foremost of these is "hitnahalut." Almost untranslatable, "hitnahalut" is a combination of settlement and messianism requiring the Jews return to the land of their heritage out of religious obligation and cultural imperative. This is no right, they argue, which can be bartered or forfeited; it is prerequisite to the Redemption.

In comparison to "hitnahalut," all other values pale. Democracy, for example, represents nothing more than an intermediary phase in the movement of the Jewish folk toward their divine destiny. It is not an end in itself nor should it be a factor in considering the holy mission at hand.

> The Jewish national renaissance is more important than democracy. Democracy can no more vote away Zionism, aliya, settlement than it can vote that people should stop breathing or speaking. The fate of Eretz Yisrael and a free and whole Jewish life in it are not subject to a majority vote. At its roots our people know this. We are a people that is especially linked to a vision.[9]

The sum of this vision is a renewal of the ancient links between the people, their heritage and the land. An end must be put to the denigrating effects of outside influences. The values of traditional Zionism and the impact of the pioneer must be placed squarely within government policy. Jewish history and Zionist thought have been taken lightly, considered a quaint oddity more appropriate to foreign fund raising and tourism.

A source of the problem was the union of Zionism with socialism in earlier times. All too often early pioneers were more involved with social experimentation than with land reclamation. Their approach was primarily secular. It was only natural that when the immediate physical problems receded and the zeal of the founders ebbed, the following generation would be left with much of the secularism and little else. A cynical materialism and weakness of resolve filled the vacuum.

This was the essential failure of labor Zionism. Thus:

> For much of the Zionist movement socialism was very important— even more important than settling the land. We have changed that order. For us, the most important thing is "hitnahalut" and the social form of our settlement is quite secondary. We exist as Jews only to fulfill our aspirations to Zion. . . . The emphasis of social form over "hitnahalut" is a foreign influence and therefore dooms labor Zionism to failure. The kibbutzim, which were its crown, have betrayed their

principles and now turn to us for spiritual inspiration. We are purifying ourselves from foreign ideologies.[10]

Ironically, new settlements are true to this emphasis, that is, the priority of settlement over social form, even when it appears to violate their religious sensibilities. Gush settlers reiterate time and again that their towns will not be kibbutzim nor do they desire isolated religious retreats. Little in them will be communal and there will be no requirements of religious observance for residence. The nonreligious are welcome to join in their attempt to build an "open city."

"Hitnahalut" is also seen as an essential to world peace. The basic ingredient of the messianic age is international harmony, a harmony that will be characteristics of the messianic age alone. Since settlement will lead to the Redemption and harken the "end of days," those truly seeking peace should do all in their power to settle the land and secure its borders. Opposition to "hitnahalut" on the grounds that it will prevent peace is predicated upon ignorance and therefore deserves little attention.

Though romantic in its thrust, the argument has a realistic, indeed almost cynical, quality as well. Peace does not appear on the horizon, argues the movement. This is a reality whether a mass program of settlement is undertaken or not. By renewing faith through the active fulfillment of the Zionist ideal, however, there may be at least a moral gain of strength and courage to withstand the ravages from without. Such strength, "whose root is the peace of justice will ultimately bring the just peace."[11]

However, the goal of "hitnahalut" and the pioneering settlements that have been undertaken in its name do not have solely spiritual ends. The movement is painfully aware of the socioeconomic problems facing the nation. The Gush claims that its prescriptions hold many of the solutions to these problems. A return to the ideals of the pioneer will resolve the effects of nonproductive labor discussed above. The issue is the priority of national over personal needs. Once the balance is set to right, morale will ascend.

By this token, emphasizing settlement does not imply neglect of pressing social and economic concerns. Rather, implicit in the call is an underlying theme.

Only the pioneering spirit can lead to a national rejuvenation which will set hearts afire. It will remove individuals, as well as the nation as a whole, from viewing only the narow, personal perspective. This will, in itself, resolve many of our social problems. The economy as well is depressed because of difficulties whose roots lie in the priority of the purely personal over that which is national.[12]

In the international realm, these arguments become still more acute. The primary raison-d'être of the Arab states, claims Rabbi Levinger, is to destroy the state of Israel and eliminate the national rebirth of the Jews on their land. The essential struggle must be against these forces and everything must be subordinated to it. The resort to force is not only legitimate but a demonstration of full devotion to the ideal. Even when peace and tranquility seem imminent, one must be ever watchful, for this has been the bitter lesson of Jewish history.

Despite charges of naïveté by opponents, Gush Emunim is well aware of the political implications of their goals and appear to be spurred by them still further. Aside from the question of settlement as a religious obligation stands the equally profound desire to prevent the weakening of government resolve. This is crucial in the matter of the conquered territories, taken to be part of historic Eretz Yisrael.

The movement is convinced that government opposition to their cause is not based upon concern for the land of Israel or its people. Rather, government leadership is interested in ends whose motivations are crassly and cynically political. It would like only to maintain an open field of options in negotiations with the United States and the Arab world. Such options are to include return of holy soil.

The movement prefers to call these areas liberated rather than occupied and realizes that they might be more easily bartered if there are few Israeli settlements there. Consequently, "hitnahalut" must also been seen in its more mundane light: as an attempt to limit options concerning the unsettled regions of "historic Eretz Yisrael." By forcing the leadership to face a mass settlement in these areas, as well as a ground swell of support within Israel proper, the alternative of relinquishing them will have been eliminated.

Finally, the government often labors under a severe misconception, it is claimed. Influenced by demands of secular politics or schooled in institutions of socialist bent, it may not fully understand what peace requires. Rather than shows of weakness, as territorial concession is seen, peace demands security. This will only come when Israel has safe and defensible borders.

STRATEGIES FOR SOCIAL CHANGE

In order to realize its goals, Gush Emunim has embarked upon a specific set of tactics designed to gain adherents and to alert the government to its ideology. In fact, the movement's tactics are often indistinguishable from its values and therein lies Gush Emunim's great strength. Aside from just preaching settlement, watchfulness, and identity with the land, the leadership has joined the rank and file in leaving comfortable city residences and moving to undeveloped areas of the West Bank.

Particularly significant in its settlement attempts have been the Biblical regions of Judea, Samaria, Hebron, and Jericho. Here new villages have been established through the efforts of the movement, generally through "squatters rallies," as in Sabastia and the military camp at Kadum. After protracted confrontations and negotiations with the government, the settlers have been given small plots of land with some meager support. In Hebron, the movement has succeeded in refounding the Jewish quarter at Kiryat Arba, brutally destroyed in an Arab pogrom in 1929.

Internally, the result of such unity of cause between leaders and subordinates is extremely egalitarian. Indeed, it may well be that attracting a leadership of high caliber, willing to work side by side with its membership, has been the movement's greatest success. Witness the following statement by an objective observer in Israel:

> It is hard to find a more authentic leadership than that of Gush Emunim and this is something to which their ideological opponents must concede. It is a leadership of personal dedication and willingness to sacrifice, a leadership of responsibility. . . . It is made up of people who not only believe in the need for settlement but who have, in fact, carried it out. Extremist politics for them is not a secondary avocation or an addition to their normal lives but rather, a part of their existence. . . . In this sence, Gush Emunim is not a protest movement, it is a movement of action and accomplishment.[13]

The self-sacrifice exhibited by its leadership has also made it the envy of other movements within the country, religious or otherwise. To the older generation, it harkens to their own pioneering days of the prestate period. To the young it is a call to action and spirit largely unknown in their urban and industrialized life styles.

In this vein, the movement has introduced a large-scale educational program by which it hopes to attract unaffiliated sympathizers as well as those now nominally members of other political organizations. Unlike other such activities, this is not perceived as a partisan ploy. Why could not those who belong to Mapam or the Labor Party participate in "hitna-halut"—which is the religious obligation of all Jews, the movement asserts. As measure of their success, Gush lecturers have been invited to speak at Kibbutz and Moshav centers in every part of the country.

Underlying this activity is a genuine desire to broaden the base of Gush support so that it may include those of secular as well as religious senti-ment. Indeed, the religious elements in its thought are also national or cultural. In one form or another, such rhetoric has been part of the Zionist movement for a century and is by no means a function of traditional religious ideology. What makes it religious here is mainly the commitments and affiliations of the group's leadership.

Therefore, it is not difficult for nonreligious portions of the Israeli population to support one or another aspect of the movement's philosophy. Simply put, one can be in favor of a harder line on territorial negotiations without feeling the need to pray three times daily. Equally, one may feel an affinity to the land and to those who have regained the pioneering spirit without being concerned with dietary practices.

By that same token, many secularists share the critique of society offered by the Gush. Much has changed, they claim; the society has lost the excitement and idealistic spirit which was once its greatest attraction.

> the strains of long ascetic dedication to an idea and a people, coupled with increasing affluence whose beneficiaries were, in the first instance the veterans themselves, have cut deeply into the simple piety and purity of earlier days. . . . And so he [the pioneer] moves first gradually and then more easily, as habit represses guilt, away from the joined dream and reality of his pioneering selflessness. . . . His movement is not in isolation. It is joined and sustained and encouraged by the movement of the whole society. . . . The wedding of personal to public life and of socialism to Jewishness, which was the core of the Second Aliyah idea, has lost its appeal[14]

To secularist supporters, Gush represents a return to that simple piety and purity. One's personal religious affiliations are quite beside the point.

In an attempt to exploit this sentiment, the Gush has embarked on a highly successful fund raising program. Parlor meetings have been ar-ranged wherein those of like mind have been persuaded to donate con-siderable sums to individual settlements. Others have made heavy equip-ment available or donated their talents in establishing small plants and commercial enterprises in new settlements. Part of the willingness stems from honest sympathy with the cause. An equal part may be the result of satisfaction derived from seeing direct results with little bureaucratic delay or political maneuvering.

Financial support has also been sought abroad. A corps of fund raisers have been trained and dispatched to various parts of the United States, for example, to elicit support from Jewish communities there. Local rabbis have sponsored dinners and lecture programs in order to familiarize their congregants with Gush activity and prepare them for the visiting representatives. In several instances, rabbis with national reputations have undertaken programs of monetary support and pressure on political figures in the form of an organization known as Emunim. [15]

Aside from settlement, the movement has also employed tactics designed to attract attention to its cause and to embarrass the Israeli government. Among these have been massive rallies—generally peaceful, although several have resulted in serious confrontations with the police and the army. A long march to Jericho attracted thousands of participants from all over the country. Similarly, a demonstration of mothers with baby carriages in front of the prime minister's office—designed to symbolize Jewish children being led to the slaughter—was widely covered by both the domestic and foreign press.

Such activities have often led to violence between Gush settlers and local Arab villagers. Religious tensions resulted from attempts to hold Yom Kippur services at the Tomb of the Patriarchs in Hebron and to establish a Jewish settlement within the town rather than only in the already Jewish suburb of Kiryat Arba. Amid claims of desecration of holy books and articles on both sides, rioting broke out throughout the West Bank and Gush Emunim members violently opposed the attempts of security forces to bring quiet. [16]

It is here that Gush differs radically from other Israeli protest groups. Unlike those which operate largely on the fringe of Israeli society, the matter of Gush Emunim has become one of national concern, debated regularly within the Halls of Knesset. Support or opposition to unauthorized settlement has become a major issue within the Israeli cabinet, dividing many of those who sought leadership in the Labor Party.

Most prominently displayed in the previous administration was the growing feud between Defense Minister Shimon Peres and Prime Minister Yitzhak Rabin. Looked upon as a covert supporter of Gush efforts, Peres was instrumental in arranging small government contracts with workers in West Bank settlements. It was also under his auspices that utilities were shared with army bases in Samaria, allowing newly established towns to have running water and electricity. Nevertheless, Peres has publicly chastised the movement when it "abuses Israel Defense Force officers, for all to see." In Hebron, he indicated that he would press charges on all who incite to riot, irrespective of their motivation.

> We shall continue extinguishing the fires of blind hatred and we are strong enough to extend protection to all citizens, no matter what their religion and their nationality.[17]

Rabin was far less amenable to the movement, criticizing it readily and emphasizing his willingness to return territories without regard to the nature or extent of settlement there. He also used the issue as an opportunity to attack Peres and the military administration on the West Bank. Rabin implied that reticence in handling illegal settlement has weakened the credibility and undermined the stated policies of the Israeli government. Nevertheless, he too saw fit to express admiration for the pioneering zeal of the movement and indicated his support for settlements in the Etzion region.

It may be that much of the confusion and rhetorical debate was a function of the desire to depose Rabin from his position as leader of the Labor Party and prime minister. A prime challenger, Peres attempted to use the settlement issue as a lever for the upcoming election. Rabin's victory in the premature Labor caucus, early in 1977, showed his tenacity though he ultimately was forced to relinquish the nomination because of a personal scandal. It may well be that precipitating an early government crisis in the last days of 1976 was a strategy to catch opponents off guard and blunt the Peres drive.

Finally, despite Gush Emunim protests to the contrary, the movement has naturally lent itself to partisan exploitation. Both the National Religious Party and the right-wing Likud bloc have attempted to win electoral support from the movement's broad popularity. Representatives of both parties make regular speeches in Knesset supporting the movement and attacking government policy to the contrary. Former Minister of Religions (NRP) Yitzhak Raphael indicated his willingness to allow Jewish settlement in Hebron proper. Similar resolutions have been introduced by Yehuda Ben-Meir (NRP).

In addition, their active endorsement of the movement's settlement policy led to bitter and virulent sessions in Knesset with Likud and MRP representatives displaying unusual disregard for the niceties of parliamentary debate. Shouting matches between Peres and Likud leader Menahem Begin led to confrontations bordering on violence. Indeed, in order to show its favor toward the settlement ideology, the Herut faction of Likud held its

1975 convention at Kiryat Arba. The action motivated mass protests from doves throughout the country who chained themselves to the roadways in order to block the convention from taking place.[18]

SUMMARY ANALYSIS

Gush Emunim is the outgrowth of a rift in the National Religious Party; the roots of this rift are to be found in the 1967 War. Its organizational structure is based at the Rav Kook School which was also the breeding ground for many of its leadership. Though much of its ideology is religious in nature, it has succeeded in attracting considerable numbers of secular followers by the pioneering aspects of its call and the hard line it espouses. An apocalyptic vision harkening to generations of Jewish hopes and mystical prayers rounds out its appeal.

The movement differs from others in Israel in several significant ways. Most protest groups base their dissent on differences with traditional Zionism. Indeed, they are either hostile to it as an ideology or reject it out of hand. Gush Emunim, however, is prototypically Zionist and personifies many of the same values that were almost universal in Israel at an earlier time. In this sense, it may fairly be stated that "hitnahalut" is little different from the spirit of the "halutz"—the pioneer—that has been part of the Zionist mainstream for a century.

Equally, its philosophy is no more naive or inflammatory than that which has sparked nation-building or change-oriented movements elsewhere. It is indicative of how far Israeli society has moved from its charismatic beginnings to its present, "rational/bureaucratic" structures (to borrow the terms of Max Weber) that such a movement has engendered so much controversy and opposition. It might properly have been redirected into the mainstream.

Like other dissenting forms, the ideology of Gush Emunim is somewhat unidimensional. It is assumed that all the nation's ills may be cured through "hitnahalut"—settlement, particularly throughout Judea and Samaria, places of religious significance. Unlike its counterparts, however, Gush offers no social prescriptions in the form that such settlement should take. The land is the overriding goal. Social experimentation is unnecessary and may well be damaging.

Gush is also unique in that it has grown quickly both in Israel and abroad. It has displayed many of the earmarks of a mass movement with grass roots appeal. More than just a question of protest, the movement probes the ability to overcome the obstacles of a highly centralized political system. Many have attacked the partisanship and clubhouse nature of

Israeli politics. Gush has stalked out on its own, disassociating itself from the party from which it was spawned. In this sense, it is the first Israeli example of a common American phenomenon, the political interest group.

The movement claims that it is merely attempting to influence the government's action, much as any interest group might. Within certain limits, the argument is sound. The crucial issue is the ability of the Israeli political system to deal creatively and flexibly with the Gush as an individual movement, with the renewed ideology of "hitnahalut" outside the official framework, and with the deep disaffections that the movement's appeal reflects. While the solutions offered by the movement are neither destructive nor nihilistic, they are more a symptom than a cause.

Evidence to this effect may be gleaned from even a cursory glance at the evaluations of other dissenting movements. Those with radically different views from Gush, members of anti-Zionist Matzpen or Natore Karta, have offered similar critiques of Israeli life. While their motivations and conclusions were poles apart, they agreed substantially on the ills they saw.

Finally, there are indications that the government and several of the parties have sensed the potentially explosive nature of the movement's success. Despite several provocations, the army has made no immediate and concerted efforts to expel the squatters. What influence has been exerted to gain economic concessions, minor though they may have been? What role might leaders of the NRP or Likud play in capturing the spirit of the movement for their electoral advantage? It is difficult to tell whether the movement will be able to steer the nonpartisan course it has so forcefully set for itself, especially as its base of support becomes broader. Will it truly motivate a renaissance or merely become a wing of an established party?

NOTES

1. This brief review of the development of Gush Emunim is based upon the following sources: the pioneering efforts of Moshe Kohn, whose study of the Gush first appeared in the Jerusalem *Post* during the summer of 1976; Rael J. Isaac, *Israel Divided: Ideological Politics in the Jewish State* (Baltimore: Johns Hopkins University Press, 1976), pp. 45–72; Janet O'Dea, "Gush Emunim: Roots and Ambiguities," *Forum on the Jewish People, Zionism, and Israel* (Fall 1976), pp. 39–50; Ehud Shprinzak, "Notes on the Nature of Extremist Politics in Israel" (Paper delivered at the Eshkol Institute of the Hebrew University, May 1976); and Avi Ben Zion, "On Fraternal Conflict in Israel," *Bitzaron* (March 1977), pp. 99–104.

2. See Don Peretz, "Israel's 1969 Election Issues," *The Middle East Journal* (Winter 1970), pp. 31–46, and Isaac, op. cit.

3. Rabbi Yochanan Fried, Gush Emunim spokesman, personal interview, August 1976.

4. Rabbi Zvi Yehuda Hacohen Kook, "Zionism and Biblical Prophecy," in *Religious*

Zionism: An Anthology, ed. Yosef Tirosh (Jerusalem: World Zionist Organization, 1975), p. 1976.

5. Rabbi Y. Fielber, *Breath to the People upon It* (Jerusalem: Emunim, 1974), pp. 3–7.

6. Kook, op. cit., p. 177. See also O'Dea, op. cit.

7. Interview with Rabbi Fried.

8. Ibid.

9. Rabbi Moshe Levinger, as cited in Moshe Kohn, "The Numbers Game," Jerusalem *Post* (August 8, 1976).

10. Personal interview with Gush Emunim settler at Elon Moreh.

11. Rabbi Moshe Levinger in Moshe Levinger, Yochanan Fried, and Hanan Porat, "Brief Answers to Timely Questions," *Gush Emunim* (March 1976), p. 36.

12. Hanan Porat in op. cit., p. 34. See also the Gush Emunim pamphlet, *What Does the P.L.O. Want* (Jerusalem, 1976).

13. Shprinzak, op. cit., pp. 10–11.

14. Leonard Fein, "The Centers of Power," in *Integration and Development in Israel*, ed. S.N. Eisenstadt et al. (New York: Praeger, 1970), pp. 51–52. See also Abba Eban, *My Country: The Story of Modern Israel* (New York: Random House, 1972), pp. 175–83.

15. Notable among these is Rabbi Fabian Schonfeld, former president of the Rabbinical Council of America.

16. Jerusalem *Post* (October 6, 1976 and November 2, 1976). See also Yehuda Litani, "The Story of Kiryat Arba," *New Outlook* (November 1976), pp. 12–14.

17. Jerusalem *Post* (October 6, 1976 and October 12, 1976).

18. Jerusalem *Post* (September 21, 1976 and October 6, 1976).

10

THE BLACK PANTHERS:
ORIENTAL JEWS AND
THE CULTURE OF POVERTY

The Black Panthers are a small group of Israeli youth who are attempting to represent the whole of Israel's Oriental population. It is variously estimated that some 60 percent of the Israeli citizenry is of non-Western descent. Largely from the Maghreb states of North Africa (Tunisia, Algeria, Morocco, and so on), or the Asian states of the Muslim world (such as Egypt, Yemen, Iraq, Iran), the bulk of this population has inferior socioeconomic status and educational opportunities in comparison with their Euro-American brothers. It is this deprivation and the prejudice it allegedly reflects that served as impetus for the creation of the Panthers, soon after the 1967 War.[1]

Cleavages between European and Oriental Jewish communities in Israel predate the creation of the state. Ironically, during much of the mandatory period, the British utilized the administrative talents of Oriental Jews, especially in municipal affairs. European immigrants, with their socialist traditions and rather crude behavioral patterns were ill-suited for this work and were often slighted by this Oriental elite. It is from these old and well-established Jerusalem families that the powerful Sefardi Community Council was formed.*

----

*Israel's ethnic cleavages are often erroneously dichotomized. The two populations are variously termed Western and Oriental, European and Islamic, Black and White, or Ashkenazi and Sefardi. Though each set of terms is less than adequate, the latter is cryptic. Ashkenaz and Sefarad mean Germany and Spain respectively and refer to those Jewish

Despite the favored positions of these Jews under British rule, as well as a thriving community of Yemenite immigrants whose skills have become synonymous with Israeli silver and metal craft, it was not here that the institutions of state were to be rooted. Of greater significance was the social and economic experimentation being carried out by immigrants from Eastern Europe. In particular, a Russian-Jewish corps was gaining valuable political experience on the councils of the Jewish Agency, the Histadrut and the political parties. Quite aside from the ethnic makeup of these institutions, their approach to political life and the ideological and cultural stamps that they bore would be indelibly East European, as indeed was political Zionism itself.

Understandably, the period of greatest strain for the Jewish national enterprise was the late forties and early fifties. Israel was forced to battle the British, the UN, and the Arab world externally. In addition, the state had to contend with a massive immigration of pitiful figures fresh from the death camps and detention centers of Europe. Their immediate acceptance and settlement—as well as their cultural, psychological, and social adjustment—were overwhelming tasks. During this period as well, because of the growing antagonisms between Israel and its neighbors, life in the Arab world became increasingly intolerable for Jews, who left their ancient homelands by the scores of thousands.

Not always was this Oriental emigration forcible, however. The Moroccan government, for example, has steered a moderate course in policy toward its Jewish citizens and some 40,000 Jews still reside in its larger cities. In addition, not all Jewish emigrants from the Arab world made their way to the Holy Land. Many of the professional and merchant classes moved to Paris, London, and New York, where they comprise an educated, prosperous, and successful community. For the more traditional and less sophisticated, however, the creation of the state of Israel and the antagonisms of the indigenous Muslim population symbolized the coming of the messianic era. To emigrate to Israel represented the fulfillment of the ancient prophecy, the harbinger of "the end of days."

The confluence of these elements made the integration of the Oriental immigrants a particular hardship. The nature of the migration was such that

------

communities that grew from the dispersions following the Crusades in Europe and the Spanish Inquisition. To refer to all Oriental Jews as Sefardim is imprecise because the latter term also includes European Jews from England, France, Italy, and Greece. Further, there are Oriental communities of North Africa or the Mideast whose histories include little contact with the erstwhile Jews of Spain. Consequently, the terms Western and Oriental will generally be used here as the best of all possible shorthands.

many of the communities' natural leaders—its professionals and educators—never came to Israel, and those who did often strained to lose their ethnic identity and melt into the mainstream. Further, these Jews manifested cultural tendencies and norms which were inappropriate to a quickly industrializing society, their other values notwithstanding. Traditionalism, familism, and a ubiquitous concern for "kavod" (personal status and self-respect), admirable as such qualities may be, did not lend themselves to a social system in which the immigrant was often asked to do work he considered beneath him, fend for himself, and watch the erosion of parental authority.

Furthermore, there was a subtle form of discrimination operative, unintentional as it may have been. Because most of the state's emergent institutions were shaped by Europeans, their ideological orientations and political culture were foreign to the Oriental newcomers. The very vision of what a Jewish state should be—in both religious and secular terms—was the product of East European Jewish life, as was much of its music, ritual, and literature. Indeed, Oriental culture was often looked at askance, as quaint and primitive at best and the culture of the enemy at worst. It is not surprising, therefore, that European immigrants adapted with comparative ease despite their harrowing experiences and the condition in which they arrived. Orientals were far less successful.

Consequently, many Oriental immigrants learned to be ashamed of their descent and imitated the Western mode. Strains on government services being severe, these immigrants were generally given a small apartment, some training, and then left to fend for themselves in a strange and threatening environment.

These problems were quite galling. The essence of Zionist ideology, the ingathering of the exiles, required that Israel be a state of social equality in which no pronounced stratification could exist. While its early egalitarianism was noteworthy, the development of distinct ethnic communities was soon visible. It was most disturbing to find ethnic origin correlating significantly with socioeconomic status, educational level, and prospects for upward mobility. To be an Oriental immigrant meant being poorer and having less chance for improvement than a European. Nonetheless, the new state's overall economic problems, compounded by its military and diplomatic vulnerability, forced domestic affairs to the background. There was simply no time nor resources with which to confront the issue.

Also, there was an innocent faith in two ameliorative factors: time and the Israel Defense Force. It was hoped that with experience and practical training, the Oriental immigrant would adapt to his new surroundings and develop sociocultural skills that might lead to success. Equally, with time, governmental and social institutions would develop, designed to accommodate the special needs of this community. Surely within a generation much of the issue would be blunted, if not totally eliminated.

In addition, it was believed that integration might be accomplished through the influences of the armed services. Israel depends upon a citizen army in which some 80 percent of the adult male population serves. Reserve duty is mandatory until the age of 50 and requires active service each year. The equality of the trenches multiplied by the mutual dependence and concern of the front line was expected to carry over into civilian life and promote understanding and respect. In this manner, a "mizug haedot"—a communal melting pot— might be created.

Such faith proved to be unfounded, however, Time did not heal, as was hoped. As hostility and war became the norm, internal problems were relegated to secondary importance and rarely confronted. The nation's priorities required physical survival and major resources were allocated to protect against the threat posed by the Arab world. Furthermore, most Israelis were poor and the common struggle, wedded to an ideology of self-sacrifice and egalitarianism, tended to diffuse the emergence of dissatisfaction. The major exception to this quiet resignation was the ethnic disturbance at Wadi Salib, a Moroccan section in Haifa, in 1959.

The army could not fulfill the integrative task to which it had been assigned. Partly, this was because hopes placed in it as a social institution were unrealistically high. The Israel Defence Force has often been cited for its open, mobile, and creative nature. It served admirably in the labor of socializing and accommodating immigrants from a score of countries to the intricacies of Israeli life. That it might overcome entirely cultural disparities and prejudice was too much to expect. Further, upon their return the pressures of poverty, poor housing, and inadequate education for jobs more than countered whatever advantages the Oriental veterans had gained in military service.

In addition, the problems facing these residents of Israel's growing slums mitigated in still other ways the positive effects of armed service. Particularly for the children of Oriental immigrants, urban poverty mean school drop outs, delinquency, and street life. Inadequate housing was exacerbated by a high birth rate and hopes for upward mobility were dim. As a result, many Oriental youths were denied acceptance to the army because of criminal records, illiteracy, or low I.Q. Thus in a country where military service is a given, yet one more stigma was added to the already deprived Oriental Israeli. Though native born, the problems inherent in immigration have now been inherited by the next generation.

The years immediately following the 1967 War were crucial to the development of ethnic concern and self-identification among Israel's Oriental poor. Until that point, the country suffered consistent recession and economic stress was commonplace. The war gave the economy a boost, raised morale, and lent a new-found respect to Israel throughout the world. Orientals, who had a considerable share in the victory, expected to share equally in increased social status and material gain. That their position did improve but not at the same rate as their Western peers underlined their plight in the years of relative calm from 1967 to 1971.

It was within this context that teenagers from the slums of Tel Aviv and Jerusalem began organizing and agitating for better housing, jobs, and education. They were spurred on by the findings of various government studies. The data indicated that, in 1968, the average family income of Western Jews in Israel was 1116 Israeli pounds (roughly $350) while that of Orientals was 470 pounds. This disparity was further aggravated by the high Oriental birth rate, almost twice that of Western families. Thus, not only were Oriental families poorer on an absolute basis but they were larger as well. The situation followed many of the same patterns of the poor in other industrialized nations and militant action was a natural concomitant.[2]

Though sporadic and often disorganized, this militancy led to major confrontations with the police in Jerusalem and Tel Aviv, some becoming large-scale riots with thousands of participants. It was from this experience that the Panthers were born, during the winter of 1970–71. Their leadership was largely Oriental teenagers, most of who neither attended high school nor were in the army and had grown up in the Hatikva section of Tel Aviv or the Musrara section of Jerusalem. They were soon joined by Shalom Cohen, former partner of Uri Avnery in *Haolam Hazeh*. The group was also influenced by contacts among government social workers and radical leftist elements of Matzpen or the New Left (Siach). As a consequence of these multiple inputs, several strains of thought have emerged as representative of the Panthers and the group has split into at least three distinct factions.

WORLD VIEW

In many ways, the Panthers represent the most intersting topic under discussion here, with the possible exception of Gush Emunim. Their leadership was small, uneducated, and inexperienced. Nevertheless, the movement has been able to muster considerable support for its rallies, if not for its membership, per se. In addition, despite its inexperience, leaders of the movement have been able to steer a course independent of the socialist and establishment influences that played a role in its formation. It can only be assumed that the disaffections it represents—the relative deprivation of the Oriental community in Israel—articulate the feelings of many Israelis, both Orientals and Westerners.

This perspective is reflected in the choice of the name Black Panthers, a title with strong negative connotations among Jews both in Israel and abroad.

> We were thinking: How can we arouse the public which has been indifferent and unconcerned and does not care about our kind of people, and which thinks we ourselves are to blame because we are backward. We said to ourselves: supposed we call ourselves "The Association of Israelis who are Wronged" . . . no one would pay attention to us. We wanted a name that gets people angry and frightened—so we got the notion of adopting the name "Black Panthers." We adopted only the name, not, God forbid, the ideology. We are good Jews and they hate Jews . . .[3]

The statement is a good reflection of the Panther world view. In the first instance, the organization believes that the Oriental community in Israel has been neglected and abandoned by the dominant Western class, despite the fact that Orientals and their children represent a majority in the country. Furthermore, even those Westerners who are sympathetic to the problem blame Oriental Jewish culture and not the Israeli social and educational systems for disparities. Consequently, the best one can do is force the Oriental child to create a poor copy of Western culture for himself and imitate the values of the norm.

By the same token, the name Black Panthers is not to be taken with undue seriousness. Members of the organization consider themselves good Jews and would like as well to be good Israelis. Allowed to enter the system, gain a marketable education and serve in the army, many of their deficiencies would dissipate and they would integrate into the general society. At base, the Panthers look upon all Israelis as one people—though they often refer to Orientals as "the second nation."

It is this disdain for Oriental culture that the Panthers perceive to be at the root of their confrontations with the Israeli government. In attempts to raise the potential and aspirations of Oriental youth, the school system has embarked upon programs alleged to divest students from poor areas of the culture of their parents. Seen as primitive and dysfunctional, even religious traditions are reshaped in the Western model. Students are taught of the history of the European Jewish communities, Russian pogroms, and the literature of the shtetl but learn little, it is claimed, of life in the Maghreb— where Jews lived for centuries.

The schools are never completely successful in their task, however, because they cannot overcome the influence of the home, or the students do not take them seriously, or because of the high rate of student drop outs. Nevertheless, the impression of the inferiority of Oriental culture does take root. The consequence is that students grow up with virtually no cultural baggage at all, except that which they gain on the streets. Along with the problems of poverty and crime, this conflict of cultures and values is self-perpetuating.

Disdain of Oriental culture has yet another impact.

> They [the Panthers] demand, on the one hand, all the accoutrements of Ashkenazi "civilized" life and on the other, respect for Sephardi traditions . . . not realizing that these traditions are part of what prevents Sephardi Jews from obtaining the economic and social benefits of Ashkenazi social life. Because of the ambivalence they feel toward their own ethnic group and the fear that they may in fact be "inferior" to their Western brothers, the Sephardim, though an oppressed majority, are the most chauvinistic Israelis to the point of jingoism and the most anti-Arab, despite the cultural affinity with Arab neighbors.[4]

More than any cultural explanations, fault is laid at the feet of the Israeli political and educational system. That Jews arriving from North Africa or Asia were inferior upon reaching Israel is a myth, the Panthers argue. One need only look at the number of North African Jews who have succeeded in Paris or New York to dispel this falsehood. Rather, it appears that it is precisely because they chose to emigrate to Israel that these Orientals and their children have suffered.

Thus:

> It is official policy that the gap between Ashkenazi and Sefardi Jews was imported. . . . Orientals were all deemed inferior and any advances made were the result of the heroic efforts of the state of Israel. This is absolutely false. Among Moroccan Jews there were four times as many physicians per thousand as among Israelis. Yet among the second generation of these emigrants there are four times fewer high school graduates than among their parents. . . . This is the result of a conscious decision by the Ashkenazi state apparatus to break all ties with Arab culture.[5]

Particularly irksome to these Oriental Jews is the special treatment that is allegedly given to new arrivals from the Soviet Union. These Soviet

Jews are often intellectuals from the big cities but also include many laborers and farmers from the Georgian and Crimean outlands. Because of the world-wide publicity given their struggles and the generally more efficient nature of Israeli institutions in comparison with twenty years ago, these new immigrants are treated to better housing and services than the Orientals ever received.

For this reason, the Panthers' ire has been particularly raised toward the government. Why, they ask, do not native Israelis receive treatment as good as these Russians? The rationale given is that the state can now afford better treatment—yet is not the state in very serious economic straits? The Panthers allege that the reason for such special treatment is the ethnic make-up of this new migration: Russian, the precise extraction of the bulk of Israeli leadership. It might be added that the Panthers are not alone in this estimation and the resentment it fosters.

In this sense, the Panthers argue that Jews of the West have been duped by Israeli propaganda. Contrary to its publicity, the Israeli state is no egalitarian homeland for the world's Jews. Those who support the United Jewish Appeal might well examine where their contributions go. Rather than for the welfare of the people, the cash gets only as far as those in power. Jews are fighting Jews in Israel, they claim, and the philanthropic agencies are supporting one side of the battle. Many Jews are opting out of organizational life only because they disagree with the policies of the Israeli government but have no legitimate means of articulating these doubts without being labeled anti-Zionist or self-hating.[6]

At their base, however, the Panthers exhibit serious ambiguities about the source of their plight. Some attribute the problem to discrimination in its simplest and barest form. Others view the issue in terms of unemployment and education—demanding that the government provide necessary services and divert monies that are being wasted in the military. A significant sector of the Panther leadership has attempted to lead the organization away from a purely ethnic orientation and toward a more radical socialist base.

As a result, a shift in the manner by which this segment defines the problem is quite noticeable.

> We do not consider this an ethnic problem but a class problem. There are wealthy Yemenites, Syrians, and Moroccans. What is important is the high correlation between ethnicity and class. We have asked for funds but we won't beg at the door of many wealthy Sefardim. We wish to change the class structure and are calling for actions that will be to their detriment. This is a political problem, not a charity issue.[7]

The response to perceived "Western oppression" has also led to radical redefinition in the area of organized religion. In general, the Oriental immigrant was far more traditionally observant upon arrival than was the European Jew. An accommodation of variants in religious practice is seen in the maintenance of two chief rabbis, one Western and one Oriental. Yet, the Panthers argue that the administration of religion and its dissemination in the schools is strictly Western.

> Certain East European modes of behavior and dress which are foreign to normative Judaism are glorified and romanticized. Parallel and similar patterns among Sefardim . . . are ignored. Sefardi children are trained in Ashkenazi Yeshivot in methods which though widespread in Lithuanian Yeshivot are foreign to the Sefardi tradition. Also, rabbis trained in Muslim countries who apply for rabbinic positions must take examinations which presuppose East European Talmudic and Halachic methodology—a methodology totally foreign to the Sefardim.[8]

As a result, some among the Panthers have called for the disestablishment of religion—to allow each culture to practice in its own way without mutual or government interference.

In sum, it may be said that the Panther world view is one of oppression, discrimination, and prejudice. The Western authorities have done little to alleviate conditions of abject poverty, low educational attainment, and crime. Whether for reasons of ethnocentric intent or simple ignorance, they have given preference to newer arrivals and the children of Orientals live in the same slums that housed their parents two decades ago. The more radical among the leadership attribute the problem to class rather than ethnic status, but invariably the organization declares itself loyal and steadfast, wishing only a "piece of the pie."

VALUES AND GOALS

Even as the general world view of the Black Panthers of Israel is simple and direct, so too are its values. Yet the simplicity is often deceptive. In desiring a "change equal to that of a comfortable Israeli," the Panthers come close to calling for a restructuring of the Israeli social system. Yet a consistent strain of thought—be it socialist, reformist, or radical—is difficult to follow in Panther literature or rhetoric. The bulk of it is couched in either negative terms of protest or highly sectarian and material demands. Thus, defining an ideology is difficult.

Nevertheless, the movement has clear societal demands:

1. To struggle as a pressure group to change government policy so as to eliminate any discrimination of a racial or ethnic type among the Jewish People, that there be one Jewish nation in Israel

2. To guarantee every child free public education from the age of four through university graduation

3. To struggle for the integration of Ashkenazic and Sefardic children in public schools

4. To demand grants of aid to large families, from public funds and governmental agencies

To set up youth clubs with leaders trained in psychology and education in poor sections

6. To build new schools in poor areas and see that they are staffed by trained and certified teachers. . . . (Author's translation)[9]

The sum of these demands are to be found in three basic requirements, the Panthers argue. They believe every Israeli is entitled to three rights: a right to "normal housing, normal standard of living and normal education." In the first instance, "normal" is defined in terms of less than three persons per room. Normal living conditions require 100 Israeli lira per family member and a normal education is one offered by experienced and trained teachers. Echoing criticism leveled at education of the poor elsewhere, the movement claims that only those teachers who do not succeed in finding employment in better schools work in poor areas.

For some sectors of Panther leadership, the problem is essentially economic and can be solved in those terms. The villain in the scenario is the Histadrut, which has ceased to represent laborers—whether employed or unemployed—and has yielded to the parties as a political forum. Consequently, there is no body that represents the working class, the bulk of which is Oriental. Nevertheless, the organization emphasizes the ethnic base of its constituency by proclaiming: "identify not as a laborer but as a Panther!"[10]

The Panthers have also expressed concern over the relatively low rate of army recruitment among their numbers. Ironic as it may sound, this protest organization has called for increased draft procedures in poor areas and a lowering of standards for recruits from poverty sections. The benefits of the army's integrative capacities will thereby be gained and the stigma of nonservice avoided. Observers see this as proof positive of the willingness of the organization to accommodate to national needs.[11]

Though not clearly articulated, it also reveals an essential aspect of the movement's values. The ultimate hope is assimilation and the elimination of any bar—be it racial or ethnic—to the integration of Jews into Israeli society. The point is reflected in the voting habits of most Orientals as well.

While economic disparities are evident, members of this group tend to support the right-wing opposition posed by the Likud bloc. Rather than stalk out on radical paths of their own, most Orientals see themselves as powerfully nationalist and patriotic.

Indeed, the alleged socialist content of the movement's ideology has been a serious point of contention within its leadership. Some view the organization as purely a protest group, representing the material and cultural needs of the Oriental community. These have insisted that demands be specific and tangible, with a minimum of rhetoric, forays into international issues, or radical prescriptions and goals. This wing of the movement has been largely represented by Panther leaders Victor Theil and Yigal Bin-Nun.

The faction led by Shalom Cohen and Sa'adia Marciano has forwarded a far more radical set of goals, conciliatory to the demands of Palestinian nationalism.

> We favor the creation of a Palestinian State next to Israel and oppose the secularization of Israel. The large portion of Oriental Jews support the right wing, not out of a sympathy with their views so much as out of sheer protest and a desire for an organized opposition. We believe that the Oriental community can be a force for peace and understanding with the Arab world. We have much in common. When Oriental Jews get together with Arabs there is an immediate affinity.[12]

This internal conflict over the movement's goals has also led to efforts of more radical groups to form coalitions with the Panthers. Sensing that they may have much to gain by lobbying among Oriental constituencies, members of Matzpen and the Israeli New Left have given much play to the "Oriental problem" and the alleged racist tendencies of Israeli capitalism. Cochavi Shemesh, a Panther founder, has had a regular column in the Matzpan newsletter and youth workers have been active in Oriental sections outside of Tel Aviv and Ramat Gan.

Nevertheless the official Panther line has been to reject these intrusions and to steer a path clear of the radical socialist tendencies of these groups:

> Our movement, the Black Panther Movement, is, was and will ever be nonpartisan in the purest form of the term. Though within our ranks we have members of every party in the land, as a group we endorse none. It has been attempted, either out of ignorance or maliciousness, to link us wth groups of the extreme left. We deny this in clear and unquestioned language: we have neither contact nor connection with them! We

emphasize that we are loyal sons of the State and we will lift a hand in favor of no one, internal or external, who calls for her detriment. (Author's translation)[13]

Nevertheless, there is implicit in all Panther literature a veiled threat toward the Western Jewish community in Israel. The movement demands the rights and privileges of all citizens for its particularly deprived constituency. It portends to speak for all Orientals. If equality is not granted, it appears, the movement's intent may be some form of separation or national liberation which would be disastrous for the state. Though no leader of the organization has ever dared raise this threat openly—nor is it likely to carry much credibility—the situation may be developing along lines parallel to those of the civil rights movement in the United States during the early sixties. The 1973 War and the economic problems that followed in its wake operate against such contingency, however.[14]

This sensitive issue notwithstanding, the organization has indicated its willingness to wrest power and influence forcibly if it is not offered peacefully. It is asserted that the tax structure falls most heavily upon laborers while capital investors are handled gingerly. This is because economic power lies in the hands of the bank rather than the government. Thus, coercion—whether physical, political, or economic, is the order of the day.

> The government fears the banks but not the Sefardi workers. We are not being represented by anyone. If the government only responds to power then we must show that the street has power too. The government seems to react only to shock and each time the shock must be harder and stronger.

The question has put the Panthers into an ambiguous position regarding the police. Large numbers of the municipal police forces and the state authorities are Oriental as is much of its leadership. Many of these are victims of the very system the Panthers are trying to change, the movement asserts, and are aware of their plight. Ultimately, the movement views its relations with the authorities as "a game: there are rules and occasional injuries but no animosity."[15]

STRATEGIES FOR SOCIAL CHANGE

Given their general feelings of despair and the deprivations that they sense within Israeli society, the Panthers are not dissimilar to other urban ethnic groups in many industrialized societies. Despite external pressures of a military and diplomatic nature, the group suffers from rising aspirations being unmatched by realistic potentials for upward mobility. They have consequently turned to the most accessible and convenient political resource at their command, violence and its threat.

Such tactics were particularly valuable during the earliest days of the movement's creation. Then its protest rallies were largely spontaneous and gained thousands of participants. While most of these Oriental protesters might never join the organization or vote for its political list, their activism reflected the frustration and despair felt by many but previously articulated by few. Born in a four-day riot in Tel Aviv, the organization has succeeded in shutting down the city's central bus terminal, protesting the rise of food costs in the Hatikva slum section as well as on Allenby Road, Tel Aviv's major thoroughfare.[16]

In addition, such massive actions also brought the plight of Israel's Oriental community before national and international audiences. In particular, it succeeded in attracting the attention of Jews of Western nations, particularly the United States, where news items and reportage tended to emphasize the ethnic and racial elements of the conflict and make much of the movement's name. In particular, analogies were drawn between the organization and the American Black Panther Party, though the Israeli group consistently disavowed any contact.

Nevertheless, the movement has renounced violence as a strategy, even while emphasizing the need for street action, for lack of an alternative political strategy of similar impact.

> We are against terrorism—holdups, kidnapping, etc., but we will use strength when necessary. At times, we must do things which are illegal but legitimate. If the police intervene with force we will respond but we have never deliberately used force as a strategy. When there is no police interference, we undertake to insure the order and peacefulness of our demonstrations.[17]

The movement has also been creative in its attempts to symbolize the problems of its constituents in reaction to official government indifference. When Minister of Religion Raphael referred to the Panthers as "parasites in Katamon (an Oriental Jewish section in Jerusalem) who prefer welfare to work" he was identified as an enemy of the cause. In retaliation, rats and mice were dumped on his doorstep. Similarly, Golda Meir has been a target of Panther ire for her offhand remarks that they are "not nice boys" and that "true Jewish identity" requires the knowledge of Yiddish. Consequently, her speeches have been interrupted by Panthers shouting—"Golda, teach us Yiddish."[18]

The Panthers have also joined with left-wing elements in their demonstrations, despite the aforementioned hesitance to form a regular coalition. To protest rising prices in commodities and the government's apparent unwillingness to subsidize the poor adequately, the movement has enlisted the support of Matzpen and Moked members. Dairy goods were stolen from trucking centers in Jerusalem and distributed among the needy of Kiryat Menahem. Similarly oil was stolen from the Shemen Company and distributed among the poor. Such "Robin Hood" tactics were followed by large-scale demonstrations over poor housing and sanitation facilities in which an Oriental buildings inspector claimed to have been brutally beaten by police for his unwillingness to cooperate in falsifying housing reports.[19]

The movement has also attempted to recruit support among Jews of Oriental descent elsewhere. In particular, a delegation of Panthers addressed the World Sefardi Federation and the World Conference of Jews of North African Origin. In a gesture of conciliation, leaders of the movement indicated their willingness to abandon violence and street actions in return for massive aid and pressure upon the Israeli government for social reform. The issue also caused consternation within the movement, especially among those more militant and unwilling to tone down in return for pledges and promises.

In addition, the Panthers have begun a massive program of fund raising and recruitment abroad. In an attempt to bring the problems of Orientals in Israel before Jews of the world, presentations have been made before councils of the United Jewish Appeal, the British United Synagogue, and various local agencies, though the reception has been less than warm. Aside from financial aid, a corps of European youth leaders have been attracted to work in poor areas and a call has been lodged to create a youth village for juvenile offenders in order to prevent their being arrested and given a criminal record. In particular, the problem of prostitution among Oriental females may be treated, it is hoped, in this fashion.[20]

In a more positive vein, the Panthers have called for significant changes in the educational system in order to offer compensatory programs for Oriental youth from poor neighborhoods.

> We ask for a change in the educational system first. Schools should be open for twelve hours a day, twelve months a year. This 12 x 12 program will enable students to gain academic enrichment yet keep off the streets. In order to publicize our position we occupy a school. We enter a school with our own staff and headmaster. When the school administration comes we "fire" them as responsible for the degradation of our children's education. This is always done with the per-

mission of the parents and the police never "reconquer" a school from us; after all, we are just insuring a quality education for our children.[21]

As might be expected, many of the internal rifts noted in reference to the movement's goals are played out in the field of tactic and strategy. In particular, the degree of radical activism and the proper stance to be assumed toward the Arab world and Palestinian Nationalism have been at issue. The movement's militant wing has joined hands with leftist elements in seeking a meaningful conciliation with the Palestinians. It has also declared its willingness to support the creation of a Palestinian national entity on the West Bank.

Arguing that "if there is peace we can spend more money on tackling poverty instead of security," three Panther leaders—Reuven Abergil, Charlie Biton and Muni Yakim—met with PLO representatives during the spring of 1975. Indeed, a plank in the movement's first national platform included support for a Palestinian state and the use of Oriental Jews "to serve as a bridge to the Arab People." In an extreme manifestation of such feeling, an expatriot Panther living in Europe was implicated in a plot to supply arms to the Popular Front for the Liberation of Palestine.[22]

Finally, the organization is subject to an institutional strategy common in response to ethnic protest groups elsewhere: cooptation. It is not unusual for the official sector to attempt to quell such dissent by bringing token members of the deprived community, especially from among the articulate leadership, into its fold. In addition, the aura of corruption has reared its head within the Panther organization. Thus, on the one hand, members of the group have been wooed by the establishment while two of its founders, the Abergil brothers, have been arrested for extortion and drug dealing among the very urban poor they claim to represent.

The movement has attempted to curb both these tendencies by tightening its internal organization and centralizing its operation, particularly under the leadership of Sholom Cohen. The result has been a competition for leadership and considerable resentment over such strictures. The very decentralization of the group was clearly expressed by Cohen at the creation of the coalition upon which the movement based its political fortunes:

> If a deprived majority in some area or development town should take it into their own hands to secure their rights, we shall not regard that as violence but as an expression of majority will.[23]

Thus the movement suffers from internal dissension and has fallen upon popular indifference due to the general economic malaise Israel presently suffers. Its direction is difficult to assess.

SUMMARY

The Black Panthers represent the manifestation of ethnic protest within Israeli society. Its emergence was a particular shock to Zionist leaders who have envisioned Israel as a place of freedom and equality for all Jews. The constituency of the organization is Israel's large proportion of Oriental Jews in the slum areas of the large cities and the development towns on the fringes. Though the movement is no more than seven or eight years old, the problems it confronts date to the founding of the state and were inherent in the conditions of emigration from the Arab states of North Africa and Asia.

Most acute are the socioeconomic problems of urban poverty. Inadequate housing, high birth rates, poor schools, and the environment of street crime and delinquency create a vicious cycle which reduces chances for upward mobility and success. Nevertheless the media and a consumer economy keep aspirations high and result in bitter frustrations. In addition, these debilities often mean rejection from the army, a virtual given in the drive for social status and economic success.

The movement's world view is simple. It is the Western Jewish establishment that dominates much of Israeli life and is in the seat of power, despite its minority status. This cultural unit has deliberately attempted to wipe out Oriental culture and life style in an attempt to remake Israel in its own image. Its perceptions of Jewish life are those of the East European shtetl, early Russian socialism, and the Lithuanian rabbinic schools. The music, culture, and values of the Oriental community have been branded as "ethnic" or foreign and prejudged to be inferior. The result is the lack of any culture for the Oriental child, other than that of poverty and crime.

The goals of the movement are simply to reverse this dangerous trend. Its rhetoric indicates a general commitment to the Zionist ideal and a hesitance to appear overly radical or militant. It is the impression that the Panthers view their role as a catlyst to create an entrée for large numbers of Orientals to the middle and upper reaches of status and power in Israeli life. Nevertheless, a more radical wing of the movement has emerged, in which socialist philosophy is apparent and an attempt is made to define the problem in class rather than ethnic terms. Support for the Palestinian cause and a generally conciliatory road toward peace has herein also been espoused.

The movement's prescriptions for change are generally negative in the sense that they call for massive protest action but little programmatic change. It appears that the primary intent was to bring the issue of Oriental deprivation in Israel forcefully before the general public and the world Jewish community. Consequently, rallies and demonstrations emphasized this desire and included thousands of participants. Though most were not actual members of the movement, their presence indicates the general sympathy of many Orientals with the cause and the concern of non-Orientals.

In addition, the movement has embarked upon "Robin Hood" tactics by which they steal goods and commodities from private businesses or government cooperatives and distribute them to the poor. Presentations have been made to international bodies of Oriental or Sefardic Jews in the hope of attracting funds for poor areas and inducing pressure upon the Israeli government to amend its policies. On occasion, overtures have been made to left-wing groups to join in protest actions and electoral coalitions, or both, though the movement has generally remained aloof in the hope of maintaining its autonomy and organizational purity.

It might be noted that inferring a consistent and clear ideology from the writings and rhetoric of Black Panther leaders has not always been a simple thing. With the exception of those socialist elements within the movement, most of the group's demands are particularistic and material, leading only to greater acceptance by the dominant Westerners. Furthermore, radical or socialist ideology that does exist is by no means representative of all or even most of the movement's leadership. The reader is cautioned to understand it in that light.

NOTES

1. The historical and social background for the development of the Panthers has been culled from the following sources: Michael Curtis and Mordecai Chertoff, eds., *Israel: Social Structure and Change* (New Brunswick, N.J.: Transaction, 1973); S.N. Eisenstadt et al., eds., *Integration and Development in Israel* (New York: Praeger, 1970); Michael Bruno, "The Social Gap Is Not Really Closing," *New Outlook* (January 1973), pp. 12–15; and Leonard Weller, *Sociology in Israel* (Westport, Conn.: Greenwood Press, 1974).

2. J. Peri, "The Black Panthers in Perspective," *New Outlook* (January 1973), p. 34.

3. Panther leader Reuven Abergil, cited in Judith Miller, "Israel's Black Panthers," *The Progressive* (March 1972), p. 35.

4. Ibid., p. 37. See also *Davar Hapenterim Hashechorim* (June 1971)—Black Panther newspaper.

5. Interview with Shalom Cohen, Black Panther spokesman, July 1976.

6. Ron Koslowe, "Will the Panthers Return," *Ha-aretz* (February 25, 1973).

7. Interview with Shalom Cohen.

8. Henry Toledano, "Israel's Sefardi Problem," *The Jewish Spectator* (April 1973), pp. 6–8; also Henry Toledano, "Time to Stir the Melting Pot," in *Israel: Social Structure and Change*, ed. Michael Curtis and Mordecai Chertoff (New Brunswick, N.J.: Transaction, 1973), pp. 333–47. It might be noted that the minister of religion in the Begin government is of Oriental extraction.

9. Reuven Abergil, Raphael Marciano, and Eliezer Abergil, "Summary of the Rules and Goals of the Black Panther Organization" (Jerusalem, 1971).

10. Sa'adiah Marciano, "What do the Panthers Want," *Ot* (March 6, 1971).

11. Shlomo Avineri, "Israel: Two Nations?" *Midstream* (May 1972), pp. 3–20.

12. Interview with Shalom Cohen. It may be further noted that the Panthers have already undergone a split over the issue of loyalty to the state, whereby the Blue-White Panthers were created, under the leadership of Eddie Malka. Blue and white are the colors of the Israeli flag. See the Jerusalem *Post* (June 19, 1974). See also the report of the movement's first national convention in the Jerusalem *Post* (September 25, 1975).

13. *Davar Hapentorim Hashechorim* (June 1971); see also Ehud Shprinzak, *The Blossoming of the Politics of Delegitimacy in Israel.* Eshkol Institute for Economic, Social and Political Research, Special Publication no. 8 (Jerusalem: Hebrew University, 1973), pp. 13–23. On contact between Matzpen and the Panthers see *Ma-ariv* (May 25, 1971).

14. Yosef Wachsman, "The Panthers Dream of Joining the Arabs in a Battle against the Establishment," *Ma-ariv* (April 11, 1972). See also Erik Cohen, "The Black Panthers and Israeli Society," *Journal of Jewish Sociology* (June 1972), pp. 93–109.

15. Interview with Shalom Cohen. See also Yitzhak Emanuel, *The Black Panthers and the State of Israel* (Holon: Ami, 1971), pp. 13–16.

16. The Jerusalem *Post* (January 30, 1974; February 1, 7, 12, and 20, 1974; November 11, 12, 1974).

17. Interview with Shalom Cohen. See also Shlomo Grudzinsky, "Comments of a Friend of the Black Panthers," *Davar* (May 28, 1971), and "Serious Warning," Special Black Panther Publication, August 25, 1971.

18. The Jerusalem *Post* (June 10, 1976 and March 13, 1974).

19. The Jerusalem *Post* (June 10, 1976; March 31, 1976; July 16, 1976; and December 10, 1975). A good summary of such Panther activism and the official response of the Israeli government may be found in Eva Etzioni-Halevy, "Protest Politics in the Israeli Democracy," *Political Science Quarterly (Fall 1975)*, pp. 497–520.

20. The Jerusalem *Post* (February 2, 21, 1975; May 18, 1975; August 14, 1975; October 28, 1975; and April 1, 1974, November 3, 5, 22, 1974). See also Amos Elon, "The Black Panthers of Israel," *New York Times Magazine* (September 12, 1971); see also Baruch Nadel, "Call-Girl," *Jerusalem Post Magazine* (November 23, 1976).

21. Interview with Shalom Cohen. On the "12 x 12" program, see Cohen's statements cited in Judy Siegel, "Year-Round Schools for Disadvantaged Youth," The Jerusalem *Post* (August 26, 1974).

22. The Jerusalem *Post* (March 31, 1975; July 2, 1975; September 25, 1975).

23. The Jerusalem *Post* (February 22, 1973); see also the Jerusalem *Post* (January 4, 1976); Yehiel Limur, "The Panther Who Returned to the Good," *Ma-ariv* (September 8, 1972).

IV

IN PERSPECTIVE

11

A COMPARATIVE ANALYSIS

Thus far, each dissenting group has been treated as an entity unto itself. Its ideology has been presented as clearly and objectively as possible, with an eye toward understanding its historical genesis, its perceptions of the universe, and the directions it would take to bring desired change. While similarities of content or source have occasionally been noted, little has been done thus far to directly compare one with the other or evaluate importance and influence within the Israeli political system. In this chapter, an attempt will be made to offer comparative insights into the thrust and development of radical protest in Israel.

It might first be noted that the organization used in this study implies that there are two major sources of radicalism in Israeli political life. The first is left-wing political ideology whose anti-Zionism is largely based upon a Marxist-socialist perspective. Certainly this typifies the thought of Matzpen, Rakah, and Moked. It is interesting to note that all three of these groups owe their beginnings, though perhaps grudgingly, to Maki, the original Israel Communist Party. Until 1962, the forerunners of these three organizations were either members or supporters of Maki.

The second major source of protest appears to be rooted in religious and ethnic identification. In the case of Natore Karta, a strong sense of Jewish tradition and custom has led the movement to rabid anti-Zionist feelings. The opposite has been the result for Gush Emunim, though the source of its right-wing Zionist pioneering is this same body of Jewish tradition. The major instance of purely ethnic political dissent, the Black Panthers, appears born from deprivation and prejudice more than from a cogent political philosophy.

177

Nevertheless, the dichotomy of socialist and ethnoreligious protest is fluid and perhaps somewhat deceptive. Though he has been here classed among the former, Uri Avnery has strongly avoided a left-wing designation. He terms his thought "post-Zionist" in that it seeks a new perspective to lay a useless ideology gently but firmly to rest. Rather than arguing for a socialist-based economy, Avnery has simply called for greater independence from the oppressive state structures, no matter what direction the change might bring. In essence, it may be possible to classify Avnery only as an iconoclast and antiestablishmentarian whose protest is based largely on a healthy sense of independence with a touch of the libertine for seasoning.

The decision to include him among the forces of the extreme left was not wholly arbitrary, however, First, no matter what Avnery's motivations, the force of his thought has been clearly of an internationalist, if not Marxist, bent. He has consistently flirted with the student Left and supported movements that call for the creation of a secular binational Palestine. As a radical peace activist, he has called for the virtual elimination of regular ties between the Jews of the world and Israel, as well as the elimination of Judaism in its established form. In addition, Avnery has supported tempering the close relationship between the United States and Israel in the name of Mideast peace and security. Finally, his electoral coalitions, first with Esther Wilenska, a former Maki leader, and more recently with Meir Peil of Moked, reflect a pragmatic sense that his place is to the left of the political arena.

Rakah, too, presents a typological problem. Because emphasis has here been placed upon the ideological prescriptions of each group, it has not been difficult to include it among the movements of the Left. As indicated, however, Rakah has recently become more identified with the needs and demands of a particular ethnic minority, Israel's Arab population. The party has strained to portray itself as the sole electoral alternative for the new generation of Palestinians under Israeli rule who will not be content with the patronage of an alignment-affiliated Arab list. Rakah has depended upon the Arab vote for some 80 percent of its electoral support and has won stunning victories in municipal elections, particularly on the West Bank and in the Galilee. The prospects of broadening that base in coming elections and becoming the major voice for Israeli Arab needs is quite good and its categorization for this study must consequently be understood within this context.

A somewhat similar but far less pronounced development may be taking place within the ranks of the Black Panthers as well. Standing primarily as a movement of ethnic protest, the Panthers seek their legitimacy in representing the deprivation and despair of Israel's Oriental population. Elements within the movement, however, have sought to define the issues in class, rather than ethnic, terms. By so doing, they have quite naturally sought justification through the use of socialist models and arguments. Though by no means universally accepted within the Panthers, these socialists have displayed values and goals similar to those of left wing groups. Roundly condemned by the movement's mainstream, some—such as Shalom Cohen—have made overtures toward New Left groups. Following this tendency to its logical extreme, former Panther Charlie Biton joined the Rakah electoral list in the 1977 national election.

These typological ambiguities notwithstanding, the categories used here do lend themselves to a direct comparison of the groups under discussion. It is clear, for example, that much of the left-wing dissent in Israel has had a common historical and institutional genesis. Though socialism and the labor orientation pervaded much of early Zionist thinking, the Palestine Communist Party was the major Jewish, non-Zionist political movement under the British Mandate. As such, it did most of its canvassing among Arab farmers and workers and was binational almost from its start.

A tradition of alienation from the legitimate Jewish forces was established early, prior to World War II, when the Party was outlawed by the British and expelled from the Histadrut. Its tradition of internal factionalization and the rift between Arab and Jewish comrades was very much part of its make-up when it became an official part of the Israeli political system with the founding of the state. Indeed, this factor was aggravated by its separation and then reunification with the Arab League for National Liberation, an offshoot of the Party, whose primary goal was not Marxist change but simply the creation of an Arab national state in Palestine.

It is no accident, therefore, that the Israel Communist Party (Maki) was the spiritual and institutional forebear of three major subjects of this study, Moked, Matzpen, and Rakah. Though never a Party member, ideological similarities between Avnery and Maki also existed, especially in the areas of binationalism, secularization, and independence from the United States. In each instance, the schismatic group, however, seems to represent one or another aspect of the tension that typified Maki during its earlier period.

Matzpen, created as a result of a rift in the early sixties, is the child of the ideological strains that have existed within the organized Communist camp in Israel. Always ambivalent about the extent of its ties of loyalty to the Soviet Union and the discretion needed to remain legitimate within a Jewish state, Maki had to temper its ideological stance with simple political pragmatism. Equally important, the diplomatic position of the Soviet Union displayed a singular lack of Marxist fervor, particularly in light of the doctrine of peaceful coexistence.

With the Cuban crisis and the growing Sino-Soviet rift in the early sixties, the younger comrades within the Israeli Party began looking for more suitable ideological lodgings elsewhere. The more internationalist and radical predispositions of the Maoist camp appealed to them. In search of a spiritual father, they lit upon Trotsky, by way of various non-Party contacts. In addition, their discontent with the rather bureaucratic and centralized mode of operation within Maki was as much a contributor to their exit as any ideological dissent.

Similarly, the 1965 rift from which Rakah was created was born of internal tensions that have been part of Israli communism from the first: the ethnic division. The bulk of the Party's ideological and political leadership had generally been in Jewish hands, although its popularity among Jewish laborers and voters was always quite limited. The thrust of its appeal, therefore, was toward the Arab voter who lived under Israeli rule and, on several occasions, the Party attempted to train Arabic cadres for positions of prominence. Nevertheless, issues of security and nationalism for Palestinians were always thorny matters by which the Party was caught in a practical and ideological bind.

The resultant schism was already apparent in 1965, although its full force did not emerge until June 1967. At that point the original Party, reduced largely to its Jewish membership, supported the Israeli war effort and defined the battle as one of self-defense. Rakah, composed mainly of the Arab members of Maki, called the action military aggression on the part of the Israelis and essentially supported the Soviet line. The USSR returned the favor by breaking diplomatic relations with Israel and transferring its recognition to Rakah as the sole representative of the peace-loving masses in Israel. The rift was now complete.

What remained of Maki floundered for the next several years with no political or ideological anchor, flirting with one or another New Left or student protest group. It lost its erstwhile leadership with the death of Moshe Sneh and the resignation of Shmuel Mikunis. Ultimately, it began a slow trek back in the direction of the political mainstream through its alignment with Meir Peil—a left-wing Zionist military hero—and his dovish student movement. The adoption of a new name, Moked, and the de-emphasis of the Party's Communist affiliations were evident in yet another rift in which the Israel Communist Opposition wing of the Party exited to join in electoral coalition elsewhere.

In a similar but far broader sense, both Natore Karta and Gush Emunim begin from a common base, the sum of traditional Jewish culture and religious thought. Yet, unlike those groups of the left, the result of this commonalty is a set of diametrically opposed political and ideological propositions. The Gush understands Jewish values in terms of a demand for immediate and dynamic settlement of all territories conquered during the 1967 War: a form of proto-Zionism, as it were. Natore Karta has interpreted Jewish values in the form of fierce and uncompromising anti-Zionism.

In part, these two movements are the logical extremes of an historical debate within the religious Jewish camp, whose roots may be sought in Eastern Europe prior to the first World War. For many, Zionism was the "first fruit of the Redemption" and participating in the rebuilding of Zion was a holy task. Centered about such religious sages as Rabbi Jacob Reines or Rabbi Abraham Kook, religious Jews were in the forefront of Zionist settlement, forming their own agricultural units and political institutions.

Fundamentally, Gush Emunim is the natural successor to the Judaism cum Zionism that was the mark of this theological position. In its original form, it was espoused by the forces of the religious Mizrahi Party, which now frames established religion in Israel. It is precisely the perceived abandonment of these original principles that irks the movement most. It sees itself largely as the extension of Judaism in Israel, reacting to the apparent indifference of the mainstream to the historic mission at hand.

By contrast, many Jewish religious leaders in Europe confronted the national movement with considerable skepticism and caution. To undertake such an enterprise without divine intervention was futile and heretic. Further, should one grant that the project was called for, it ought to be led only by religious leaders and masters of the tradition. Zionist spokesmen did not qualify on these grounds. Consequently, the move toward Jewish nationalism was opposed by many of Jewry's leading religious figures prior to World War II.

Natore Karta views itself as the spiritual descendant of this opposition and has oriented its entire existence about this principle. It considers life in Israel, religious or secular, as an abomination and stringently opposes the continued autonomy of the Jewish state. In this vein, it has sought leadership outside the country, in the form of Rabbi Joel Teitelbaum, head of the Satmar Hassidic dynasty, located in Brooklyn.

WORLD VIEW

It is interesting to note that the groups under discussion here share many similar perceptions of their political environment. There is a common view, for example, that Israel has failed to fulfill its purpose as standard-bearer for world Jewry. Further, it is argued that Israeli society by no means represents the best in either Jewish values or tradition. Rather, varying forms of materialism and the mundane nature of daily life are the mark of the nation.

The ubiquitous bureaucracy is blamed for much that is wrong with Israeli institutions. From Gush Emunim on the Right to Matzpen on the Left, responsibility for the expiration of spirit and idealism is placed on or near the development of a heavy-handed institutional structure. For some, the ideal lost is Zionism, for others, socialism, but that ideals have been lost is generally agreed.

There is also a consensus over the contribution of specific institutions within the state. Perhaps more than any other, the Histradrut plays the role of villain. Intended to represent the needs of the workers, it has become one of Israel's major employers. Intended to negotiate disputes democratically, it has become an oligarchic structure whose major purpose is the pursuit of state policy. Intended to unify labor under the rubric of socialist Zionism, it has created a fragmented work force whose discontent is reflected in the number of unauthorized strikes regularly undertaken.

The party system has also been blamed for much of the unhappiness within the state. Here too the heavy-handed and highly centralized structure is attacked as antidemocratic and purposefully oligarchical. The parties have abandoned what they originally stood for, so that the voter is all but unable to make an intelligent decision at the polls. Yet, these partisan institutions often dominate the welfare and livelihoods of their supporters and electoral decisions are made on the basis of patronage and largess—that is, the politics of the clubhouse.

However, distinct differences exist as to the content of those ideals that have been lost and the impact of ideals upon institutional structures. For the movements of the Left, the most fundamental problem of all is Zionism. To Matzpen it was never justified while for Avnery or Peil it had (or may still have) some value. Yet its transformation into a state religion and especially its identification with the very practical political goals of Israeli politicians is quite dysfunctional. The only hope for peace in the Middle East is for Israel to abandon most of these ideological components and secularize.

The extent of the secularization and its particular form will be discussed below. At present, suffice it to say that Zionism has created an inherent and unjustified hatred and mistrust for the Arab world, the very neighbors with which Israel must learn to live if it is to integrate itself into its region. It has also caused an inordinate dependence upon the United States and the world's Jewish communities. This still further alienates the state from its neighbors. As Avnery has put it, Israel is a European nation in a Third World setting.

Another aspect of this secularization process is the disestablishment of religion in Israel. This would mean the acceptance of civil procedures for marriage and divorce, as well as the elimination of rabbinic positions under government jurisdictions in municipalities, as well as business and social enterprise. Most significantly, in the formulation of these dissenters, it would also mean the possibility of a non-Jewish demographic complexion in Israel. Considering the large minority of Arabs already living under Israeli jurisdiction, a binational state is the natural extension of this hypothesis.

For Natore Karta, Zionism has always been the villain. It is this heresy that has led the people astray and robbed Judaism of its distinctive character. That institutional life in Israel is inappropriate and oppressive is a concomitant of the entire national enterprise which attempts to make Jews like any other people. Not only has the state not succeeded in bringing the millenium and with it divine favor, but it has caused still greater estrangement from religious faith and given the people an ungodly sense of independence and liberty. The only hope is the elimination of Zionism as a political force and its replacement by secular authority. Though Nature Karta and the various left-wing groups begin from very different points, their views coincide in this important area.

The stance of the Black Panthers is far less inclusive; indeed it may be considered parochial by comparison. Rather than blame either socialist or Zionist ideals for its discontent, the views of this movement are framed by largely ethnic considerations. It is not Zionism but its domination by European Jewish leaders that causes problems. Precisely because the view of Arabic culture is denigrating, those who have been raised in it are looked upon as inferior or culturally deprived. Precisely because much of Zionist thinking was formulated in the Jewish sections of Eastern Europe, little serious consideration is given for the plurality of Jewish life. It is discrimination, both conscious and unconscious, that structures the relationships between the Western and Oriental Jew in Israel. Only an equalization of opportunity will quell the discontent which grows stronger each day in the poverty-stricken slums of Israel's major cities and development towns.

Seeking a natural ally in the poor and deprived, many leaders of left-wing protest in Israel have attempted to enlist the support of Oriental Jewish spokesmen, particularly among the Panthers. For the most part, these overtures have been resisted. This may reflect the fact that the Oriental Jew of Israel is by no means anti-Zionist. Indeed, they are often supporters of the right-wing Likud Party. For the Panthers to present themselves as avowedly anti-Zionist might well separate them from their constituency. Equally, it may be that the Panthers' protest is more purely material and less ideological than that of many socialist or New Left organizations.

Yet, given the factionalization of the movement, there is an affinity between certain leaders and movements of the Left. In 1977, some four distinct Panther groups stood for election independently or in coalition with others. Operating on the fringe, it was still clear that the main differences between these Oriental lists was the degree to which they adhered both practically and ideologically to a socialist line. Panther representatives were to be found in alignment with Rakah as well as leading a Zionist Panthers list, reflecting the diversity of views expressed by Orientals generally and Panthers in particular in assessing the political universe in which they operate.

Finally, Gush Emunim stands apart both in terms of its assessment of Zionism and its ideas on the direction of state policy. Rather than assign its discontent to Zionist principles, Gush is unhappy about their deemphasis within Israeli society. It is precisely because the pioneering spirit and self-assurance of an earlier day are no longer evident that Israel suffers as it does. Dependent upon the good will of others and lacking a vital sense of sacrifice, the people seek only to "gain the highest wage for the least work." A renewal of original Zionist values might well cause a renaissance of Israeli Jewish culture, therefore.

More than anything, Gush Emunim exhibits complete confidence in its cause. Unlike those within the Avnery or Peil camp who call for greater experimentation and liberalism, the Gush views its course in unilateral terms. The weakness of Zionism, they claim, has been undue social experimentation and a liberal perspective. The youth, in particular, must be imbued with the confidence and vision for which the state was once noted. Indeed, in almost mystical proportion, the movement's leadership claims that peace will come not by international negotiation or big power manipulation, but through the secure settlement of the Jews in their land, all of it.

VALUES AND GOALS

As has been noted in previous chapters, it is not always easy to differentiate between the various ideological components being discussed here. At the very least, values are the direct outgrowth of the movement's perceptions of its environment. Nevertheless, while similarities have been described in terms of respective world views, the values that grow from them are a good deal more disparate.

For the movements of the left there seems to be considerable consensus over the demands for regional peace. The single means to bring security and calm to the region is to confront Palestinian nationalism. Settlement of this vital issue will allow the Israeli people to concentrate their efforts and resources on pressing internal problems. In one form or another, each of these groups calls for the formation of a Palestinian state on the West Bank and in the Gaza Strip.

Motivations for this move vary. Avnery sees it as the utmost in practicality. The manner by which one eliminates terrorism, he argues, is by separating the militants from the community whose demands they express. Concretely, were a Palestinian state created, it is likely that it would be led by moderates who would view terrorism as dangerous and would try, along with the Israelis, to eliminate it. Moked leaders add that Israeli military superiority can easily insure the integrity and security of any territorial negotiation that is made.

Rakah, partly out of loyalty to the Soviet Union but more as a response to its Arab constituency, has assumed a moral posture, arguing that essential rights of Palestinians are and always have been denied by the Israelis. This denial has been all the more emphatic in the years since the 1967 War, with Israel presiding over a massive Arab minority in East Jerusalem and the conquered areas. Creating a Palestinian homeland and compensating those who have suffered losses over the past three decades is a minimal requirement toward the development of mutual trust in the region.

Matzpen, characteristically, is far more radical in its prescriptions. Nothing short of a socialist revolution will effectuate desired change. The revolution need not start in Israel, indeed it is likely to begin elsewhere in the Middle East, with no help from outside revolutionary forces. The movement takes exception to the thrust of the Palestinian struggle, which it understands to be far too national, giving little consideration to the concerns of class and economics. In addition, a basic requirement of any such radical change is that the victorious rebels also consider the needs of the Israeli people living in the Middle East, an aspect noticeable by its absence in most Palestinian rhetoric.

Interestingly, Natore Karta—beginning as it does from a strictly religious and traditional base—has also called for such a radical political change. Arguing that the essence of Arab-Israeli conflict is not fundamentally Jewish but Zionist, the movement points to centures of alleged trust and friendship between Jews and Arbs in the Holy Land before the advent of Zionism. What is now called Israel should be transformed, they argue, into a secular or Arab state or both, under the protection of the UN. This would satisfy the needs of the Palestinians as well as those of "truly believing" Jews, whose nationalist demands await the coming of the Messiah. In this sense, the demands of this traditionally religious sect may be the most radical of all.

With the exception of Moked, this assessment of Zionism is also common to the movements of the Left. It is at the root of the difficulties in the Mideast and a form of institutional or ideological racism. Matzpen has euphemistically called for the de-Zionization of Israel, while Avnery attacks the Law of Return which enforces legal idfferences between Jew and non-Jew in the matter of citizenship. In its essentially anti-Zionist stance, Rakah is following in the path of the various Communist movements that preceded it, including Maki. Peil has proclaimed Moked, however, a Communist Party which still accepts Zionism as the Jewish movement of national liberation and divorces itself from the "Soviet Church."

For the Black Panthers, life appears much simpler. Their perceptions of the universe are largely dichotomous, Sefardi-Ashkenazi or Western-Oriental. The movement represents a specific constituency, Israel's Oriental poor, and its prescriptions are consequently quite simple. In the first instance, changes are needed in the way Oriental Jews, particularly those of Arabic heritage, are viewed by the dominant Western community. It is destructive for these Orientals to be torn from their traditions, which are every bit as Jewish as those of Eastern Europe.

Further, steps must be taken to insure the elimination of conscious and unconscious discrimination in education, housing, and conscription. It is ironic and telling that a group that has wrought violent dissent within Israeli society calls for increased and equal conscription. This is a reflection of its view toward Zionism. By no means opposed to the state ideology, the Panthers demand only that they (the Oriental Jewish community) be given an equal opportunity to succeed and indeed to die for their country. It is the perceived denial of this right that frustrates them.

Also interesting in this regard is that the bulk of Israel's Oriental Jewish community votes for neither the Panthers nor the various anti-Zionist groups of the Left. Rather they are generally supporters of the movements of the Right, particularly the Likud, the nation's erstwhile right-wing opposition party. This is for two reasons. It is not uncommon for those on a lower rung of the social ladder to demand harsh treatment for those who sit yet one step lower, that is, the Arab minority. Furthermore, Likud has traditionally been the single viable alternative to the Labor Alignment. Support for Likud may not have been so much out of sympathy with its platform as a rational mode of protest. In any event, it reflects the generally positive stance of the Orientals toward Zionism as an ideology.

The values of Gush Emunim stand apart among the groups being discussed for both their orientation and the mystical fervor with which they are applied. At best, these values may be summed up by the term "hitnahalut," i.e., settlement of the land. The motivations for such action, taken especially in the occupied regions of the West Bank, are both religious and practicasl. In an attempt to fulfill the perceived biblical requirements incumbent upon each Jew, the movement has called upon countrymen to help people regions with largely Arab populations. By so doing, Gush Emunim looks toward a revitalization of Israeli institutions and the long-awaited Redemption.

In addition, there is a clear understanding that such action may limit the options of the administrations in negotiating peace with the Arab world and the super powers. The existence of new settlements, whether under government sanction or in spite of it, will force the foreign ministry to be cautious in concessions it may be prepared to make. With a sincere belief in the holiness of the land, no matter who holds its title, the leaders of the movement have declared their willingness to remain on their new settlements even should the territory be returned to Arab jurisdiction.

STRATEGIES FOR SOCIAL CHANGE

As there have been similarities in the perceptions and prescriptions of each movement, so too similarities exist as to the tactics employed to bring about desired change. For most, these tactics are practical and grow from the directions implicit in the values expressed. For Natore Karta, for example, tactics and strategies appear to take two distinct directions. Their protest is largely a response to the very existence of a Jewish state contrary to biblical and rabbinic edict and the perceived desecration of Jewish life through lack of observance, alleged immorality, and public indecency.

Consequently, depending on the desired goal, the strategy is made to fit appropriately. On the occasions that the movement wishes to express its disapproval of the Jewish national enterprise it has made representation to the councils of the UN, the Vatican, U.S. presidents, and various Arab leaders. In addition, periodic announcements are made to the American people through the secular press as well as media run by supporters in Europe and North America. In each instance, the attempt is to separate Zionism from Judaism, claiming that the former is a debaser of religion and the latter has no particular quarrel with the Arab people.

When, however, the perceived sanctity of public morals is at stake, especially in close proximity to the Natore Karta quarter of Jerusalem, the sect is not beyond violent street demonstrations. Whether the issue is the building of a stadium in which exhibitions will take place on the Sabbath, the rerouting of buses, or electioneering in earshot of their homes, these bearded religious zelaots have clashed with police and security forces alike. Known to use rocks, bottles, and sticks, their confrontations have often been violent and have resulted in arrests and recriminations on both sides.

Interestingly, radical groups of the Left, as well as the more militant wings of the Black Panthers, have also taken to street demonstrations in support of their cause. Not having a natural constituency, those protests organized by Matzpen or Moked (and its predecessor Maki) have not generally met with much success. It is the ethnic sentiments expressed or channeled by the Panthers that has led to massive demonstrations in the streets of Tel Aviv and Jerusalem. These have often lasted for days, broken the normal flow of business and trade, and caused severe injuries. Consequently, left-wing elements often attempt to claim the Panthers protest as their own and to merge their forces with those of the Orientals.

Generally the Panthers have resisted these efforts at merger, especially when it appears that such radical leftist groups intend only to tap the strength of Oriental discontent and protest for their own designs. In addition, it should be noted that the Panthers are by no means the sole or even major representatives of the Oriental cause in Israel, though they may well be the most vocal and volatile. Perhaps the large turnouts at such protest rallies are an expression of the extent of Oriental discontent and deprivation without reflecting any degree of Panther strength or support.

The same may be the case in discussing the strategies employed by Rakah. Its future depends upon its role as a legitimate conduit for the expression of Palestinian demands within the Israeli political system. Increasingly, its lot has been cast with the Arab minority, reflected in the ethnic content of its support. Violent expressions of dissent on the West Bank, Gaza, East Jerusalem, and the Galilee have been used to focus the discontent of Arab residents in the direction of the Communist Party. A measure of the success of this tactic is the surprising victories of Communist-supported lists in municipal elections in major Arab towns.

This development is epitomized in the general strike call over alleged land expropriations and other discriminatory actions. While Communist theory and doctrine are largely foreign to Arab villagers, the integrity of land title is universally understood. Consequently, Land Day, in March 1976, was a major effort to protest such actions and rally support for the Party. It left violent eruptions, confrontations with security forces, blood, and death in its wake.

By contrast, Gush Emunim has emphasized the natural extension of its value system as the cornerstone for desired change in Israel. "Hitnahalut"—settlement out of religio-cultural imperative—is taken not just as a rhetorical ideal, but as a matter of practical concern. The movement has organized settlements throughout the West Bank with no purpose other than peopling the area with Jews. Its new towns are built on no social or economic principle other than establishment for its own sake.

It is not meant to imply, however, that Gush Emunim has not also taken to the streets to express its position. Rallies have been organized in major cities as well as long marches to points of particular contention, such as Hebron, Nablus, and Jericho. Of all those under discussion, this movement has succeeded in winning considerable support from the mainstream both within and without its own religious camp. It has also gained concessions from both the Ntional Religious Party and the erstwhile ruling Labor coalition, making it the most significant of all subjects in terms of quantitative political influence and appeal.

Finally, it is to be noted that among the movements of the Left, attempts have been made by Gush to develop contacts abroad. These include the establishment of units or wings in foreign cities as well as cooperative ventures with like-minded student and Arab organizations. Matzpen, for example, maintains an independent wing named the Israel Revolutionary Action Committee Abroad (ISRACA) led by expatriate Israelis in Europe. Either alone or under the auspices of the Bertrand Russell Peace Foundation, the group publishes position papers, policy statements, and so on, and runs seminars in which its radical and socialist ideology is disseminated.

Somewhat similarly, both Uri Avnery and Meir Peil participated in high level talks with representatives of the Palestine Liberation Organization in Paris during the fall of 1976. The talks also included leading members of the Israeli economic establishment and caused a furor in Jerusalem. In both instances, the Israeli government has undertaken to curtail the freedom of political activity of its citizens abroad. Bills have been presented in the Knesset and the Justice Ministry has moved to gain criminal indictments. Yet never has the legality of such actions been clarified and consequently the official response has been ineffectual. It is unlikely that the actions of these dissidents have much impact other than publicity or propaganda value.

A FINAL NOTE

It appears that, despite the breadth of their views and the disparity of their ideologies, significant similarities emerge among the subjects of this study: Israeli dissidents. Their perceptions of the political universe are strikingly similar. They see much the same problems in much the same manner. In turn, each decries the materialism and lack of moral strength that allegedly characterizes Israeli society. Whether the values are socialist or religious, the consensus that early values have been abandoned seems universal.

Yet there is significant divergence, particularly over specific prescriptions for change. The most significant issues are not those of ideology so much as those of constituency, to the extent that the two can be easily separated. The important questions are seen in ethnic terms by the Panthers and largely by Rakah with the critical differentiation there being Jewish identification, i.e., Oriental Jews vs. Palestinians. They are viewed in terms of traditional religious belief by both Natore Karta and Gush Emunim though the results are poles apart, reflecting a history of religious conflict over the value of Zionism. The important issues are matters of militant socialism in the perceptions of the movements of the Left, with the degree of radicalism reflecting the nature of the membership of each group and who it attempts to attract.

It is also interesting to note that dissident groups on the radical fringe appear to conform to an iron rule of factionalism—such groups often seek ideological purity over practicality and are willing to subdivide rather than strike an ideological compromise. Matzpen sports at least four distinct wings within Israel, Israeli Communists have a history of internal strain dating back half a century, and the Panthers are constantly in a state of flux refected in the disparate units bearing their name in the 1977 election.

This has not been the case with Natore Karta and Gush Emunim, however. Perhaps their apparent unity of action may be attributed to the monolithic and religious nature of their base. Both movements follow the teaching of a specific sage or council of sages who, it is claimed, holds the secret of a truth, divinely revealed. In addition, both are largely one-dimensional in their quests, the one anti-Zionist, the other proto-Zionist. Finally, it may well be that much of the fractionalizing within the ideologies of other movements reflects less the purity of their thought than the personal dispositions of the given wing and its leadership. Within movements such as Natore Karta and Gush Emunim there is little room for such personal differences because of the nature of the leadership and the truth it claims to hold.

In this chapter a summary analysis and comparison has been presented to clarify the main strains of thought attributable to our subjects. Through such comparisons, similarities and divergencies of thought have been discussed and outlined. It remains now to discuss the implications of these movements for the Israeli political and social system, the nature of their impact within Israel and abroad, the response of the system to such ideologies, and perhaps a brief word about the importance of ideology and dissent in modern political life. This will be attempted in the final chapter, particularly in light of the results of the Israeli elections of May 1977 and the political maneuverings in their wake.

12

1977: THE YEAR OF
THE EARTHQUAKE

Much of what has preceded was researched or written prior to May 1977, a landmark date in Israeli political history. On the seventeenth of that month, what some Israelis call the earthquake, others the hurricane, occurred. For three decades of statehood, the Israel Labor party stood at the center of government. Despite its various rifts and permutations, the party had been senior partner to every Israeli government. Though never able to win a clear majority of its own, it supplied the nation with all its prime ministers and most of its national heroes. Internal ruptures notwithstanding, it had well withstood the tests of time.

Yet, in May 1977, the impossible occurred. Burdened by equal parts of corruption, indifference, and loss of voter confidence, the Labor Alignment lost its hold on Israeli leadership. Its successor was the Likud bloc, perennial rival and stronghold of the right-wing opposition. With this unexpected turnabout, Menahem Begin—former guerrilla leader and spokesman for the hawkish annexationist position—was named prime minister and asked to form a new government. It is auspicious for our purposes to review the events that led up to the Likud victory and the changes that the new government has wrought. By this means, a concluding statement regarding the role of dissent in the election and projections for the future may be made.

It is important to note that several of our subject groups played a significant part during the new election and beyond. Some formed a variety of new coalitions during the campaign, although few were particularly successful. In the case of Gush Emunim, however, the Likud victory may be seen as vindication of their annexationist position. Their status was significantly advanced nationally, as well as within the National Religious Party. The machinations of these groups and the stances they took during and since the election will form part of our discussion.

The 1977 election was actually premature. Since Israeli elections generally take place four years apart, it was expected that the campaign would be held during late 1977 or 1978 at the earliest, and most party lists were prepared with that in mind. In what still appears to be a bizarre series of events, however, a government crisis was precipitated over the issue of Sabbath observance.

In early December 1976, several American-made F-15 jets were delivered to Israel and accepted with considerable fanfare after the onset of the Sabbath. Four days later a "no confidence" vote was entered against the government by Agudat Israel, the strictly religious party, in protest of the action. Several leftist elements joined in the move, though for various reasons having little to do with religious observance. The Knesset debate was vitriolic. Yet Prime Minister Rabin was able to stave off the drive, the no confidence motion being defeated 55 to 48. Crucial in the matter, however, was the abstention of nine Knesset members of the National Religious Party, partner to the government coalition.

By the strict definition of collective responsibility, it is required that members to the coalition vote with the government on motions of no confidence. Their failure to do so implies their own default from the partnership. With the abstention of the NRP, therefore, the initiative rested with the Labor Alignment to react. It was not fully expected, however, that the prime minister would take advantage of his option, thereby bringing down his own government. Nevertheless, on December 19, Rabin ousted the NRP from the government coalition, dissolving the Knesset and tendering his resignation the following day.[1]

For the next several months, a "care taker" government was formed, largely by shuffling vacant cabinet ministries among those of the Labor Alignment already holding government portfolios. The party was ailing, however, both internally and externally, its maladies coming to the fore as it prepared for an early campaign. Its most serious conflicts arose over the issues of corruption and the competition for party leadership.

In the first instance, two of its leading figures proved closely related to national scandals. Asher Yadlin, a former chairman of the Israel Health Organization (Kupat Cholim), had been accused of assorted charges of bribery and misuse of public funds. In early February, he pleaded guilty to four counts of bribery and one of income tax evasion, being subsequently remanded for a prison term. Parallel to these investigations stood charges of embezzlement leveled against Minister of Housing Abraham Ofer.

These latter charges were never substantiated, as Ofer committed suicide and the prime minister declared that investigation into his actions should be officially closed. The cabinet confirmed this decision, announcing, however, that investigations of other government officials would continue.

It was within this context of exposé and scandal that the Labor Party held its nominating convention on February 22–23, 1977. Although Abba Eban had announced his candidacy for leadership, he withdrew in favor of Defense Minister Shimon Peres. A favorite of the bureaucracy, Peres had a reputation for implementing policy and was reputed to have been the prime mover behind the Entebbe raid of July 1976. Rabin had suffered for his lackluster approach to leadership and his inability to inspire confidence. The convention vote was expected to be close. Rabin was barely able to beat off the Peres candidacy, winning the Labor nomination by a mere 41 votes (1445–1404).[2]

The matter of corruption was to haunt the Labor Party at yet another level, however. In March of 1977 it was revealed that the prime minister and his wife jointly held an American bank account violating Israeli currency laws. It was later learned that the Rabins held some $27,000 in such accounts, a fact conceded to by the prime minister. The Finance Ministry fined Rabin $1,500 and he resigned his position as leader of the Labor Party, accepting an extended leave of absence on April 22.

Peres was confirmed as Labor's nominee for the prime ministry and took Rabin's office upon his leave. Adding frosting to the cake, it was announced on April 23 that the Finance Ministry was also investigating similar charges of currency violation against Abba Eban. In the meanwhile, one of Labor's most celebrated members, former Defense Minister Moshe Dayan announced that he would not run for Knesset on the Labor ticket although he would consider supporting the party in its electoral bid.

Yet, one of the most significant events of the campaign occurred outside the Labor camp: the development of the Democratic Movement for Change (DMC). As has been noted, new party lists and independent political configurations do not generally meet with much success in Israel. Because the established parties are well-entrenched and their hold on material benefits for members is extensive, individual voters are hesitant to stray. The growing rift and daily scandals within the Labor Party made a fresh political presence attractive to a variety of constituencies, however.

With this in mind, high-level members of Israeli government and administration rallied behind former war hero and chief of staff Yigal Yadin in late 1976. Yadin had remained impervious to the lure of politics previously, contenting himself with a world-wide reputation as an archeologist and scholar. He gathered about him a cross-section of both hawks and doves, Laborites and independents, military leaders, intellecuals and industrialists whose common thread appeared to be only the desire for meaningful change.

The new list included Amnon Rubenstein, a law professor and leader of Shinnui, the change-oriented movement of academics and activists created after the 1973 War. It also held Shmuel Tamir of the Free Center Movement, a right-wing faction whose three Knesset seats were split from the Likud bloc as issues of personality and ideology overrode basic similarities of policy. In addition, former Labor figures Meir Zorea (head of the Israel Land Authority), Shmuel Toledano (advisor on Arab affairs), and Meir Amit (former military chief of intelligence and director of the industrial complex Koor) were offered DMC candidacy—making the new party truly broad and interpartisan.*

By its own concession, the DMC was offering little new in the crucial arenas of foreign policy and defense. Its platform contended that Israel's eastern border should be the Jordan River, allowing that withdrawal from occupied territories there "should be rejected unless it would be an integral part of a full treaty." The party also rejected an independent Palestinian state as a danger to Israeli security. Rather, the Palestinian question should be solved within the context of one Arab state roughly equivalent to the present kingdom of Jordan, providing self-determination for all its various constituencies on territory *east* of the Jordan. So similar, in fact, was the DMC stand to that of both leading parties, that each of the latter regularly accused the former of prearranging a coalition agreement with their rival.[3]

Yadin preferred to concentrate his attack on domestic issues. These were broadly defined as economic questions of inflation and labor unrest, the social questions of the disadvantaged, and the political aspects of governmental effectiveness. While offering such social amelior4tives as preferential aid to the disadvantaged, Yadin struck a hard economic line, requiring a limit to wage agreements, legislation to forbid strikes in critical occupations, and a firm commitment to curb inflation.

A parallel thrust of his program was the issue of government corruption and administrative inefficiency. The DMC called for a reduction in the

---

*It should be noted that despite several attempts, it was not possible to lure members of other factions to join the new list. These included the Citizens Rights Movement, the Independent Liberals, and Shlomzion, who were unwilling to eliminate their organizational structures and resign their Knesset seats as Yadin insisted. The decision proved unfortunate for the first two, who subsequently lost five of the seven seats held in the previous Knesset.

number of ministries and a program to cut the effects of an overbearing bureaucracy—often the result of inflationary governmental employment programs. Finally, it based a good portion of its appeal on a long-debated issue in Israeli political affairs: electoral reform. Yadin demanded a new regional constituent plan to replace that of proportional representation within two years.[4] Put simply, the DMC attempted to portray itself less as a formal party with commitments in the vital areas of defense and security. It would rather appeal to the voter as a movement of reform and government efficiency at whose base lay the ideal of change.

The campaign proceeded apace with vitriolic attacks leveled by the Labor alignment and Likud mutually. The former charged that a Likud victory would be a threat to democracy in Israel, while the latter challenged the Labor willingness to offer territorial concessions in return for peace. Various possible coalition formations were bandied about and, despite the acid of their invective, both leaders were alleged to be considering a broad-based government led by a Labor-Likud coalition similar to the "government of national unity" created on the eve of the 1967 War.

Whatever the outcome, it was clear that the DMC had gained strength and might well play the crucial role of "balancer." Yadin, for his part, emphasized that he would stay out of a coalition should the alternative require significant compromise of principle. In his words: "the DMC did not come into being just to join a government but to bring about changes in all areas of life. If our conditions are not met, we can also remain in the opposition."[5]

THE ELECTION

The campaign ended with an unprecedented television debate in which Begin and Peres faced each other over questions moderated by a local newsman. Their positions remained essentially the same, appearing to be separated more by degree than by kind, more by approach and personality than by substance. Polls available on election eve generally awarded a slight victory to the Labor Alignment, never amounting to more than five or six seats and clearly insignificant to the job of coalition formation. More crucially, it was indicated that some 20 percent of the electorate was undecided.[6]

The final election results were rather curious in a number of important ways. Most spectacular, of course, was the victory of the right-wing Likud Party, ending 30 years of Labor hegemony and bringing to a close the era of essentially one-party rule in Israel. Likud leader Menahem Begin had patiently awaited his opportunity to hold office, serving as the autocratic mainstay of the loyal opposition for three decades. Far from a majority, however, it would be his formidable task to force a viable coalition reflecting his own right-wing leadership.

Significantly, though, Likud's gains were less than overwhelming. In 1973, it had garnered 30.2 percent of the popular vote and was awarded 39 seats in the eighth Knesset. Its 1977 share of the popular vote was 33.4 percent, reflecting a net gain of no more than 3.2 percent over the previous election. Similarly, in 1977 Likud was awarded 43 parliamentary seats, only 4 more than it had held previously. By no means could this be described as a decisive victory.

More than Likud's success, it may be that the electoral turnabout was the result of the failure of the Labor alignment. The Peres-led list was able to win only 24.6 percent of the popular vote—32 seats in the upcoming ninth Knesset. The alignment had lost 15 percent of its 1973 constituency and 19 places in its parliamentary delegation.[7] As discussed above, the debacle could surely be attributed to many short-term factors, that is, such as corruption, internal conflicts, and defections.

Yet it may be seen as the capstone to a long-term trend as well. This is reflected in the data presented below for Labor alignment electoral results:

	1965*	1969	1973	1977
Percent of vote	51.2	46.2	39.6	24.6
Number of seats	63	56	51	32

*Mapai and Achdut Avoda in alignment, Mapam, and Rafi.

As indicated, in the elections to the seventh Knesset of 1965, the parties that presently constitute the Labor alignment were able to gain a slim majority of both the popular vote (51.2 percent) and seats in the Knesset (63). Through a gradual process of erosion in the following two elections and the defeat of 1977, Labor's constituency was actually cut in half over the short span of 12 years. Being turned out of office appears in this light to have been a matter of time—short-term factors making the time ripe.

Precisely where the Alignment votes went is a matter of some debate. The most obvious drain on their constituency appears to have been the DMC. With the exception of Menahem Begin, Yigal Yadin as head of the DMC list surfaced as the election's "big winner." Though he was a political newcomer heading a party with no formal institutional affiliations or prior electoral record, Yadin and his party were able to gain 11.6 percent of the popular vote, being awarded 15 Knesset seats. This made the DMC Israel's third largest parliamentary delegation.

Wherein lay its constituency has been a matter of controversy, however. That there was considerable disaffection from Labor is, of course, clear, Aside from its preelection difficulties, it suffered several other debilities. As the party in power, it was held responsible for a myriad of social and economic ills, that is, galloping inflation met by regular devaluations of the pound, rising crime rates, income disparities and a general decline in the quality of life.

Further, this was the first election since the major investigations of the alleged security and intelligence failures of the 1973 War. The revelations had shaken major Labor figures from public life and the aura of military defeat still hung over the alignment. Finally, the electorate seemed impatient with the lackluster and indecisive leadership that Labor offered. Unable to successfully wage war or keep peace, its direction inspired little confidence.

It has been argued, therefore, that the DMC represented a suitable alternative for many of Labor's traditional supporters. Almost indistinguishable from it on questions of security and foreign affairs, the DMC offered a fresh approach to major domestic concerns as well as a change from tired personalities of little charisma. Secular and professional, such a list might well initiate structural change and infuse new life in a system that had grown hard and inflexible with age. The presence of leading candidates previously associated with the alignment on the DMC list made the switch somewhat less painful. Thus, the theory goes, the bulk of Labor's loss can be attributed to the success of the Democratic Movement for Change.[8]

For some, however, such a formulation is deceptively simplistic. Many Likud figures, along with Laborites, appeared on the DMC list. If the new list was indistinguishable from the alignment on foreign policy, neither was it that far removed from the more liberal sectors of the Likud. Its very novelty might well be an attraction to long-time Likud supporters, who despaired of ever seeing Begin as prime minister and were searching for an alternative. To argue that the 1977 election was largely a repudiation of Labor, in which Likud's victory was inadvertent, ignores the real possibility that many Likud voters were also attracted to the DMC.

In addition, the appeal of Yadin's list, almost by its very nature, was to the more affluent and politically sophisticated. Discussions of electoral reform or change in political structure are not generally attractive to those uninitiated to their ramifications or to whom a primary concern is financial insecurity. In a society of which some 50 percent of the electorate is under the age of thirty and a large proportion subsists at or near the poverty level, it may be erroneous to attribute an electoral shift to the appearance of a new party whose basic thrust is procedural change.

In fact, both preelection and postelection data indicate that, though Likud's gains were not impressive over previous years, the party did well in areas of traditional Labor strength. In addition, its gains reflect popularity among future strategic voter populations—the young, the poor, and the Oriental. In a preelection newspaper poll, for example, the Likud held a plurality among younger voters, doubling those who expressed preference for the DMC. There appeared to be an inverse relationship between such factors as age, education, and income on the one hand and support for Likud on the other. As the former fell, the latter rose. Stated preference for the DMC, however, was related positively to income, no matter what the previous affiliation. This, the DMC appeared to be sapping the strength of both parties at the upper income levels, though not necessarily equally.[9]

The election itself seems to have borne out these tendencies. Among those in the armed services, Likud polled nearly half the total vote, more than Labor and the DMC combined. Similarly, in development towns and cooperative settlements—both traditional Labor strongholds, with large contingents of Oriental Jews—Likud's margin rose sharply while the alignment suffered a serious decline. This is particularly interesting in that those often characterized as most alienated from established political life have chosen this right-wing bloc as the vehicle for their protest. In sum, it is equally possible that, quite apart from the repudication of Labor, the 1977 election may be seen as the genesis of a right-wing ruling coalition with sufficient vitality to hold power for some time.[10]

Yet, even such a conclusion may not be fully warranted. Some two weeks after the parliamentary elections, a second, less sensational, election was held, for delegate seats to the Histadrut, Israel's labor federation. Here too, Likud expected to repeat its Knesset successes and end Labor's traditional domination. Though it was able to increase its vote by 5.5 percent over 1973 (28.2 percent in 1977 from 22.7 percent in 1973), almost doubling its Knesset gains, Labor managed to hold 55.3 percent of the vote and carried the election.

The alignment victory was not an unconditional success, as it reflected a loss of roughly 5 percent from its 1973 vote, continuing a long-term decline beginning in 1965 and paralleling its loss of Knesset seats over the past twelve years. In addition, a good part of Labor's victory was the result of a stepped-up campaign in the various kibbutzim and agrarian settlements whose past participation in the Knesset election was haphazard and somewhat complacent. Likud continued to carry the lower-class urban vote and that of the Oriental development towns.

While its Histadrut victory was not unqualified, Labor was able to regain its losses and maintain power in one of the country's most crucial institutions, possibly implying a revival of alignment power. As such, it has been interpreted as the result of "voters shocked by what they had wrought" in the Knesset elections the previous month. It may also be the foundation of a bipolar system: a Parliament with right-wing leanings and a labor federation whose values are those of the liberal Left, not unusual in societies where labor unions are not quasi-government agencies. Such a duality may prove unworkable in Israel, as the bitter and stormy outbreaks at the Histadrut convention in November 1977 attest.[11]

THE NEW GOVERNMENT

A final curiosity is the coalition which Begin proceeded to forge upon his accession to power. A first initiative was offered to the religious parties and to the Shlomzion faction whose two seats had been earlier split from Likud behind the leadership of military hero Arik Sharon. The National Religious Party had been the alignment's traditional ally, while the more strictly Orthodox Agudat Israel and its worker's branch had largely eschewed government participation on ideological grounds. However, both found it relatively easy to enter into coalition with Likud.

In the case of the Agudat bloc, its five seats were offered to the coalition on the basis of an extensive agreement which cedes considerable advantage to the cause of organized religion in Israel. Its stipulation includes extension of Sabbath restrictions by law, added support for both governmental and nongovernmental religious schools and seminaries, exemption of religious women from military conscription, expansion of the power of religious courts, and increased censorship of literature and the arts. It also includes a pledge to attempt repeal of the liberalized abortion law, passed after the NRP was ousted from the government by Prime Minister Rabin.

For the National Religious Party, coalition partnership was more dependent upon questions of security and settlement policy. Quite germane to our purposes here, it should be noted that the spectacular popularity of Gush Emunim—in both ideological and practical terms—was a considerable threat to the party, which still served as its political parent. Gush leadership was bent on an independent stand, separating themselves from the party and either offering their own list or, more likely, supporting another existing one, probably Likud. Either consequence might have been disastrous for the NRP.

In a late decision, the NRP was able to stave off the large-scale exodus of its fiery youth faction by choosing Rabbi Haim Drukman, a Gush Emunim sympathizer and favorite of Rabbi Tzvi Yehuda Kook, its spiritual director, for the second position on its party list. Somewhat mollified, Gush Emunim did not formally break its ties with the NRP and Rabbi Kook endorsed the list. Thus, the party based its appeal largely on settlement and security grounds, rather than on religious issues.

Due in no small part to this move, the NRP won twelve seats, an increase of two over 1973. With its newly found mandate and a change in its constituency to the Right, the party joined with Likud. One of its younger members, Zevulun Hammer, was appointed minister of education and culture. It is no coincidence that Hammer was among those who supported the original formation of the Gush in 1974.[12] Subsequent developments between Gush Emunim and the new government will be discussed below.

In a second bold move, Begin turned to Moshe Dayan, elected to the Knesset on the alignment's list, to serve as his foreign minister. In accepting the position, Dayan declared himself independent of the Labor Alignment, indeed of any formal partisan affiliation. As might be expected, this elicited storms of protest from his party colleagues, who demanded that by resigning from the party list on which he was elected, Dayan was in effect resigning his Knesset seat. Nonetheless, Dayan entered the government as an independent, claiming that he had actually been ejected from the alignment for considering a cabinet ministry.[13]

As a result of these negotiations, the new Begin-led government held the barest of coalition majorities. It was clear that, to have a viable base, Likud would have to negotiate elsewhere for parliamentary support. For this purpose, Begin opened talks with the newly-formed Democratic Movement for Change, through its leader, Yigal Yadin. The negotiations, which were long and arduous, and which broke down at several points, took more than five months. It was not until late October 1977, that a political agreement was reached.

The agreement opened ruptures within the DMC that had been festering for some time. The Begin initiative caused conflict within the DMC as early as the summer, when Yadin was criticized by his membership for maintaining an aloof and autocratic attitude within the party council. Indeed, the very democratic nature of council decision making under Yadin—something precious to the DMC's reform-oriented constituents—had been called into serious question. Amnon Rubinstein, one of the party's most popular members, absented himself from the final coalition vote, considering the details of the proposed partnership a retreat from DMC principle.

Despite internal pressure, the new list joined the government—accepting a negotiation offer it had earlier rejected. Yadin was named deputy premier and DMC members were awarded the Ministries of Justice, Transport, and Communications and Labor-Social Betterment, a newly-created department. In addition, the party retained freedom of expression on matters relating to West Bank settlement policy, won a commitment for electoral reform and freedom of vote on all religious matters. Finally, the creation of the new ministry—a combination of the former Ministries of Labor, Social Welfare, and the National Insurance Institute—is coordinated by Yadin who also controls budgetary allocations. Thus was formed the new Begin Government.[14]

IDEOLOGY AND DISSENT IN 1977

It remains to document the activities of our subject groups during the earthshaking events of the 1977 election to the point of this writing. In many ways, it may be construed that the election stands as evidence of the resurgence of ideology as a variable in Israeli electoral politics. However it is interpreted, the defeat of the alignment may appear as a retreat from the politics of pragmatism and flexibility, or indecisiveness and boredom, depending upon one's point of view.

Instead, the voter chose two figures whose public personalities fall more in line with perceptible ideological positions. Menahem Begin has always portrayed himself as a staunch promponent of the Right. He consistently favored a hard line toward the Arab world, disengagement from labor or socialist economic commitments, and the annexation of some conquered territories, more from considerations of divine right than practical security.[15] It might be recalled that he led his then-opposition Herut faction to its annual convention at Kiryat Arba, a Jewish settlement on the West bank, in 1975.

Equally important, Yigal Yadin represents a more definitive political style, if not a systematic ideological position, than might be attributed to Labor alignment activity. He has taken pains to maintain partisan independence on the interrelated issues of territorial concessions and organized religious values, implying a softer or more flexible position on both. Further, Yadin represents a secular, reformist nonestablishmentarianism that might fit easily with the stance of the Israeli peace position. By no means is ideology a dead issue, therefore, in Israeli politics.

The subjects of our study assumed a variety of positions during and since the election. In addition, many participated actively—some with substantial success—on party lists, while others disdained political activity, true to their ideological positions. Still others appear to have moved little during or since the election, possibly indicating internal difficulties or temporary demise.

One of the latter was Matzpen. Representing the most extreme position on the political spectrum, it appears that the movement has become little more than a curiosity in Israeli politics. Its influence in Israel, never impressive, has been dissipated by other pressing events, while its activism abroad seems to have declined, possibly because of further fractionalizing. It may be reasonably hypothesized that Matzpen members will seek other outlets for their intellectual and ideological activity, possibly through the formation of new organizations or in coalition with already existing ones.

It may be noted that still another option exists for Israelis of radical ilk, that taken by those unhappy—no matter what their political stripe: emigration. At this writing, one of Israel's most serious social problems is "yeridah"—the migration of many of its native born or naturalized to Western countries, particularly the United States. It is not altogether unlikely that those who persist in their disdain for Israeli institutions but are frustrated in their attempts to protest and organize in dissent will leave, seeking happiness elsewhere. Evidence exists, however, that many Israelis who have emigrated are able to increase their fortunes materially but are often unhappy with the life styles that are required of them abroad.[16]

As might be expected, a second group of our subjects disdained from any form of participation in the elections: Natore Karta. As in the past, voting was strictly forbidden. On principle, Natore Karta publicly denounced all parties and passionately warned against their collective evil to all who would listen. The sect has been quite active, however, since the election.

The accession of Menahem Begin to political leadership has by no means pleased its leadership. Indeed, in one important way, they might well have preferred an Alignment victory. Given its avowedly non-religious, quasi-socialist stand, it was quite simple to separate between Labor Zionism and traditional Judaism. One could easily argue that such a brand of nationalism had neither roots nor sympathies in Jewish piety. Begin, however, has attempted to portray himself as a deeply religious individual with a sense of divine command that contributes to his values and policies. This appears as a particular affront.

In response, the sect has taken a firm position attempting to uncover Begin's atheist past. Its publications are filled with historical analyses purporting to show the antiorthodoxy equally evident in the thought of

Begin and his spiritual progenitor Zev Vladimir Jabotinsky. A letter containing such arguments was forwarded to President Carter after Begin's initial visit to the United States, to correct the "mistaken" impression of Begin as sincere and well-meaning. His pious demeanor, it was charged, was little more than a "clerical disguise," intended to mislead "those uninitiated to his real political aims."[17]

Particularly irksome, in this regard, has been the decision of Agudat Israel—the most strictly Orthodox of Israel's parties—to join the Likud coalition. That the National Religious Party has joined appears to raise little comment from Natore Karta. Its history has been one of coalition partnership while the sincerity of its Orthodox commitments has often been suspect in Israel's most traditionally observant circles. Agudat Israel, however, represents a serious threat.

Consequently, Natore Karta has unleashed a barrage of vehement protest at the party and its leadership. Agudat Israel is variously accused of "blasphemy toward heaven," allowing themselves to "praise the wicked and help to establish a regime of evil doers." The religious parties have accepted bribes, it is alleged, as well as material concessions, for their apostasy. In so doing, they have "fallen lower and lower," even turning on those who have innocently protested their actions. In their sin, they "reproached [those who dissent] with scorn and didn't hesitate to use all the low methods of coercion at their disposal."

There is, therefore, but one path for the true believer. He must protest all such actions of collaboration and cooptation. He must separate himself from the community of evil and especially from "these flatterers who sold themselves to the atheistic regime." All must raise their voices and declare loyalty to the ancient traditions of Judaism."[18]

It is likely that Nature Karta will continue its lonely fight to oppose the foundation and operation of a Jewish national enterprise. The very unique nature of its stand and the consistency in which it has been manifest underwrites ready publicity in the forums and the columns of world opinion. Its impact among the various Arab states should not be discounted, either. Further, the movement has a captive constituency due to the very nature of the pious life that its adherents lead. Its anti-Zionist stand offers a raison d'être that many religious sects might well envy and it is about this issue that it rallies support internally as well as abroad.

Ironically, despite the treasonous nature of its stance, official posture toward Natore Karta has been little more than condescending amusement. The movement has been permitted to rally, protest, and organize, almost unfettered by the authorities, unless it incites violence outside its particular residential quarters, possibly because Natore Karta harkens back to a life of simplicity and piety with which many Israeli leaders can identify. Natore Karta will probably be allowed to pursue its goals more as a curiosity than as a political force.

Not all dissidents were quite so circumspect about their participation in the 1977 elections. Sensing a fiery campaign and the air of impending change, many entered the foray, as they had in the past. With the hope of expanding their constituencies and broadening their appeal, they entered into coalitions with personalities of like mind who headed party lists. To some, this appeared a compromise, yet the purity of principle may be worthless if it falls on deaf ears. In the main, however, such maneuvering and manipulation was of little avail.

A prime example of dissident coalitions was the formation of Sheli (a Hebrew acronym for "Peace on Israel"). At its head stood Arie Lova Eliav, a popular spokesman for the "soft line," who left the Labor alignment to create the Independent Socialist Party in 1975. Eliav was joined by Meir Peil whose Moked Party was merged into the new list and who was subsequently offered its second position. Third position went to Uri Avnery, in return for his Haolam Hazeh group, which ran as Meri (Israel Radical Party) in 1973. Sa'adian Marciano, a founder of the Black Panthers and leader of its Jerusalem branch, was listed fourth. Sheli represented a cross-section of Israeli protest with natural appeal to several populations: alignment malcontents, the military, literary and intellectual dissidents, and the Oriental poor.

The new list supported the establishment of an independent Palestinian state on the occupied West Bank. It implied that the Palestine Liberation Organization must be a participant in any peace negotiations and with the exception of minor modifications (subject to mutual agreement), Israel must return to its pre-1967 borders. A united Jerusalem would serve as capital for both Israel and the new Palestinian state.

Reflecting the general swing toward the Right, Sheli did not do well at the polls. The Israeli voter appears to have had little interest in dovish solutions to its security problems. The list won 27,281 votes, primarily in large urban centers. This was some 5,000 fewer votes than Moked and Meri polled together in 1973. Sheli was awarded two seats in the new Knesset—going to Eliav and Peil. True to its platform, the new party wasted little time before attacking the government. Claiming that intransigence and annexationism would lead to a clash with the United States, Eliav argued that the new prime minister might progressively alienate Israel from the few friends it had left.[19]

The participation of Sa'adiah Marciano on the Sheli List also reflected a chronic ailment in the Black Panther organization. Whatever was their influence in terms of shock value and consciousness-raising, the group has been unable to sustain a unified and cohesive front. Consequently, due to internal bickering, personality conflict, flirtation with socialist ideologies, and militant dissent, or simple naïveté, the Panthers increasingly disqualify themselves as spokespersons for the plight of the Oriental. Even many who displayed sympathy have become impatient and disillusioned. Indeed, their natural constituency, the Oriental poor, often express little confidence in their ability to bring change.

In 1973, two Panther lists appeared on the ballot: the regular party, led by Shalom Cohen, and a splinter group known as the "Blue-White" Panthers, who expressed their greater Zionist loyalties by including the Israeli colors in their title. Running separately, the Cohen-led group won over 13,000 votes, while the latter gained almost 6,000. While neither was sufficient for a Knesset seat, a combined total of 19,000 votes would have placed at least one Panther, probably Cohen, in Knesset. In 1977 this unfortunate situation was multiplied, for Panthers were to be found on four disparate lists.

As noted, Sa'adiah Marciano failed to gain a seat behind Eliav on the Sheli list. Similarly unsuccessful was senior statesman Shalom Cohen. In an attempt to unite with an established and well-articulated interest group, Cohen joined with Yehoshua Peretz, fiery leader of the Ashdod dock workers council. Known for their militancy and strength, the dock workers include large numbers of Orientals and have always agitated for improved social benefits and living standards. Together they created Hofesh (Freedom), known also as the Neighborhood and Labor Front. The experiment proved disastrous, netting less than 2,500 votes.

Rather sadly, Voctor Tayer—who figured prominently in the aforementioned Blue-White Panther rift—was forced to create his own Zionist Panther list in 1977. His original intent was to joint with Yigal Yadin's Democratic Movement for Change, on the assumption that the new list would be glad to offer a safe seat to an Oriental leader. In its zeal to initiate electoral reform, however, the party eschewed the backroom caucus in favor of an internal election. The vote was based on traditional proportional lists, Yadin's desire for a geographic constituency election notwithstanding.

As a result, none of the Oriental delegates was placed and they left the party in protest. When Yadin refused to tamper with the results, Tayer and his Panther followers created the Zionist Panther list. Not surprisingly, their efforts were futile, having come late to the campaign and lacking a real constituency. The list polled less than 1,800 votes and will probably evaporate as a political presence.[20]

Ironically, the only Panther to win a Knesset seat actually left the Panther fold and joined a new Communist list called the Democratic Front for Peace and Equality. There could be little doubt that the new list was led and directed by Rakah personnel. Its first position was held by Meir Wilner and its second and fourth by Tawfiq Tubi and Tawfiq Ziyyad, all Rakah dignitaries. In an attempt to broaden its appeal to the Jewish poor and the non-Communist Arab villagers, however, the party changed its image somewhat.

As part of this face lift, a safe position (third) was offered to Charlie Biton, Panther organizer and ex-convict. It was through this unlikely path of Communist affiliation that the Panthers placed a member in Knesset. A second member, Cochavi Shemesh, failed to win a seat. In addition, the new front included Hanna Mo'is of the Arab local councils, who had previously avoided Communist affiliation.

In sum, the Rakah front polled over 80,000 votes and was awarded five Knesset seats. Some 90 percent of its vote came from the Arab population. This comprised roughly 50 percent of the total Arab vote. Therefore, alignment-affiliated Arab lists and the National Religious Party—both traditional favorites among many Arab villagers—did quite poorly. It may reasonably be expected that the Communist share of the Arab vote will continue to increase.

Interestingly, many had predicted even a greater success for Rakah in the 1977 election. Perhaps the very inclusion of Oriental Jews and non-Communist Arabs gave Rakah a less militant look, which alienated many of the younger Arab voters. It is quite possible that these, who did not vote for Rakah (and probably did not vote at all), might have, if Biton and the others had not been included. The lesson for Rakah is that its victories will be all the more impressive if it concentrates on its Arab constituents and up-grades nationalist appeals. This, of course, it does at the risk of incurring the wrath of Isareli authories.[21]

Far and away the most influential of all our subjects since the 1977 election has been Gush Emunim. As noted, Menahem Begin has always expressed sympathy with movements of settlement and is an avowed defender of the annexationist position. In addition, he has presented himself as a deeply religious individual with a sense of transcendence. His concern for territories is attributed as much to a religio-national mission as to the practicality of politics. At the very least, the Gush would now be faced with a sympathetic government and a cognate spirit at its head.

More parochially, its stock rose within the National Religious Party. It was only after an ideological sympathizer, Rabbi Chaim Drukman, was allotted the second position on the NRP list that Rabbi Kook and his Gush followers decided not to bolt the party. The NRP gained two Knesset seats in the election and increased its popular vote by some 30,000 over 1973. This success has been largely attributed to the popularity of the Gush and its members have won new respect among NRP regulars.

The movement has also been gratified by another development within the new government. As noted, a small splinter faction, Shlomzion (Peace for Zion), broke from Likud prior to the election. Despite last moment efforts to rejoin, the list ran independently, with military leader Arik Sharon at its head. Its two seats were incorporated into the new coalition and Sharon was subsequently named minister of agriculture and chairman of a joint government-Jewish Agency committee on settlement.

In this capacity, he has been an unstinting friend and supporter of the Gush settlement efforts. He has praised their actions in Parliament, arguing that, rather than question Gush motivation, Israelis should be proud. In fact, he has claimed, encouragement would be a natural response were not Israelis bent on "abasing themselves before the Gentile." In effect, Gush Emunim is fulfilling "the most important political activity possible, under present-day circumstances." The movement could not have asked for a more fertile political environment.[22]

As if to punctuate the close relationship envisioned, the new prime minister visited Elon Moreh on the West Bank immediately after his election. The site was particularly significant in that it was founded by squatters who lived at the nearby military base, Kadum. The new settlement had been a cause célèbre and characterized the poor relationship between the Gush and the Labor government. That the latter opposed the settlement but took no action to remove it also epitomized the government's weakness and indecisiveness.

In a moving ceremony, Begin stood at the town's center, Sharon to his left and a Torah scroll in his arms. He lauded the idealism, self-sacrifice, and tenacity of the settlers and made his support for their actions clear. More significantly, he announced that there would be many more Elon Morehs. True to his word, Begin legalized three West Bank settlements established despite the opposition of his predecessors and indicated his intentions to found three more in the immediate future. All this happened in the first three months of his tenure in office. Inferring this to be a mandate for their own initiative, Gush leaders announced that they planned twelve new "garinim" (seed groups for preliminary settlement) by September of 1977.[23]

Despite such auspicious beginnings, the relationship between the new government and Gush Emunim was not without strain. The movement criticized the Begin regime for "dragging its feet" on settlement. In particular, the new settlements promised by Gush for September were never established and the time of their founding was left purposefully vague. Ironically, his own visions of a "Greater Israel" notwithstanding, Begin found the first challenge of his government to come from the annexationist right.

The issue appears to be less one of substance than of timing. The prime minister early became involved with delicate negotiations with the United States and later in the historic mission of Anwar Sadat to Jerusalem. Gush pressure for new settlements in the fall of 1977 were a particular nuisance. Yet, precisely because of his own sympathies with their cause, Begin was much embarrassed by their statements and actions.

On a broader field, one might also interpret the conflict as one of credibility and authority, that is, who should have the final word about so crucial an issue as West Bank settlement. To a large degree, the popularity of the Gush is based upon the apparent idealism and spontaneity of its actions. Having to defer their goals in the name of political sensitivity, timing, and the partisan views of any government leader appears as an affront to their values. It is clear, however, that even an agreeable prime minister cannot allow actions of such consequence to take place without his clear authorization, nor can he be faced with a fait accompli. It might be added that Mr. Begin may have erred in his overt enthusiasm for the Gush so early in his administration.

The conflict also revealed strains within the Gush organization. Whether or not such fissures existed earlier is unclear. Certainly they were kept well hidden and it is only the issue of a relationship with the friendliest of governments that brought them into full view. In response to threats that adherents would soon carry out settlement actions with or without government approval, Rabbi Kook, the movement's spiritual head, took a dim view. He exhorted the group not to ruin its relationship with so warm a friend as Mr. Begin.

Several long and tiresome meetings between Begin and Gush leaders ensued. Rabbi Kook's words obviously put the movement into an embarrassing position and it was finally conceded that the movement would take no action without government authorization; final authority for settlement would lie within government prerogative. Nonetheless, a group of Gush settlers, apparently dissatisfied with what appeared to be a sellout, attempted their own action near the ancient site of Jericho on the West Bank.

Faced with what might be a major crisis so early in his regime, Mr. Begin acted swiftly and forcefully. The army was ordered to removed the settlers before the entire issue might gain national interest and international publicity. Thus, irony was heaped upon irony. It was not the "dovish" (the term is used advisedly) Labor Alignment but a right-wing administration that used army forces to remove would-be settlers on the West Bank. In addition, the selfsame ideals and motives that were extolled by Gush leaders under the Rabin government were discouraged under Likud.[24]

A second source of conflict arises from an interesting strategy (or coincidence—depending upon one's position) regarding security forces on the West Bank. It was revealed that Gush settlements, notably the Kiryat Arba group near Hebron, have advertised for "religious young men seeking interesting security work in the Judea-Samaria area." Though the action was taken without any formal identification with the movement, the minister of police came under serious criticism for allowing the creation of a private Gush Emunim force within his jurisdiction.

The new program called for enlistment in a special police detachment which would allow volunteers to study part time at the religious schools at Kiryat Arba. Indeed, interviews were being carried out by Rabbi Zvi Eideles, head of the academy. It was denied that members of the new patrol would be permitted to choose their own areas of operation and police spokesmen argued that all those who enlisted passed the same rigorous tests without regard to their political beliefs or religious commitments and affiliations.

The issue was the cause of an acerbic Knesset debate in which several opposition members left the hall in protest. Tempers flared over the question of whether the new unit was at the disposal of Gush settlers and the extent of control that was being exercised over it by regular police authorities. The program was defended, significantly, not by a cabinet minister, but by NRP whip Yehuda Ben-Mier, who had been a moving force in the creation of Gush Emunim. Finally, in response to a motion for the agenda tendered by the alignment, Mr. Begin himself took the floor in defense and the motion was struck down, 42–19.

It may be expected that such strains will continue. Even the friendliest government must exercize its own prerogative and cannot allow a group of zealots to wrest control from it. Yet Begin is in a delicate position, caught between his mandate and the pressure it implies. The Gush is clearly gaining in popularity and his past position supports their actions. Yet, the leadership of a modern nation and the careful negotiations he has himself set into motion make it necessary to delay, if not compromise, the very principles he held when in the opposition.

Similarly for the Gush. Its position and the monolithic internal support it received may have been a reaction to a foe that was common to all, the Labor alignment. That fissures have opened within its ranks only underlines the very new environment with which it is faced. The movement must face a crucial issue; shall it remain ever in the opposition, shall it become involved in the political game only partially, or shall it offer its whole-hearted support to one or another partisan leader. Each option implies several disadvantages; yet some stance must soon be chosen lest the movement flounder, lose some of its freshness and appeal, and allow internal strain to overtake its mission.

It is interesting to note that some arena of compromise has been reached between the government and the Gush over the question of settle-ment. Several settlement groups have received government approval from the Ministry of Defense. The new groups, however, would be settled at government direction either on formal military and security encampments or on those used for such activities on a temporary basis. The settlers would be offered government jobs, thus removing from them the appear-ance of "civilian settlements" in occupied areas. Eventually, the govern-ment conceded, the military establishments would be removed in favor of the new settlers. Thus, the government appears to have capitulated but in a quiet and nonspectacular manner.[25]

CONCLUDING STATEMENT

The foregoing has been an insight into a unique phenomenon. To the extent that democracy can be defined as that form of government which permits dissent of even a radical and extreme nature, Israeli political institutions must be judged democratic. Most new or developing nations have not been able to afford the luxury of such open protest. Intent upon economic mobilization and the growth of heavy industry, even the most radical of such societies is often ideologically monolithic in both form and direction.

At the risk of generalizing, several similarities can be inferred from the stated positions of these groups. Though moving toward a variety of goals, their world views, that is, their perceptions of the social and political universe, are often strikingly parallel. Many bemoan the growing insti-tutionalization of the state and the awkward bureaucracy that is its re-flection. Materialism and a lack of idealistic spirit are concomitants of this ailment. Each emphasizes, in some form, matters less formal and rational in its yearnings for a charismatic past.

So, too, the nature of their goals and values. Whether socialist, annexationist, religious, or ethnic, the analyses are remarkably unidimen-sional. Salvation, in whatever incarnation, hangs on the emergence of one factor: renewed settlement, socialist revolution, or Sefardic awareness. While the content of these goals differ—radically, in some instances—the thrust appears to stem from the same romantic spirit, the same idyllic nihilism that has been noted above.

Strategies and tactics are far more down to earth. At times they recognize the multiplicity of resources available, as in the formulations of Haolam Hazeh or Gush Emunim. Nevertheless, the threat of violence, street action, and confrontation is never far from the surface. It may well be that the adventurous and exciting nature of such action is precisely what galvanizes those attracted to the ideologies in the first place. In pointed terms, confrontation is one more prop in the romantic imaginations of those who radically dissent.

In terms of formal membership, the ideologies here outlined represent a small fraction of the Israeli polity. Even in the days of protracted negotiation and diversity of approach in the wake of the Sadat peace offensive, Israelis posit a surprising consensus in support of their government. Nonetheless, it would be a mistake to dismiss these radicals as the lunatic fringe, operating only at the very edge of the political parameters.

Numbers may be a poor barometer of ideological impact. A body of thought can have considerable influence in an indirect and subtle manner. Despite the consensus, a moderate peace faction exists in Israel under the administration of Menahem Begin, no less. Drawing from intellectuals, students, Labor politicians and military leaders, strength has been marshalled in favor of a "soft line" and territorial concessions. This move has met its parallel among powerful American Jews including Senators Jacob Javits and Abraham Ribicoff. The ideological lines of Avnery and Peil are to be found within this camp.

By the same token, Gush Emunim has met with a ground swell of grass roots support both inside of Israel and abroad. Many of its settlements have been legitimated and others nurtured under the benevolent aegis of Prime Minister Begin and Agriculture Minister Sharon. The movement has captured the imagination of a broad cross-section of Israelis who will offer support in the event of serious confrontation. Only a last minute concession by the National Religious Party prevented a Gush exodus from its ranks in 1977 and it is not altogether clear that this can be prevented forever.

So it is too with the Black Panthers. Though their influence as a movement has run its course, the problems that its original organization reflected, that is, ethnic deprivation and socioeconomic disparity, remain, The slums, drug abuse, crime, and poverty will not disappear. While most Orientals were neither formal members nor overt supporters of Panther action, the level of their frustrations made them easy targets for participation in large-scale rioting and violence, particularly in the slum areas of Tel Aviv and Jerusalem. In the event of peace—and even in its absence—violence can be expected to continue until this fundamental social problem is faced and progress is made toward its solution.

A far more complex issue inheres in the ideology of Rakah. As the party moves toward becoming the established representative of Palestinian Arab interests within Israel, its position poses an ever more serious threat. The high Arab birth rate, the real possibility of an eventual Jewish minority in Israel, regular acts of terror and brutality, and outward pressure from the United States make Israel's choices the more difficult. The younger Arab generation is less likely to cooperate with alignment-affiliated lists or to be coopted by small political handouts. Unless serious steps are taken, Rakah's small membership will swell, its ideology will grow increasingly radical, and the chances for cooperation will become even more dim.

Our journey in this work has been an exploratory one, intended to be neither exclusive nor conclusive. Yet there is a chronic danger in attempting a study of this type. There is the real fear that the material will be dated before the ink is dry. Even as these words are written, dramatic peace initiatives are being launched and capsized daily throughout the Middle East. Leaders appear at once magnanimous and intransigent, sincere and cynical. Dissenters lose their passion; their support, fluid from the outset, fluctuates and ebbs.

Yet the issues they espouse exhibit surprising tenacity, outliving the political lives of their exponents. Much is yet to be said about ideology, radicalism, and dissent in both a singular and comparative context. Study will continue in developing polities as well as in the "older" states, in the mainstream and at the radical fringe. It is in the spirit of such ideological tenacity and its pursuit that this study is presented.

NOTES

1. Jerusalem *Post* (December 14–20, 1976).
2. New York *Times* (February 24, 1977).
3. See the review of the party platforms reprinted in *New Outlook* (April-May 1977), pp. 20–23.
4. See Yosef Goell, "All Eyes on the Party Leadership," Jerusalem *Post* Weekly Edition (May 17, 1977).
5. Ibid. For an analysis of the possible coalitions being considered on the election eve, see David Shaham, "Elections in Shadow of Doubt," *New Outlook* (April-May 1977), pp. 17–18, 28.
6. Goell, op. cit.

7. For a detailed outline of the election results see the Jerusalem *Post* (May 27, 1977).

8. For an explication of this view, see Don Peretz, "The Earthquake—Israel's Ninth Knesset Elections," *Middle East Journal* (Summer 1977), especially pp. 252557. To bolster the analysis, it is noted that, of the kibbutz vote, traditional backbone of the Labor coalition, some 20 percent was diverted to the DMC.

9. The poll appeared in *Ma-ariv* (March 31, 1977).

10. This perspective is cogently argued in Eric and Rael Jean Isaac, "The Earthquake: Israeli Elections, 1977," *Midstream* (August-September 1977), pp. 3–10.

11. The Jerusalem *Post* (June 28, November 8, 11, 1977); see also David Shaham, "Labor Revival in the Histadrut," *New Outlook* (August 1977), pp. 33–36.

12. See Yehudit Buber-Agasi, "A Clericalist Coalition," *New Outlook* (August 1977), pp. 38–40. It is ironic to note that Rabbi Kook, spiritual leader of the Gush, was not in favor of Hammer's cabinet appointment.

13. See Mosehe Kohn and Asher Wallfish, "Spirited Opposition Greets New Government," Jerusalem *Post*, Weekly Edition (June 28, 1977). In Dayan's own words, "I did not resign from the Alignment. I was expelled from it . . . following my agreement to Prime Minister Begin's request to serve the nation in this most critical hour."

14. On the difficulties of bringing the DMC into the government, see the Jerusalem *Post* (June 28, 1977; July 26, 1977; October 25, 1977; and November 1, 1977).

15. See the Jerusalem *Post* for the week of November 1, 1977. Begin has proven true to his word. His finance minister announced far-reaching changes in the structure of the Israeli economy. The long-range effects of these changes will move Israel far closer to Western capitalism than it has ever been. More immediately, however, it has meant rising prices and consumer and labor unrest.

16. On this issue, see, for example, David J. Schnall, "Yored Is Also a Noun," *Midstream* (February 1978), pp. 73–78; and James Feron, "The Israelis of New York," *New York Times Magazine* (January 16, 1977).

17. Jerusalem *Post* (July 27, 1977). See also David Landau, "The Anti-Zionist Publicist from Jerusalem's Meah Shearim," *Jerusalem Post Magazine* (October 28, 1977).

18. See the statement of the Edah Haredit reprinted as "A Call to the Jewish People Everywhere," and Moshe Sternbuch, "Agudas Israel Joining the Government," in *The Jewish Guardian* (July 1977); also see "Call from the Central Rabbinical Congress of the United States and Canada," *The Jewish Guardian* (September 1977).

19. On the Sheli platform, see "Elections 1977—Who, What, and Why," *New Outlook* (April-May 1977), p. 23.

20. For a discussion of the influence of the Panthers on social change in Israel, see Gideon Levitas, "Social Policy and Elections," *New Outlook* (April-May 1977), pp. 24–25, 28.

21. See the discussion of the 1976 convention of the Communist Party of Israel in Meir Wilner, "Peace in the Middle East—Sheet Anchor for Israel," *World Marxist Review* (April 1977), pp. 32–40; on Rakah's perceptions of the election see Emil Touma, "The Ultra-Right in Power: Causes and Consequences," *World Marxist Review* (August 1977), pp. 76–82. On Biton in the Knesset, see "Prison is Hell, Biton Tells Fellow MK's," in the Jerusalem *Post* (July 26, 1977).

22. Jerusalem *Post* (October 18, 1977).

23. Yosef Goell, "Visions, Plans, and Realities," *Jerusalem Post Magazine* (September 16, 1977).

24. The entire issue is described in the Jerusalem *Post* (September 20–29, 1977); see also Mark Segal, "Golem and Gush Emunim," *Jerusalem Post Weekly Edition* (October 18, 1977).

25. Jerusalem *Post* (October 18–25, 1977).

GLOSSARY

Achdut Avoda: Left-wing Labor faction now included in the Labor alignment

Agudat Yisrael: Strictly Orthodox movement whose philosophy was initially ambivalent toward Zionism

Ahad Ha'am: "One of the folk," pen name for nineteenth-century essayist Asher Tzvi Ginsburg

Aliyah: Ascendance or emigration to the Holy Land

Asefat Hanivharim: The elected assembly; National Council of Jews in Palestine prior to 1948

Ashkenazim: Jews of European or Western descent

Avodah Ivri: "Hebrew Labor," Histadrut policy of servicing and extending labor among Jewish immigrants

Ayn Breira: "We have no alternative," Hebrew phrase which describes need to cooperate and remain united

Breira: Dovish group of American-Jewish dissenters from official Israeli policy

Edah Haredit: Organized religious community of Jerusalem

Gush Emunim: "Bloc of the Faithful"

Halutz: Pioneer, particularly referring to the settlers of the late nineteenth and early twentieth century

Haolam Hazeh: "This World," title of magazine edited by Uri Avnery

Hafarperet: The Mole, youth wing of Matzpen

Haganah: Major military wing of the Jewish Agency prior to 1948

Herut: Right-wing political faction now included in the Likud bloc

Hevrat Ovdim: A cooperative holding subsidiary of the Histadrut

Histadrut: Israel's Labor Federation

Histnahalut: Settlement of land based on religious zeal

Hovivei Zion: Lovers of Zion, major nineteenth century Zionist organization in Eastern Europe

Irgun Tzvai Leumi (Etzel): Militant band of terrorists operating with semi-autonomy during the Israeli War of Independence

Kibbutz: Communal agricultural settlements attached to one or another political movement

Knesset: Israeli Parliament

Kupat Holim: Israel Health Organization

Likud: Right-wing coalition of Israeli parties led by Menahem Begin

Lohamei Herut Yisrael (Lehi): See Irgun Tzvai Leumi

Mafdal: National Religious Party, successor to Mizrahi

Maki: Acronym for the original Israel Community Party—broke with USSR in 1967

Mapai: Acronym for the Israel Labor Party, the central coalition party through 1977

Mapam: United Workers Party, Marxist-Zionist movement aligned with the Labor Party

Matzpen: The Compass, popular title for the Israel Socialist Organization

Meri: Acronym for the Israel Radical Party

Mizrahi: Religious Zionist movement founded in 1902

Moked (The Focus), result of alignment between parts of Maki and left-wing student groups

Natore Karta: Guardians of the City

Palmach: Special shock troop from which grew the officer corps of the Haganah

Rakah: Acronym for the New Communist list

Siach: Acronym for the Israeli New Left

Sefardim: Jews of Oriental descent

Tchelet-Adom: The Blue-Red, left-wing student and youth faction aligned with Maki to form Moked

Va'ad Leumi: National Council, executive committee of Asefat Hanivharim

Yishuv: Jewish settlement in Palestine prior to 1948

Yored, Yerida: Immigration from Israel

Zahal: Acronym for the Israel Defense Force

BIBLIOGRAPHY

BOOKS

Abcarian, Gilbert. *American Political Radicalism*. Waltham, Mass.: Xerox, 1971.

Abramov, Yigal. *Perpetual Dilemma: Jewish Religion in the Jewish State*. Jerusalem: World Union of Progressive Judaism, 1976.

Allon, Yigal. *The Making of Israel's Army*. London: Vallentine and Mitchell, 1970.

Apter, David, ed. *Ideology and Discontent* New York: Free Press, 1964.

Avnery, Uri. *Israel Without Zionists*. New York: Macmillan, 1968.

Becker, Aharon. *Histadrut: Program, Problems, Prospects*. Tel Aviv: International Department of the Histadrut, 1966.

Bell, Daniel, ed. *The End of Ideology*. Glencoe, Ill.: The Free Press, 1960.

Benewick, Robert, et al., eds. *Knowledge and Belief in Politics: The Problem of Ideology* New York: St. Martin's, 1973.

Bernstein, Marver. *The Politics of Israel*. New York: Greenwood Press, 1959.

Birnbaum, Ervin. *The Politics of Compromise: State and Religion in Israel*. Rutherford, N.J.: Fairleigh Dickinson University Press, 1970.

Birnbaum, Philip, ed. *Daily Prayer Book*. New York: Hebrew, 1949.

Blau, Amram. *Kingship Shall Revert to Apostasy*. Jerusalem: Hamakor, 1970. (Hebrew.)

Borochov, Ber. *Nationalism and the Class Struggle*. New York: Young Poale Zion Alliance of America, 1937.

Brandeis, Louis. *Brandeis on Zionism: A Collection of Addresses & Statements*. Washington, D.C.: Zionist Organization of America, 1942.

Burstein, Moshe. *Self-Government of the Jews in Palestine since 1900*. Tel Aviv, 1934. (Hebrew.)

Curtis, Michael, and Mordecai Chertoff, eds. *Israel: Social Structure and Change*. New Brunswick, N.J.: Transaction, 1973.

Czudnowski, Moshe, and Jacob Landau. *The Israeli Communist Party and the Elections for the Fifth Knesset*. Stanford, Calif.: Hoover Institute, 1965.

Denisoff, R. Serge. *The Sociology of Dissent*. New York: Harcourt, Brace & Jovanovich, 1974.

Dolbeare, Kenneth, and Patricia Dolbeare. *American Ideologies: The Competing Beliefs of the Seventies*. Chicago: Markham, 1971.

Domb, Yerahmiel. *The Transformation*. London: Tomchei Natore Karta, 1958.

Eban, Abba. *My Country: The Story of Modern Israel*. New York: Random House, 1972.

Eisenstadt, S.N., et al., eds. *Integration and Development in Israel*. New York: Praeger, 1970.

Elizur, Yuval, and Elihu Salpeter. *Who Rules Israel*. New York: Harper & Row, 1973.

Emanuel, Yitzhak. *The Black Panthers and the State of Israel*. Holon: Ami, 1971. (Hebrew.)

Filber, Yehuda. *The Soul of an Ascendant Nation*. Jerusalem: Emunim, 1974. (Hebrew.)

Halevi, Nadav, and Ruth Klinov-Malul. *The Economic Development of Israel*. New York: Praeger, 1968.

Hertzberg, Arthur, ed. *The Zionist Idea*. New York: Atheneum Press, 1975.

Hilberg, Raul. *The Destruction of European Jewry, 1933–1945*. Chicago: Quadrangle Books, 1971.

Horowitz, David. *The Economics of Israel*. London: Pergamon Press, 1967.

Isaac, Harold. *American Jews in Israel*. New York: John Jay, 1967.

Isaac, Rael. *Israel Divided: Ideological Politics in the Jewish State*. Baltimore: Johns Hopkins University Press, 1976.

Isaac, Rael Jean. *Breira: Counsel for Judaism*. New York: Americans for a Safe Israel, 1977.

Israel. Knesset. May 31, 1966. *Divrei Ha Knesset*. 6th Knesset, 63rd sess., p. 1576.

Kohn, Moshe. *Who's Afraid of Gush Emunim?* Collection of a series originally published in the Jerusalem *Post*. Jerusalem: Jerusalem Post, 1977.

Landau, Jacob. *The Arabs in Israel: A Political Study*. London: Oxford University Press, 1969.

Lane, Robert. *Political Man*. New York: Free Press, 1972.

Laquer, Walter. *Communism and Nationalism in the Middle East*. New York: Praeger, 1957.

——————. *A History of Zionism*. New York: Holt, Rinehart and Winston, 1972.

Leslie, S. Clement. *The Rift in Israel*. New York: Schocken Books, 1971.

Levin, Nora. *The Holocaust*. New York: Thomas Y. Crowell, 1968.

Lewisohn, Ludwig, ed. *Theodor Herzl: A Portrait for This Age*. New York: World, 1955.

Lichtheim, George. *The Concept of Ideology*. New York: Random House, 1967.

Lipset, Seymour M. *Political Man*. Garden City, L.I.: Doubleday, 1960.

Marmorstein, Emile. *Heaven at Bay*. London: Oxford University Press, 1969.

Natore Karta. *A Clarification*. Pamphlet. Jerusalem, 1960. (Hebrew.)

——————. *An Insight toward Independence*. Jerusalem, 1970. (Hebrew.)

Peres, Shimon. *David's Sling: The Arming of Israel*. London: Weidenfeld and Nicolson, 1970.

Perlmutter, Amos. Military and Politics in Israel. New York: Praeger, 1969.

Rackman, Emanuel. Israel's Emerging Constitution. New York: Columbia University Press, 1955.

Rejai, Mostafa, ed. *Decline of Ideology?* Chicago: Aldine/Atherton Press, 1971.

Sachar, Howard M. *A History of Israel*. New York: Alfred A. Knopf, 1976.

Sargent, Lyman T. *Contemporary Political Ideologies*. Homewood, Ill.: Dorsey, 1972.

Teitelbaum, Joel. *Studies in Redemption*. New York: 1967. (Hebrew.)

——————. *The Ascent of Moses*. New York: 1959. (Hebrew.)

Waxman, Chaim, ed. *The End of Ideology Debate*. New York: Funk & Wagnall, 1968.

Weisgal, Meyer, ed. *Chaim Weizmann*. New York: Dial Press, 1944.

Weller, Leonard. *Sociology in Israel* Westport, Conn.: Greenwood Press, 1974.

Zohar, David M. *Political Parties in Israel: The Evolution of Israeli Democracy*. New York: Praeger, 1974.

ARTICLES

Avineri, Shlomo. "Israel: Two Nations?" *Midstream*, May 1972, pp. 3–20.

Avnery, Uri. "Fighting for the Peace: The Silent Majority." *New Middle East*, March–April 1972.

——————. "Jerusalem is Not Saigon." *New Outlook*, May–June 1975.

——————. "The New Leaders." *New Outlook*, July–August 1976.

——————. "The Palestinian Option." In *The Palestinians: People, History, Politics*, ed. Michael Curtis et al., New Brunswick, N.J.: Transaction, 1975.

——————. "Reflections on Mr. Hammami." *New Outlook*, January 1976.

——————. "The Third Year of the Six Days' War." In *Reflections on the Middle East Crisis*, ed. Herbert Mason. Paris: Mouton, 1970.

——————. "Unofficial and Unrepresentative: Transcript of an Interview at the Hague." *New Middle East*, September 1969, pp. 23–28.

Bailey, Clinton. "The Communist Party and the Arabs in Israel." *Mid-stream*, May 1970.

——————. "The Soviet Involvement in Egypt: A Dilemma for Rakah." *New Outlook*, July–August 1970.

Berkowitz, Gila. "Madam Rabanit." *Israel Magazine*, December 1972, pp. 71–75.

Brannegan, William. "The Communist Parties of Israel." *The Nation*, October 25, 1970.

Brecher, Michael. "Images, Processes, and Feedback in Foreign Policy: Israel's Decision on German Reparations." *American Political Science Review*, March, 1973, pp. 73–102.

Brownstein, Lewis. "Decision-Making in Israeli Foreign Policy: An Unplanned Process." *Political Science Quarterly*, Summer 1977.

Bruno, Michael. "The Social Gap Is Not Really Closing." *New Outlook*, January 1973, pp. 12–15.

Buber-Agasi, Yehudit. "A Clericalist Coalition." *New Outlook*, August 1977, pp. 38–40.

Cohen, Erik. "The Black Panthers and Israeli Society." *Journal of Jewish Sociology*, June 1973, pp. 93–109.

Domb, Yerahmiel. "Neturei Karta." In *Zionism Reconsidered*, ed. Michael Selzer. New York: Macmillan, 1970.

Elon, Amos. "The Black Panthers of Israel." *New York Times Magazine*, September 12, 1971.

Feron, James. "The Israelis of New York." *New York Times Magazine*, January 16, 1977.

Goell, Yosef. "All Eyes on the Party Leadership." *Jerusalem Post Weekly Edition*, May 17, 1977.

Halevy, Eva Etzioni. "Protest Politics in the Israeli Democracy." *Political Science Quarterly*, Fall 1975, pp. 497–520.

Halpern, Ben. "The Role of the Military in Israel." In *The Role of the Military in Underdeveloped Countries*, ed. John Johnson. Princeton: Princeton University Press, 1962.

Hasenson, David, Rachel Nitzan, and Aaron Rahmat. "Natore Karta: An Extremist Group." Senior thesis, Hebrew University, 1974. (Hebrew.)

Isaac, Eric, and Rael Jean Isaac. "The Earthquake: Israeli Elections, 1977." *Midstream*, August–September 1977, pp. 3–10.

Isaac, Erich, and Rael Isaac. "Israel's Dissenting Intellectuals." *Conservative Judaism*, Spring 1972.

Isaac, Rael Jean. "The Rabbis of Breira." *Midstream*, April 1977, pp. 3–17.

Khenin, David. "For a Policy of Reason." *World Marxist Review*, February 1975.

———. "Israel after the October War." *World Marxist Review*, February 1974.

Lamm, Norman. "The Ideology of Neturei Karta: According to the Satmerer Version." *Tradition*, Fall 1971.

Landau, Jacob. "A Note on the Leadership of Israeli Arabs." In *Political Institutions and Processes in Israel*, ed. Moshe Lissak and Emanuel Guttmann, pp. 383–94. Jerusalem: Hebrew University, 1971.

La Palombra, Joseph. "Decline of Ideology: A Dissent and Interpretation." *American Political Science Review*, March 1966.

Levinger, Moshe, et al. "Brief Answers to Timely Questions." *Gush Emunim*, March 1976.

Levitas, Gideon. "Social Policy and Elections." *New Outlook*, April/May 1977.

Lipset, Seymour M. "The Changing Class Structure and Contemporary European Politics." *Daedalus*, Winter 1964.

Marmorstein, Emil. "Religious Opposition to Nationalism in the Middle East." *International Affairs*, July 1952.

Miller, Judith. "Israel's Black Panthers." *The Progressive*, March 1972.

Mullins, Willard. "On the Concept of Ideology in Political Science." *American Political Science Review*, June 1972, pp. 498–510.

Novak, William. "The Breira Story." *Genesis 2*, March 16, 1977.

O'Dea, Janet. "Gush Emunim: Roots and Ambiguities." *Forum on the Jewish People, Zionism, and Israel*, Fall 1976, pp. 39–50.

Parekh, Bhiku. "Social and Political Thought and the Problem of Ideology." In *Knowledge and Belief in Politics: The Problem of Ideology*, ed. Robert Benewick et al. New York: St. Martins, 1973.

Peled, Matityahu. "The Cure for Nazareth." *New Outlook*, January 1976, pp. 35–38.

Peretz, Don. "The Earthquake—Israel's Ninth Knesset Elections." *Middle East Journal*, Summer 1977.

—————. "Israel's 1969 Election Issues." *The Middle East Journal*, Winter 1970, pp. 31–46.

Peri, J. "The Black Panthers in Perspective." *New Outlook*, January 1973.

Putnam, Robert. "Studying Elite Political Culture: The Case of 'Ideology'," *Political Science Review*, September 1971.

Sartori, Giovanni. "Politics, Ideology, and Belief Systems." *American Political Science Review*, June 1969, pp. 398–411.

Schnall, David. "Dialectic Zionism." *Judaism*, Summer 1973, pp. 334–41.

—————. "Notes on the Political Thought of Dr. Moshe Sneh." *Middle East Journal*, Summer 1973, pp. 342–52.

—————. "The Super Powers and the Middle East." *Tradition*, Fall 1975.

——————. "Territoriality and the Jews, 1924–1936: A Case Study of Soviet Minority Group Policies." *The Helderberg Review*, Spring 1972, pp. 49–59.

——————. "Yored Is Also a Noun." *Midstream*, February 1978, pp. 73–78.

Shaham, David. "Election in the Shadow of Doubt." *New Outlook*, April–May 1977, pp. 17–28.

——————. "Labor Revival in the Histadrut." *New Outlook*, August 1977, pp. 33–36.

Shils, Edward. "The End of Ideology?" *Encounter*, November 1955.

Shprinzak, Ehud. *The Blossoming of the Politics of Delegitimacy in Israel.* Eshkol Institute for Economic, Social, and Political Research, Special Publication no. 8. Jerusalem: Hebrew University, 1973. (Hebrew.)

——————. "Notes on the Nature of Extremist Politics in Israel." Paper read at Eshkol Institute of Hebrew University, May 1976. (Hebrew.)

Slann, Martin. "Ideology and Ethnicity in Israel's Two Communist Parties: The Conflict Between Maki and Rakah." *Studies in Comparative Communism*, Winter 1974, pp. 359–74.

Tartakover, Arieh. "The Making of Jewish Statehood in Palestine." *Jewish Social Studies*, July 1948.

Toledano, Henry. "Israel's Sefardi Problem." *Jewish Spectator*, September 1972, pp. 6–8.

Touma, Emil. "Limits of Partnership in U.S.-Israeli Relations." *World Marxist Review*, June 1975.

——————. "The Ultra-Right in Power: Causes and Consequences." *World Marxist Review*, August 1977, pp. 76–82.

Weiner, Herbert. "The Case for Natore Karta," *Jewish Digest*, March 1964, pp. 59–64.

Wilner, Meir. "Peace in The Middle East—Sheet Anchor for Israel." *World Marxist Review*, April 1977, pp. 32–40.

NEWSPAPERS AND PERIODICALS

Al-Ittchad

Arakhim: Problems of Peace and Socialism

Ba-Moked, Bitzaron

Davar

Davar Hapanterim Hashechorum

Haolam Hazeh

Hatzofeh

Information Bulletin of Communist Party of Israel (IBCPI)

Jerusalem *Post*

Jerusalem Post Weekly Edition

The Jewish Guardian

Kol Ha'am (English translation: Israel at Peace)

Ma-ariv

Mishmeret Homotenu

New York *Times*

Yediot Achronot

Zu Haderekh

INDEX

Va'ad Leumi, 34ff

Wachsman, Yosef, 167f
Wallfish, Asher, 201n
War of Independence (1948), 56-57,
    134, 140-41
Weiner, Herbert, 134n
Weissfisch, Label, 130n, 131n
Weizmann, Ezer, 48
Weizmann, Chaim, 18n, 33
Weller, Leonard, 31n, 156n
Wilenska, Esther, 67, 109, 116n, 178
Wilner, Meir, 74, 77, 78n, 79n, 81n,
    88n, 207, 207n
World Zionist Organization, 12, 32,
    83

Yadin, Yigal, 194ff
Yadlin, Asher, 193
Yakim, Muni, 170
Yom Kippur War (1973), 111, 141,
    144, 167
Yuval, Davis, Nira, 89n

Zadok, Haim, 117
Zionism, 10ff, 50, 156, 182ff; and Gush
    Emunim, 125ff; and Haloam
    Hazeh, 59-60; and the Israel
    Socialist Organization, 92ff; and
    Moked, 109ff; and Natore Karta,
    125ff; and Rakah, 81ff
Ziyyad, Tawfiq, 79n, 107, 207
Zohar, David, 40n

ABOUT THE AUTHOR

DAVID J. SCHNALL is Associate Professor of Political Science at the College of Staten Island, City University of New Work. Professor Schnall has taught at Brooklyn College, Fordham University, Long Island University, and Rockland Community College. He resides in Brooklyn with his wife Tova and their son Eliezer Hillel. He holds B.A. and M.S. degrees from Yeshiva University where he received his rabbinic ordination. Professor Schnall also holds an M.A. and Ph.D. from Fordham University, where he was inducted into Phi Beta Kappa.

An active author, Dr. Schnall has published widely in the areas of urban affairs, Middle East politics, and Jewish life. His last book was *Ethnicity and Suburban Local Politics* (New York: Praeger, 1975), and he has contributed to the *Middle East Journal, Asian Profile, The Annals,* The *Journal of Social History,* The *Review of Politics* and the *Policy Studies Journal.* His articles and reviews have also appeared in *Judaism, Tradition,* and *Midstream,* as well as in several popular magazines and journals.